INQUIRY JOURNAL

UNITED STATES HISTORY:
Voices and Perspectives

Mc
Graw
Hill

About the Cover: Edward C. Gleed, Tuskegee pilot

Cover Credits: (Left) FatCamera/E+/Getty Images, (right) Library of Congress Prints and Photographs Division [LC-DIG-ppmsca-13269]

mheducation.com/prek-12

Send all inquiries to:
McGraw Hill
8787 Orion Place
Columbus, OH 43240

ISBN: 978-0-07-699989-7
MHID: 0-07-699989-0

Printed in the United States of America.

2 3 4 5 6 7 8 9 SOH 27 26 25 24 23 22

Table of Contents

Dear Student,

Most of us are curious, and we have many questions about many things. We have the more personal questions, such as, "Will my favorite book be made into a movie?" or "Why does my former best friend not want to hang out with me anymore?" to questions of a larger nature about the world around us. These might include questions such as, "What does being treated like an adult mean?" "Why can't people share?" "Why do countries go to war?" "How do I understand what I see or read about in history books, online, or in the news?" and "Why is the peace process so difficult?"

Asking good questions helps us take charge of our own learning. Learning to ask good questions is a process, as "yes" or "no" types of questions do not get us very far in discovering why events happened or why people behave as they do. Once we master this process, however, we become better thinkers and researchers and can find out more about the subjects that interest us. Asking good questions is also important if we want to understand and affect the world around us.

In this Inquiry Journal, there are "Compelling Questions" that you will research. These types of questions concern all people—those who have lived, those who are living now, and those who will live in the future. Examples of these questions include: "How do beliefs shape cultures?" and "How are laws and policies reflective of a society's values?" You will create some of your own Supporting Questions to help you answer the Compelling Question.

As you move through the study of history, you will be reading primary and secondary sources about a specific time period. Primary sources—whether they are diaries, poetry, letters, or artwork—were created by people who saw or experienced the event they are describing. Secondary sources—whether they are biographies, history books, or your student text—are created after an event by people who were not part of the original event. Create the **Foldables® Inquiry Journal Study Guide** in this book and use it to help you analyze different types of primary and secondary sources.

Once you have completed the readings and answered the questions, you will evaluate the sources and use evidence to explain how they help you answer your Supporting Questions and the Compelling Question. Then you will be given the opportunity to take informed action. This means that you will use what you have learned and apply it to a current issue in a way that interests you. You will share this information with other students or with people outside of the classroom.

Name _____ Date _____ Class _____

Innovative Technology in the Lives of Native Americans

 COMPELLING QUESTION

What are the effects of technology on society?

Plan Your Inquiry

In this Inquiry Activity, you will develop Supporting Questions about technologies used by Native Americans based on the Compelling Question and examine primary and secondary sources. Finally, you will answer your Supporting Questions, communicate your research conclusions, and take action based on what you've learned.

Background Information

When you hear the word *technology*, you may think of smartphones, tablets, and other modern devices. Today, new digital technologies like these continue to change our lives at an astounding rate—in ways that our ancestors never even imagined. But technology has played a central role in the lives of Americans ever since the first humans arrived in North America nearly 15,000 years ago.

Technology can be defined as the use of knowledge to invent new tools, systems, or ways of doing something. Throughout human history, people have developed and used technology to meet their needs and make their lives easier. More than two million years ago, early humans started to make tools and weapons from stone. Our ancestors may have started building fires as many as one million years ago. Early Native Americans carved spears to hunt mammoths and constructed stone hoes to till soil. Later Native Americans developed sophisticated systems for irrigation and drainage, farming, and transportation.

Native Americans lived in harmony with their environment, but they also modified it to enable them to survive and thrive wherever they lived—from the rocky mountains of Peru to the frozen tundra of the Arctic.

The Ancient Puebloan were Native Americans who built dwellings in the sides of cliffs, an example of innovative ways that early Americans changed their environment through the use of technology. The Mesa Verde cliff dwellings were built in what is now Colorado in the late 1190s.

Develop Supporting Questions About Technology in the Lives of Native Americans

 COMPELLING QUESTION

What are the effects of technology on society?

Talk About It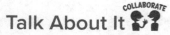

Discuss with a partner what type of information you would need to know to answer this question. For example, one question might be: How is *technology* defined?

Directions: Write down three additional questions that you need to answer to be able to determine the effects of technology on native peoples in North, Central, and South America.

Supporting Question 1:

Supporting Question 2:

Supporting Question 3:

Apply Historical Concepts and Tools

Directions: As you read and work with primary and secondary sources, use the graphic organizer to take notes and organize information.

Organizing Source Information		
Source	**Title and Author/ Creator**	**Notes**
A	Olmec Drainage System	
B	Inca Terrace Farming and Irrigation	
C	Inuit Snow Goggles	
D	Chacoan Road System	
E	Aztec Causeways at Tenochtitlán	

Analyze Sources

Review and analyze Sources A–E. There are questions that accompany each source to help you examine the source and check for historical understanding.

Olmec Drainage System

The Olmec people lived between 1200 and 800 B.C.E. in what is now Mexico. They lived in hot, tropical lowlands along the Gulf of Mexico, where they grew crops such as maize and beans. In this region, rain was not always predictable and the land frequently flooded. These stone tiles, discovered by archaeologists in 1967, provide clues about how the Olmec developed a water and drainage system to alter to their environment.

PRIMARY SOURCE : ARTIFACT

EXAMINE THE SOURCE

1. Describing Describe the tiles shown in the photograph.

2. Making Connections What modern technologies do the tiles remind you of? How are they similar and different?

3. Making Inferences What might the Olmec have used the tiles for?

4. Analyzing What do these tools tell you about how the Olmec could manipulate their environment?

Need Extra Help?

Many of the sources in this Inquiry Journal are photographs, which means they don't necessarily give clear information about how the technology was used or how it affected society. To interpret the sources and answer the Compelling Question, you will need to make inferences, or conclusions drawn from known facts, about each technology. Start by closely examining the image. What do you notice about it? Then, connect what you see in the image with what you already know. You may find it helpful to make connections between the ancient technologies and modern technologies. How is the technology in the photograph similar to a modern technology you know about? How does that modern technology affect our society? Based on what you know about the past, what inferences can you make about how the ancient technology affected society?

B

Inca Terrace Farming and Irrigation

The Inca Empire flourished in the Andes Mountains of South America in the 1400s and 1500s C.E. The Inca built their empire by conquering neighboring communities who did not agree to Inca rule. The economy of the Inca was based on agriculture, and farmers grew a large variety of crops including maize, sweet potatoes, squash, and cotton.

The Inca used highly advanced farming methods. They farmed on broad, flat platforms called terraces that they cut into the mountainsides. To help direct water for irrigation, or watering crops, and drainage, they carved water channels into the sides of the terraces. At the height of the Inca civilization, this network of terraces covered approximately 3,861 miles (6,214 km) across the vast empire.

PRIMARY SOURCE : PHOTOGRAPH

EXAMINE THE SOURCE

5. Describing Describe what you see in the photograph.

6. Contrasting How are the terraces different from the surrounding land?

7. Making Inferences Why do you think the Inca built terraces?

8. Analyzing How might the design of the terraces have helped direct water for irrigation?

9. Drawing Conclusions What do the terraces reveal about the Inca civilization?

C

Inuit Snow Goggles

The Inuit are an indigenous people who live in parts of Alaska, northern Canada, and Greenland. They adapted their culture to survive in the extremely cold and snowy conditions of the Arctic. For food, the Inuit depended on animals, moving seasonally to temporary hunting camps. In summer, Inuit hunters traveled by kayak and used harpoons to hunt seals and walrus. In summer, they hunted caribou with bows and arrows.

For thousands of years, the Inuit have made snow goggles to protect against snow blindness, a painful eye condition caused by overexposure to ultraviolet light from the sun. The condition is often caused by sunlight reflecting off the snow, making it a serious problem on sunny days in the Arctic. The goggles pictured below are from the 1800s, but they are similar to the goggles that the Inuit have used since before Europeans came to the Americas.

PRIMARY SOURCE : ARTIFACT

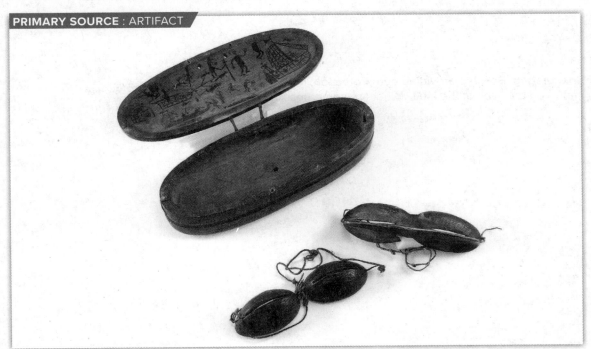

EXAMINE THE SOURCE

10. Describing Look carefully at the photograph. Describe the objects you see.

11. **Making Inferences** How might the snow goggles have protected the wearer against snow blindness?

12. **Speculating** Besides providing eye protection, how else might the goggles have improved the lives of the Inuit? What are some possible effects of this technology?

D

Chacoan Road System

The Ancient Puebloan people thrived from about 1 C.E. to 1300 in what is now the American Southwest. Early Puebloan people moved from place to place, hunting and gathering wild foods. Later, they began building more permanent communities. They developed farming methods to grow maize, squash, beans, and other crops in the dry climate.

In these communities, the ancient Puebloan people built and lived in elaborate villages called pueblos. Visitors to the Chaco Culture National Historical Park in New Mexico can see the remains of some of these pueblos, which are still linked by a complex network of ancient roads and stairways. The first photograph below shows an aerial view, or a view from above, of this road network. Chacoan roads ranged from 12 to 20 feet wide. They were designed to both avoid major obstacles like rivers and to cut through smaller landforms such as low hills.

PRIMARY SOURCE : PHOTOGRAPH

13. **Describing** Describe the Chacoan road system as shown in the two photographs.

14. **Comparing and Contrasting** How are the Chacoan roads similar to and different from modern roads?

15. **Speculating** Why do you think the Ancient Puebloan built such an extensive network of roads?

E

Aztec Causeways at Tenochtitlán

In the 1300s, a Native American culture called the Aztec built their capital city, Tenochtitlán (present-day Mexico City), on an island in the middle of a lake, accessed only by causeways, or roads built above water. It became the largest city in the Americas and one of the largest in the world. Tenochtitlán served as a center of trade, and thousands of merchants visited its outdoor marketplaces.

Rumors of gold and stories about the splendid city dazzled Europeans. In the 1500s, the Spanish explorer Hernán Cortés led an expedition to Mexico. During his journey, he wrote letters to the Spanish king detailing his observations of Tenochtitlán and the Aztec people and culture. He included the map below, which shows a complex and thoughtfully designed city.

PRIMARY SOURCE : MAP

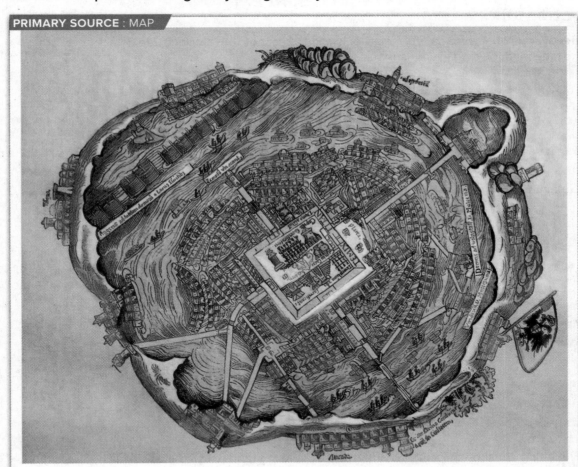

This map of Tenochtitlán created by Hernán Cortés in 1520 is considered the first European image of the city.

" This great city of Temixtitan [Mexico] is situated in this salt lake. . . .   There are four avenues or entrances to the city. . . . All the streets at intervals have openings, through which the water flows, crossing from one street to another; and at these openings, some of which are very wide, there are also very wide bridges. . . . [On] many of these bridges ten horses can go abreast. Foreseeing that if the inhabitants of this city should prove treacherous, they would possess great advantages from the manner in which the city is constructed, since by removing the bridges at the entrances, and abandoning the place, they could Leave us to perish by famine without our being able to reach the main land. "

— Hernán Cortés, letter to Emperor Charles V of Spain, 1522

---

treacherous untrustworthy

> EXAMINE THE SOURCE

16. Identifying What were the main distinguishing features of Tenochtitlán? Use details from the letter and the map in your answer.

17. Explaining According to Cortés, what is a "great advantage" of the city's design?

18. Making Inferences What is another possible advantage of the city's design?

19. Evaluating What do these sources reveal about the strengths of the Aztec? Explain.

Evaluate Sources and Use Evidence

20. <u>Citing Text Evidence</u> Review the Supporting Questions you developed at the beginning of the topic and the evidence you gathered and recorded in the Graphic Organizer. Which sources will help you answer the Supporting Questions? Circle or highlight those sources in your Graphic Organizer. Looking at the subset of sources you have chosen, be prepared to explain why you chose each source.

	Supporting Question	Primary Source and Notes
1		
2		
3		

Challenge

Using reliable print or online resources, conduct research to identify other technologies used by Native Americans. Select one of them that you think will help you better answer your Supporting Questions, and conduct further research to find out more about the technology. Why was it developed? How did it function? How did it affect the lives of the Native Americans who used it? Incorporate this research into your response.

21. Directions: Now, answer the Supporting Questions that you developed at the beginning of the activity to help guide you in answering the Compelling Question.

Answer for Supporting Question 1:

Answer for Supporting Question 2:

Answer for Supporting Question 3:

Communicate Conclusions

Talk About It

22. Collaborating Work in small groups. With your group, discuss specific examples of technologies used by Native Americans and how these technologies may have changed their lives. What conclusions can you draw about the role that technology plays in society more generally? Consider each row in your Graphic Organizers as you talk about which sources offer the best evidence to support your conclusions. Take notes about your discussion and choose one person in the group to share your conclusions with the class.

Write About It

23. Argumentative Writing Consider the advantages and limitations of the sources that you used to answer the Supporting Questions you developed. What makes the sources reliable or unreliable? How did the sources help you answer the questions? What information was missing that could have helped you answer the questions more completely and accurately? Which sources were the most and least helpful? Write a few paragraphs evaluating and critiquing the sources.

24. Answering the Compelling Question What do you think? What are the effects of technology on society? Write a two-minute speech using evidence from at least three sources to support your argument.

Take Informed Action

25. Making connections Think about a new technology that is affecting society today, or a technology in development that may affect society in the near future. For example, you might choose smartphones, self-driving cars, or robots. Conduct research to determine how the new technology may affect society in both positive and negative ways. From the results of your research, develop and support an argument about the technology. In your opinion, is the new technology good or bad for society overall? What should be done to either promote the technology or prevent its negative impacts?

✓ YOU CHOOSE

Select one of these Take Informed Action products to apply what you've learned.

A. Write a newspaper editorial sharing your opinion about the technology.

B. Write and produce a podcast or video sharing your opinion.

C. Write a letter to a government official sharing your opinion and urging them to take action.

Take Informed Action Rubric: Argument

Self-Evaluation As you develop your argument, think about the following criteria. These are the criteria your teacher will use to evaluate your Take Informed Action activity.

Peer Review Use this rubric to grade the argument and product developed by another classmate or group of classmates.

	Argument	Supporting Evidence	Historical Accuracy	Organization
4	The argument is strong, focused, and clearly communicated.	Comprehensive evidence from primary and secondary sources is included. References are relevant and specific.	The argument is well-researched and factually accurate.	The argument is exceptionally well-organized and focused and demonstrates a thorough and deep understanding of the issue.
3	The argument is clearly communicated.	Adequate evidence is included. Some references may be general.	The argument is well-researched but contains some factual mistakes.	The argument is well-organized and focused and demonstrates an adequate understanding of the issue.
2	The argument is somewhat unclear.	Some evidence from sources may be weakly integrated, imprecise, repetitive, or vague.	The argument is not well-researched and contains some factual mistakes.	The argument is organized but is inconsistent in focus and demonstrates an inadequate understanding of the issue.
1	The argument is missing, confusing, or ambiguous.	Evidence is minimal or irrelevant. References may be absent or incorrectly used.	There are many factual mistakes.	The argument lacks organization, focus, and a basic understanding of the issue.
SCORE				

TOPIC 2 • EXPLORATION AND COLONIZATION, 476–1718 C.E.

Rewards, Dangers, and Effects of Early Exploration

 COMPELLING QUESTION

What were the rewards, dangers, and effects of exploration?

Plan Your Inquiry

In this Inquiry Activity, you will develop Supporting Questions about the rewards and dangers of early exploration based on the Compelling Question, and examine primary and secondary sources. Finally, you will answer your Supporting Questions, communicate your research conclusions, and take action based on what you've learned.

Background Information

European exploration of lands and waterways beyond Europe was motivated by the growing trade between Europe and Asia. Explorers set out looking for sea routes that would take them to Asia, which held the promise of silk, spices, and other valuable goods. Monarchs of Spain, Portugal, France, and England funded the travels. Finding a sea route to Asia would give the founding country an advantage. Great profits could be made from selling these goods throughout Europe.

Europeans had learned about the attractive resources of Asia in a round about way. Beginning in the 1090s, Europeans launched military attacks, called the Crusades, against Muslims in Southwest Asia. The Europeans, who were Christians, wanted to regain control of the Christian Holy Land of Jerusalem from the Muslims, who were followers of Islam. Ultimately, Europeans were unsuccessful in doing this. However, in the process of trying, they began a brisk trade with the Muslims who had been trading with merchants in Asia for centuries.

At the time of European contact, the native people in North, Central, and South America lived in societies with their own religions, economies, languages, customs, agricultural practices, and technology. For example, the Taíno were the people who Christopher Columbus met when he landed on the Caribbean island of Guanahaní in 1492, and historians estimate that there were over one-hundred thousand Taíno living on the island. Instead of honoring the Taíno society, Columbus and his men viewed them as resources to get what they wanted. They forced the Taíno to work in gold mines and produce food for them. Columbus and his men also brought diseases to the Americas, which eventually destroyed native populations.

Sailors and explorers thought that sea monsters were an actual threat that would hinder their exploration in uncharted areas around the world, as depicted in this illustration by German mapmaker Sebastian Münster around 1550. After more ships ventured west, sea monsters began disappearing from maps.

Develop Supporting Questions about the Rewards, Dangers, and Effects of Early Exploration

 COMPELLING QUESTION

What were the rewards, dangers, and effects of exploration?

Talk About It COLLABORATE

Discuss with a partner what type of information you would need to know to answer this question. For example, one question might be: What effects did exploration have on European explorers and the people they encountered?

Directions: Write down three additional questions that you need to answer to be able to determine the rewards, dangers, and effects of European exploration.

Supporting Question 1:

Supporting Question 2:

Supporting Question 3:

Apply Historical Concepts and Tools

Directions: As you read and work with primary and secondary sources, use the graphic organizer to take notes and organize information.

	Organizing Source Information	
Source	**Title and Author/ Creator**	**Notes**
A	Extracts from Columbus's Journal	
B	Select Letters of Christopher Columbus: With Other Original Documents, Relating to His Four Voyages to the New World	
C	Antonio Pigafetta's Journal of Magellan's Voyage	
D	Letter from John Day About Cabot's Voyage	
E	Cortés Letter to Emperor Charles V of Spain	

Analyze Sources

Review and analyze Sources A–E. There are questions that accompany each source to help you examine the source and check for historical understanding.

Extracts from Columbus's Journal

Italian sailor Christopher Columbus wanted to reach Asia by sailing west, not east, from Europe. After several attempts, he found a sponsor to finance his voyage—the king and queen of Spain. On August 3, 1492, Columbus and his crew set sail from southern Spain in search of a route to Asia. Columbus commanded three ships, the *Niña*, the *Pinta*, and the *Santa Maria*, and he kept a journal of the voyage. He had planned the voyage for four weeks, but it continued longer. Finally, on October 12, 1492, a sailor on the *Pinta* spotted land. Little did Columbus know that he had not arrived at Asia but rather to a land unknown to Europeans. This voyage would be the first of four voyages that Columbus would make to what is now known as the Americas.

   This entry from Columbus's journal describes events that took place during his first voyage. Notice that in this version of the journal, which was created later by a historian, Columbus is referred to in third person as "the Admiral." There is no known copy of Columbus's original journal.

PRIMARY SOURCE : JOURNAL

66 Monday, 6th of August
The **rudder** of the caravel *Pinta* became **unshipped**, and Martin Alonso Pinzon, who was in command, believed or suspected that it was by **contrivance** of Gomez Rascon and Cristóbal Quintero, to whom the caravel belonged, for they dreaded to go on that voyage. The Admiral says that, before they sailed, these men had been displaying a certain backwardness, so to speak. The Admiral was much disturbed at not being able to help the said caravel without danger, and he says that he was eased of some anxiety when he reflected that Martin Alsonso Pinzon was a man of energy and ingenuity. They made, during the day and night, 29 leagues. ...

Sunday, 9th of September
This day the Admiral made 19 leagues, and he arranged to reckon less than the number run, because if the voyage was of long duration, the people would not be so terrified and disheartened. In the night he made 120 miles, at the rate of 12 miles an hour, which are 30 leagues. The sailors steered badly, letting the ship fall off to N.E., and even more, respecting which the Admiral complained many times. 99

— Christopher Columbus, Journal of the First Voyage, 1492

rudder the steering part of a ship

unshipped unloaded or removed from a ship

contrivance a plan or scheme

1. Identifying Why did the rudder become "unshipped"?

2. Explaining Why would a broken or missing rudder present a dangerous situation?

3. Identifying Cause and Effect What effect did knowing that the captain of the *Pinta* "was a man of energy and ingenuity" have on Columbus?

4. Making Inferences What did Columbus mention on Sunday that was done to help make the voyage more bearable? Why might this have helped lessen a dangerous situation?

5. Summarizing What are some dangers related to exploration that are revealed in these journal entries?

B

Select Letters of Christopher Columbus: With Other Original Documents, Relating to His Four Voyages to the New World

On October 12, 1492, Christopher Columbus and his crew landed on an island near the Caribbean. They spent about five months exploring the area and meeting many of its indigenous people, whom he called Indians because he believed he had landed in the Indies—the islands off the coast of China. In this excerpt of a letter written to the treasurer to King Ferdinand and Queen Isabella of Spain, Columbus explains his interactions with the island people. He also provides insights into Spain's motives for the voyage.

PRIMARY SOURCE : LETTER

66 Knowing that it will afford you pleasure to learn that I have brought my undertaking to a successful termination, I have decided upon writing you this letter to acquaint you with all the events which have occurred in my voyage, and the discoveries which have resulted from it. . . .

As soon however as they [the inhabitants] see that they are safe, and have laid aside all fear, they are very simple and honest, and exceedingly liberal with all they have; none of them refusing any thing he may possess when he is asked for it, but on the contrary inviting us to ask them. They exhibit great love towards all others in preference to themselves: they also give objects of great value for **trifles**, and content themselves with very little or nothing in return. I however forbad that these trifles and articles of no value (such as pieces of dishes, plates, and glass, keys, and leather straps) should be given to them, although if they could obtain them, they imagined themselves to be possessed of the most beautiful trinkets in the world. It even happened that a sailor received for a leather strap as much gold as was worth three **golden nobles**, and for things of more trifling value offered by our men, especially-newly coined blancas, or any gold coins, the Indians would give whatever the seller required; as, for instance, an ounce and a half or two ounces of gold, or thirty or forty pounds of cotton, with which **commodity** they were already acquainted. Thus they **barterd**, like idiots, cotton and gold for fragments of bows, glasses, bottles, and jars; which I forbad as being unjust, and myself gave them many more beautiful and acceptable articles which I had brought with me, taking nothing from them in return; I did this in order that I might the more easily **conciliate** them, that they might be led to become Christians, and be inclined to entertain a regard for the King and Queen, our Princes and all Spaniards, and that I might **induce** them to take an interest in seeking out, and collecting, and delivering to us such things as they possessed in abundance, but which we greatly needed. 99

— Christopher Columbus, Select Letters of Christopher Columbus, March 14, 1493

trifles unimportant things

golden nobles English gold coins

commodity an article to trade, buy, or sell

barterd to exchange goods or services for other goods or services; bartered

conciliate to win over; to try to gain friendship

induce to persuade

6. Describing How does Columbus describe the indigenous people he meets? What are examples of words Columbus uses that indicate his attitude toward the inhabitants?

7. Drawing Conclusions What does Columbus hope to gain when he gives the inhabitants items he considers beautiful and to have more value? Why do you think he does this?

8. Analyzing Point of View What perspective is missing from Columbus's letter? Why is it important that historians consider missing perspectives, such as these, when examining primary sources?

9. Inferring How do you think the inhabitants felt about being forced to change their religious belief system?

Antonio Pigafetta's Journal of Magellan's Voyage

News of Columbus's voyage inspired other explorers to head out over the oceans. Ferdinand Magellan, from Portugal, explored mainly for Spain. He sailed around South America and across the Pacific Ocean in search of a westward route to Indonesia in the Pacific. In 1521, he and his crew of 240 men, which included Antonio Pigafetta, became the first Europeans to land in the Philippines. Magellan became friendly with one Phillipines king, who agreed to convert to Christianity.

Pigafetta was a scholar from Italy. He kept a journal in which he detailed the voyage with Magellan as well as a view of the people and languages spoken in the Philippines. Pigafetta was one of the lucky 18 men from the voyage to make it back to Spain. Magellan died in a battle after ordering his men to burn down the village of another Phillipines king, who refused to convert to Christinity. His remaining crew became the first people, to circumnavigate, or travel entirely around, Earth.

PRIMARY SOURCE : JOURNAL

> 66 Pieces of gold of the size of walnuts and eggs are found by sifting the earth in the island of that king who came to our ships. All the dishes of that king are of gold and also some portion of his house, as the king himself told us. According to their customs he was very grandly **decked out**, and the most handsome man that we saw among those people. His hair was exceedingly black, and hung to his shoulders, with a silk veil on his head and two large golden earrings fastened in his ears; he wore a cotton cloth all embroidered with silk, which covered him from the waist to the knees; at his side hung a dagger, the handle of which was very long and all gold, and its **scabbard** of carved wood; he had three spots of gold on every tooth, and his teeth appeared as if bound with gold; he was perfumed with **storax and benzoin**; he was olive-skinned and tattoed all over. That island of his was called **Butuan and Caraga**. When those kings wished to see one another, they both came to hunt in that island where we were. The name of the first king is Rajah Columbu, and the second Rajah Siaiu. 99

— Antonio Pigafetta, The First Voyage Around the World, March 1521

decked out decorated or dressed elaborately

scabbard a case for the blade of a dagger or sword

storax and benzoin fragrant resin that comes from trees

Butuan and Caraga islands in the Philippines

10. **Identifying the Main Idea** What key point does the author make in his journal entry?

11. **Interpreting** How does Pigafetta describe the gold he observes on the island? Why does he focus on this information?

12. **Analyzing Point of View** What is the author's attitude toward the king? Explain your answer.

13. **Drawing Conclusions** Why is the description of the king important to understanding the author's purpose?

D

Letter from John Day About Cabot's Voyage

After learning about the early ocean voyages, rulers throughout Europe began to send other explorers in search of lands. They hoped the explorers would be able to claim land in their name and possibly find a new route to Asia. England's ruler in 1496 was Henry VII, and he provided Italian navigator John Cabot with funds for an expedition. Cabot made several trips to North America searching for a route to Asia. Like Columbus, he found no route. Instead, he located land in present-day Canada, claiming it for England. In late 1497 and early 1498, an English merchant named John Day wrote a letter to the "Lord Grand Admiral," believed to be Christopher Columbus. In the letter, Day provided information he had regarding John Cabot's voyage in 1496.

SECONDARY SOURCE : LETTER

❝ I am sending the other book of Marco Polo and a copy of the land which has been found [by John Cabot]. I do not send the map because I am not satisfied with it, for my many occupations forced me to make it in a hurry at the time of my departure; but from the said copy your Lordship will learn what you wish to know, for in it are named the capes of the mainland and the islands, and thus you will see where land was first sighted, since most of the land was discovered after turning back. . . .

In that particular spot, as I told your Lordship, they found a trail that went inland, they saw a site where a fire had been made, they saw manure of animals which they thought to be farm animals, and they saw a stick half a yard long pierced at both ends, carved and painted with brazil, and by such signs they believe the land to be inhabited. Since he was with just a few people, he did not dare advance inland beyond the shooting distance of a crossbow, and after taking in fresh water he returned to his ship. . . .

They left England toward the end of May, and must have been on the way 35 days before sighting land; the wind was east-north-east and the sea calm going and coming back, except for one day when he ran into a storm two or three days before finding land; and going so far out, his compass needle failed to point north and marked two **rhumbs** below. They spent about one month discovering the coast and from the above mentioned cape of the mainland which is nearest to Ireland, they returned to the coast of Europe in fifteen days. They had the wind behind them, and he reached Brittany because the sailors confused him, saying that he was heading too far north. . . .

It is considered certain that the cape of the said land was found and discovered in the past by the men from Bristol who found 'Brasil' as your Lordship well knows. It was called the Island of Brasil, and it is assumed and believed to be the mainland that the men from Bristol found. ❞

— John Day, from James A Williamson,
The Cabot Voyages and Bristol Discovery Under Henry VII, 1962

---

rhumbs any of the points found on a compass

14. Identifying What are the signs that Day describes that indicate the land Cabot explored was inhabited?

15. Summarizing What does John Day's letter suggest about problems, or dangers, Cabot faced while on his voyage?

16. Speculating From examining the letter, what can you conclude about the meaning of the line, "They had the wind behind them, and he reached Brittany because the sailors confused him, saying that he was heading too far north"?

17. Citing Text Evidence What point is Day making in his argument related to the land that was found by Cabot? What evidence from the passage suggests that Day had knowledge about the discovery?

Cortés Letter to Emperor Charles V of Spain

Spanish explorers, called conquistadors, began to search for riches they believed could be found in the Americas. One conquistador named Hernán Cortés, also known as Fernando Cortés, arrived in Mexico in 1519. There, he encountered the people of the Aztec Empire who had built a large city in the middle of Lake Texcoco. He was amazed by the native people's wealth in gold and hoped to acquire it for himself and his homeland of Spain. He conquered the Aztec Empire, and took their land and riches for Spain. This letter from Cortés to Spanish emperor Charles V accompanied a sampling of those riches.

PRIMARY SOURCE : LETTER

66 Which petition and requirement we send with these, our **procurators**, to Your Majesties, and we all humbly **supplicate** Your Royal Highnesses, that you will grant not only this, but all the other favours, which in the name of this council and town may be petitioned by the said procurators, and that you will regard us as your most loyal **vassals**, such as we have been and always will be. The gold, and silver, and jewels, and valuables, and the *rodelas*, and the wearing apparel, which we send by the procurators to Your Royal Highnesses, and which, over and above the one-fifth which belongs to Your Majesty, Captain Fernando Cortes, and this council, pray you to accept, go with this memorial, signed by them and by the said procurators, as Your Royal Highnesses may see from it.

The first treasure sent to Spain contained the following curious objects:

A gold necklace composed of seven pieces, with 185 small emeralds set in it, and 232 gems, like rubies, from which hung 27 small bells of gold, and some pearls.

Another necklace of four pieces of gold with 102 red gems, like rubies, 172 emeralds, 10 fine pearls, set in it, and 26 little golden bells pendant.

Two wheels, one of gold representing the sun, the other of silver bearing the image of the moon, 28 hands in circumference, and bearing various figures of animals, and other devices, beautifully worked in relief.

A head-dress of wood, decorated with gold and gems, with 25 golden bells pendant; instead of a plume it had a green bird, whose eyes, beak and feet were made of gold. 99

— Hernán Cortés, letter to Emperor Charles V of Spain, 1522

Copyright © McGraw Hill   Cortes, Fernando (Hernán Cortés), Fernando Cortes: His Five Letters of Relation to the Emperor Charles V, Volume 1, by Francis Augustus MacNutt. Cleveland: The Arthur H. Clark Company, 1962.

procurator a person authorized to act on behalf of another

supplicate to ask for or to beg

vassal servant

rodela a shield or buckle that is round

Need Extra Help?

You may find reading this passage especially difficult. After all, the language used in the 1500s was very different than language used today. To better understand the passage, look at each sentence one at a time to determine its meaning. Some words in the passage are already defined. Use a print or online dictionary to look up any other words that you do not understand. Use your own words to paraphrase what you think the sentence means. Once you have paraphrased all the sentences in the passage, you should have a better idea of the passage's meaning.

Some historians believe that this feathered, golden headdress was given to Cortés by Aztec ruler Montezuma.

EXAMINE THE SOURCE

18. **Identifying** Which words or phrases from the first sentence help support the meaning of the word *supplicate*? What tone does the author create by choosing to include these words? Why?

19. **Making Connections** Explain the relationship that Cortés had with Charles V and the relationship that Cortés felt that he had with the Aztec people.

20. **Inferring** What do you think happened to the indigenous people that Cortés conquered?

Evaluate Sources and Use Evidence

21. Citing Text Evidence Review the Supporting Questions you developed at the beginning of the topic and the evidence you gathered and recorded in the Graphic Organizer. Which sources will help you answer the Supporting Questions? Circle or highlight those sources in your Graphic Organizer. Looking at the subset of sources you have chosen, be prepared to explain why you chose each source.

	Supporting Question	Primary Source and Notes
1		
2		
3		

22. Directions: Now, answer the Supporting Questions that you developed at the beginning of the activity to help guide you in answering the Compelling Question.

Answer for Supporting Question 1:

Answer for Supporting Question 2:

Answer for Supporting Question 3:

Communicate Conclusions

Talk About It

23. Collaborating Work in a group of six students. Have three students take on the role of explorers. The other three students should play the role of the explorers' friends or family. Then imagine that you are a group of Europeans deciding whether to set out to explore the Americas. The explorers should point out the rewards. The explorers' friends and family should make everyone aware of the risks and effects. Next, have one person from each group share his or her arguments with the class. Then, take a class vote to see whether the exploration should proceed.

Write About It

24. <u>Informative Writing</u> Choose two sources that you recorded in the graphic organizer that helped you answer the Supporting Questions you developed. Then write a few paragraphs comparing and contrasting those two sources. Be sure to include information on how the historical background and arguments for exploration are similar or different in these sources.

25. <u>Answering the Compelling Question</u> What do you think were the rewards, dangers, and effects of exploration? Make a list of rewards of early exploration and a list of dangers. Refer to the sources and your notes about them as you create your two lists. Then, create a digital presentation that describes the rewards and dangers of exploration. Be sure to cite at least two sources. Add images and music to your presentation to add interest.

Challenge

Conduct research to find out more about three Europeans not mentioned who explored the Americas. Focus your research on the following: dates and places of exploration, sponsor, reasons for exploration, dangers encountered, rewards of exploration, and consequences of exploration. Then create a chart that describes your findings about each explorer you researched.

26. Making Connections Early explorers had to judge whether the rewards of making sea expeditions were worth the dangers. Today, there is little unknown land left on Earth to explore. However, there are other new frontiers, such as space and the deep sea, that continue to be explored. Think about these questions: Why do countries today want to explore the unknown? What are the rewards of modern-day explorations? What risks are involved? Conduct research to find out more about either space or deep-sea exploration to answer these questions. Then decide whether you support or oppose future exploration. Be sure to think of at least three reasons to support your position. Make a detailed outline that tells how you might defend your position in writing.

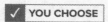 **YOU CHOOSE**

Select one of these Take Informed Action products to apply what you've learned.

A. Write a letter to a government official explaining whether you think space or deep-sea exploration should continue and why you think this.

B. Write an article for a school newsletter that explains your position on future exploration.

C. Create a podcast that argues for or against future exploration.

Take Informed Action Rubric: Detailed Outline

Self-Evaluation As you defend your position on future exploration, think about the following criteria. These are the criteria your teacher will use to evaluate your Take Informed Action activity.

Peer Review Use this rubric to grade the outline and final product developed by another classmate or group of classmates.

	Organization	Historical Accuracy	Logic	Writing/Editing
4	The outline is extremely well-organized as is the final product.	The final product shows clear evidence of research.	Extreme thought was put into the defense of the position taken.	The final product is exceptionally well-written and includes no errors.
3	The outline is well-organized, as is the written product.	The final product shows evidence of research.	Sufficient thought was put into the defense of the position taken.	The final product is well-written and includes few errors.
2	The outline and the written product are somewhat organized.	The final product shows some evidence of research.	Limited thought was put into the defense of the position taken.	The final product is adequately written and includes a number of errors.
1	Neither the outline nor the written product are organized.	The final product does not show evidence of research.	Little thought was put into the defense of the position taken.	The final product is not well-written and includes multiple errors.
SCORE				

TOPIC 3 • ENGLISH COLONIES ARE SETTLED AND GROW, 1607–1754

Freedoms and Democracy in Colonial America

 COMPELLING QUESTION

Was colonial America a free society?

Plan Your Inquiry

In this Inquiry Activity, you will develop Supporting Questions about democratic principles in early colonial America and whether they were intended for everyone living in or near the colonies based on the Compelling Question, and examine primary sources. Finally, you will answer your Supporting Questions, communicate your research conclusions, and take action based on what you've learned.

Background Information

In 1620 the *Mayflower* left Plymouth, England, headed for North America. The passengers on board were Protestant Separatists, and they wanted a new life away from England. They had permission to set up a colony between what is today the Chesapeake Bay and the Hudson River. There these Pilgrims hoped to live a peaceful life practicing the religion of their choice. However, because of rough weather the *Mayflower* ran off course, and the ship landed closer to what is today Cape Cod. The group forged ahead and named their colony Plymouth.

Soon more colonists came to North America. Puritans founded the Massachusetts Bay Colony in 1630. The colony grew to be large and successful. However, disagreements over religious beliefs forced members of the colony to leave. This included Roger Williams who later founded Rhode Island.

Plymouth, the Massachusetts Bay Colony, and Rhode Island were not the first settlements by the English. Years before, in 1607, the English had settled in Jamestown, Virginia. Leaders in all of these early colonies set up plans for government. They wrote documents that conveyed the freedoms and democratic principles the colonists were to abide by. Democratic principles include rule by the people, free and fair elections, all people being bound by the same laws, and the government's obligation to keep its citizens informed. However, these freedoms were not intended to include everyone living in or near the colony. Native Americans and enslaved African Americans were not treated the same as white male settlers.

Residents of colonial towns used meeting houses for religious, political, and social reasons. Some of these meeting houses, such as this one in Williamsburg, Virginia, are still standing today.

Develop Supporting Questions about Democratic Principles in Colonial America

 COMPELLING QUESTION

Was colonial America a free society?

Talk About It

Discuss with a partner what type of information you would need to know to answer this question. For example, one question might be: Were all people in colonial America treated in the same way?

Directions: Write down three additional questions that you need to answer to be able to determine whether colonial America was a free society.

Supporting Question 1:

Supporting Question 2:

Supporting Question 3:

Apply Historical Concepts and Tools

Directions: As you read and work with primary sources, use the graphic organizer to take notes and organize information.

	Organizing Source Information	
Source	**Title and Author/ Creator**	**Notes**
A	Mayflower Compact	
B	Fundamental Orders of 1639	
C	A *Plea for Religious Liberty* by Roger Williams	
D	An Ordinance and Constitution of the Virginia Company in England	
E	A Proposal for Subjugating the Indians, December 15, 1622 by John Martin	

Analyze Sources

Review and analyze Sources A–E. There are questions that accompany each source to help you examine the source and check for historical understanding.

Mayflower Compact

In November of 1620, just before landing at Plymouth, Massachusetts, adult male passengers on the *Mayflower* signed the Mayflower Compact. The document was created out of necessity because the original charter for the colony was to have been closer to the Hudson River. Instead, the passengers found themselves near Cape Cod. With no real legal status and the threat of arguments erupting onboard, Pilgrim leaders wrote a plan for government for the colony. The document is considered the first written constitution in the Americas and established the idea of self-government and consent of the people.

More settlers soon came to what is today Plymouth County. In 1635, a group of Puritans built a settlement called Hingham. They built a meeting house soon after their arrival that was later replaced by one built in 1681 that still stands today. This meeting house, called the Old Ship Church, was used to discuss civic issues and as a place of worship on Sundays.

PRIMARY SOURCE : DOCUMENT

66 IN THE NAME OF GOD, AMEN. We, whose names are underwritten, the Loyal Subjects of our dread **Sovereign** Lord King James, by the Grace of God, of Great Britain, France, and Ireland, King, Defender of the Faith, &c. Having undertaken for the Glory of God, and Advancement of the Christian Faith, and the Honour of our King and Country, a Voyage to plant the first Colony in the northern Parts of Virginia; Do by these Presents, solemnly and mutually, in the Presence of God and one another, **covenant** and combine ourselves together into a civil Body Politick, for our better Ordering and Preservation, and Furtherance of the Ends aforesaid: And by Virtue hereof do enact, constitute, and frame, such just and equal Laws, Ordinances, Acts, Constitutions, and Officers, from time to time, as shall be thought most meet and convenient for the general Good of the Colony; unto which we promise all due Submission and Obedience... 99

— male settlers at Plymouth, the Mayflower Compact, 1620

The Old Ship Church is a colonial meeting house established by Puritans that still stands in Hingham, Massachusetts.

Sovereign a supreme ruler

covenant to promise by a binding agreement

1. **Explaining** Why does the Mayflower Compact include the word *covenant*?

2. **Identifying** To whom were the signers declaring their loyalties?

3. **Describing** What were the signers agreeing to in the Mayflower Compact?

4. **Identifying** What do you notice about the people who signed the Mayflower Compact? What might this indicate about the role of women during early colonial America?

5. **Citing Text Evidence** What is shown in the photograph of the Old Ship Church? What democratic principles does the photo illustrate?

6. **Analyzing** How does this document demonstrate democratic principles?

B

Fundamental Orders of 1639

In 1638 Reverend Thomas Hooker, a Puritan leader and the founder of Connecticut, explained in a sermon that government authority should rest with the people. He believed that God allowed the people the right to choose their leaders and to set limits on their authority. Hooker's idea was not something Puritans had heard before. Most ideas in their lives came from the Bible or the monarchs and other rulers. However, the idea interested other Puritan leaders. These leaders were from the towns of Hartford, Windsor, and Wethersfield in the Connecticut colony. They created a document based on Hooker's ideas. It had a preamble, which is an introduction that explains the document's purpose, and 11 orders, or laws, that established the right of the people to create a government they would live by. The freemen, or white, land-owning men, of the towns agreed to the document.

PRIMARY SOURCE : LAW

66 Forasmuch as it hath pleased Almighty God by the wise **disposition** of his divine **providence** so to order and dispose of things that we the Inhabitants and Residents of Windsor, Hartford and Wethersfield are now cohabiting and dwelling in and upon the River of Connectecotte and the lands thereunto adjoining; and well knowing where a people are gathered together the word of God requires that to maintain the peace and union of such a people there should be an orderly and decent Government established according to God, to order and dispose of the affairs of the people at all seasons as occasion shall require; do therefore associate and conjoin ourselves to be as one Public State or Commonwealth;. . . .

4. It is Ordered, sentenced, and decreed, that no person be chosen Governor above once in two years, and that the Governor be always a member of some approved Congregation, and formerly of the Magistracy within this Jurisdiction; . . . .

In which Court the Governor or Moderator shall have power to order the Court, to give liberty of speech, and silence **unseasonable** and disorderly speakings, to put all things to vote, and in case the vote be equal to have the casting vote. But none of these Courts shall be adjourned or dissolved without the consent of the major part of the Court.

11. It is Ordered, sentenced, and decreed, that when any General Court upon the occasions of the Commonwealth have agreed upon any sum, or sums of money to be **levied** upon the several Towns within this Jurisdiction, that a committee be chosen to set out and appoint what shall be the proportion of every Town to pay of the said **levy**, provided the committee be made up of an equal number out of each Town. 99

— Fundamental Orders of 1639

disposition character	**unseasonable** happening at an inopportune time
providence fate	**levied** imposed; charged
	levy a tax

7. Identifying What did the preamble of the Fundamental Orders of 1639 create? Who did the residents of Connecticut believe they were following by creating this?

8. Drawing Conclusions What rule is stated concerning the colony's leadership? Why might leaders have included this rule?

9. Analyzing What right is established by the 11th Fundamental Order? Use words from the document in your answer.

10. Making Generalizations According to the Fundamental Orders of 1639, what did the people of colonial Connecticut believe about government?

11. Making Connections How is the document the Fundamental Orders of 1639 similar to and different from the Mayflower Compact? How do these documents show change and continuity?

C

A Plea for Religious Liberty

Roger Williams was a religious leader who was banished from the Massachusetts Bay Colony. Leaders in that colony did not approve of his views on religious freedom. They also did not like his idea that magistrates, or officials who carry out the law, had no right to be involved in religious matters. Upon leaving Massachusetts Bay, Williams headed to Providence and founded the colony of Rhode Island. The colony welcomed people who followed religions that were not welcomed in other colonies, such as Anabaptists and Quakers. Williams supported religious tolerance, but he believed that Protestantism as preached by theologians like John Calvin, John Cotton, and Theodore Beza (all of whom are referenced in the following excerpt) was the only true religion. In 1644, while he was in England obtaining a charter for his colony, he wrote this work.

PRIMARY SOURCE : BOOK

66 First. That the blood of so many hundred thousand souls of protestants and **papists**, spilt in the wars of present and former ages, for their respective consciences, is not required nor accepted by Jesus Christ the Prince of Peace.

Secondly. **Pregnant** scriptures and arguments are throughout the work proposed against the doctrine of persecution for cause of conscience.

Thirdly. Satisfactory answers are given to scriptures and objections produced by Mr. Calvin, Beza, Mr. Cotton, and the ministers of the New English churches, and others former and later, tending to prove the doctrine of persecution for cause of conscience.

Fourthly. The doctrine of persecution for cause of conscience, is proved guilty of all the blood of the souls crying for vengeance under the altar.

Fifthly. All civil states, with their officers of justice, in their respective constitutions and administrations, are proved essentially civil, and therefore not judges, governors, or defenders of the spiritual, or Christian, state and worship. 99

— Roger Williams, *A Plea for Religious Liberty,* 1644

papists Roman Catholics

Pregnant full of meaning; significant

12. Identifying What point does the author make about religious wars? Why is this an important point?

13. Explaining Why does the author include references to scriptures, Calvin, Beza, Cotton, and New English church ministers?

14. Making Inferences The author uses the phrase "persecution for cause of conscience" several times. Why might he include this phrase so often?

15. Interpreting What argument does the author make related to keeping the government out of issues that have to do with religion?

D

An Ordinance and Constitution of the Treasurer Council, and Company in England, for a Council of State and General Assembly

The first House of Burgesses in Virginia met in 1619. This group passed laws to better serve the people from the colony including the different geographic areas its members represented. The early lawmaking group was unicameral, or made up of one body, and it was a self-governing body. It paved the way for a self-governing assembly in Virginia. However, the group disbanded after six days. Then in 1621 the Virginia Company of London issued a new ordinance. The government's legislature would be bicameral, or made up of two bodies. The lower house would be the General Assembly, or House of Burgesses. The upper house would be the governor and his Council. The lower house is described in this excerpt.

SECONDARY SOURCE : LAW

❝ The other Council, more generally to be called by the Governor, once yearly, and no oftener, but for very extraordinary and important occasions, shall consist for the present, of the said Council of State, and of two **Burgesses** out of every Town, **Hundred**, or other particular Plantation, to be respectively chosen by the inhabitants: Which Council shall be called THE GENERAL ASSEMBLY, wherein (as also in the said Council of State) all Matters shall be decided, determined, and ordered by the greater Part of the Voices then present; reserving to the Governor always a Negative Voice. And this General Assembly shall have free power, to treat, consult, and conclude, as well of all emergent Occasions concerning the Publick **Weal** of the said Colony and every Part thereof, as also to make, ordain, and enact such general Laws and Orders, for the **Behoof** of the said Colony, and the good Government thereof, as shall, from time to time, appear necessary or requisite; ❞

— An Ordinance and Constitution of the Virginia Company in England, July 24, 1621

Burgesses inhabitants of a town; representatives of a town

Hundred a subdivision of a county

Weal well-being

Behoof advantage or benefit

Copyright © McGraw-Hill Thorpe, Francis Newton, ed. The Federal and State Constitutions, Colonial Charters, and Other Organic Laws of the States, Territories, and Colonies, Now or Heretofore Forming the United States of America. Vol. 7. Washington: U.S. Government Printing Office, 1909.

16. Identifying Who made up the General Assembly, referenced as the "other council" in the excerpt, and how were its members chosen? How often did it meet?

17. Summarizing What was the purpose of the council?

18. Analyzing How does this law reflect democratic principles?

19. Making Connections Which document, the Fundamental Orders of 1639 or the Mayflower Compact, is this law most like? Why?

E

A Proposal for Subjugating the Indians, 1622

Long before colonists settled in Jamestown, for more than 12,000 years, the Powhatan people lived near the eastern part of the Chesapeake Bay in what is now part of Virginia. They became known as the Powhatan Confederacy, which was made up of about 30 tribes. This alliance was formed by a chief known as Powhatan. The Powhatan grew many crops including maize, melons, beans, and vegetables. From the earliest days of colonial settlement in Virginia, relations between settlers and Native Americans were difficult and uneasy. In 1622 after years of struggles between settlers and Native Americans in Virginia, Opechancanough (spelled "Opichankanoe" in the excerpt below), the Native American leader who succeeded Powhatan, attacked the Jamestown colony, which encroached on the land that Native Americans used for hunting and farming. More than 340 colonists working on plantations and in other areas along the James River were killed. People began to fear more Native American attacks. This led to the creation of documents suggesting ways to defend against the Native American population.

PRIMARY SOURCE : DOCUMENT

Printing Office, 1906, 1953.

Copyright © McGraw Hill   Martin, John. "The Manner Howe to Bringe the Indians Into Subjection, December 15, 1622," in Virginia Company Of London, and Library Of Congress, The Records of the Virginia Company of London, edited by Susan Myra Kingsbury. Washington: U.S. Government

66 The manner howe to bringe in the Indians into [**subjection**] wthout makinge an vtter **exterpation** of them together wth the reasons.

First By disablinge the mayne bodie of the Enemye from haueinge the **Sinnewes** of all expediccons. As namely Corne and all manner of **victualls** of anye worth.

This is to be acted two manner of wayes.

ffirst by keepeinge them from setteing Corne at home and fishinge.

Secondly by keepeinge them from their accustomed tradinge for Corne.

For The first it is pformed by haueinge some 200 Souldiers on foote, Contynuallie harrowinge and burneinge all their Townes in wynter, and spoileinge their weares. By this meanes or people seacurely may followe their worke. And yet not to be negligent in keepeinge watch.

For the seacond there must provided some 10 **Shallopps**, that in May, June, Julye and August may scoure the Baye and keepe the Rivers yt are belonginge to Opichankanoe. . . .

Reasons why it is not fittinge vtterly to make an exterpation of the Sauages yett. . . .

Holy writt sayeth . . . not to vtterly distroy the heathen, least [lest] the woods and wilde beasts should ouer runn them

My owne observaccon hath bene such as assureth me yt if the Indians inhabitt not amongst vs vnder obedience And as they haue ever kept downe ye woods and slayne the wolues, beares, and other beasts . . . we shalbe more opressed in short tyme by their absence, then in their liueing by vs both for or owne securitie as allso for or Cattle. 99

— John Martin, A Proposal for Subjugating the Indians, December 15, 1622

Need Extra Help?

You may find reading this passage difficult because of the language and spellings. Many words are spelled in a way that is different from what you are used to. Reread each sentence aloud one at a time. Notice any unfamiliar words. Ask yourself: Does this word look like a word I know? If so, identify its meaning and use it in the sentence. Also, you can use other words around a confusing word to help figure it out. If that doesn't work, use a print or online dictionary to help you.

subjection the act of forcing another person or group to be controlled

exterpation **(extirpation)** the act of elimination

Sinnewes **(sinews)** the parts of a thing that bind it together

victualls food

Shallopps ships

EXAMINE THE SOURCE

20. Explaining What is John Martin's proposed plan for subjugating Native Americans?

21. Explaining Why doesn't Martin want to fully destroy the Native Americans?

22. Drawing Conclusions What can you conclude about the motivations of these colonists?

Evaluate Sources and Use Evidence

23. <u>Citing Text Evidence</u> Review the Supporting Questions you developed at the beginning of the topic and the evidence you gathered and recorded in the Graphic Organizer. Which sources will help you answer the Supporting Questions? Circle or highlight those sources in your Graphic Organizer. Looking at the subset of sources you have chosen, be prepared to explain why you chose each source.

	Supporting Question	Primary Source and Notes
1		
2		
3		

Challenge

The selected primary sources touch on only some aspects of people's rights and freedoms in early colonial America. Conduct research to find out more about early colonial governments and the freedoms enjoyed by some groups or denied to other groups. Look for primary and secondary sources that help answer one or more of your Supporting Questions. Include your research by citing articles and books in your response.

24. Directions: Now, answer the Supporting Questions that you developed at the beginning of the activity to help guide you in answering the Compelling Question.

Answer for Supporting Question 1:

Answer for Supporting Question 2:

Answer for Supporting Question 3:

Communicate Conclusions

Talk About It

25. Collaborating Work in a small group. On a large sheet of paper, draw a concept web with a center oval and six surrounding ovals. Write the Compelling Question in the center oval. Take turns adding source evidence that helps answer the question. As you write your evidence, explain why it helps to answer the question. Continue taking turns until everyone has had at least two turns. Then, as a group, identify the three most helpful pieces of evidence from your concept web. Discuss how these sources help answer the Compelling Question. Share your conclusions with the class.

Write About It

26. Informative Writing Choose two or three sources you recorded in the graphic organizer that helped you best answer your Supporting Questions. Prepare a multimedia presentation in which you summarize the content and identify the most significant facts that answer your Supporting Questions. Be sure to incorporate key facts and ideas from the sources as well as from the background information about each source.

27. Answering the Compelling Question What do you think? Was colonial America a free society? In this case, the question cannot be answered with a simple yes or no response. Of course, the colonies were not a completely free society, but colonists did try for some degree of democracy. Write a three-paragraph essay that provides examples of how colonists intended to apply the principles of democracy and ways they failed at doing this. Be sure to include evidence from the various sources in your writing.

Take Informed Action

28. Making Connections People living in early colonial America set up governments according to their beliefs and needs. They included only certain groups in the establishing of laws, and some of those laws did not protect all groups. Some people enjoyed more freedom than others. Today, laws are designed to be fair for all people regardless of race, gender, age, and religion. But do laws give people all the freedoms they want or need? In his State of the Union message in 1941, President Franklin D. Roosevelt said that Americans have four basic freedoms—freedom of speech, freedom of religion, freedom from want, and freedom from fear. Think about how these freedoms affect you today. In a chart, define and write examples of each type of freedom mentioned by President Roosevelt. Then think about an issue today in which you believe one of those freedoms is being violated or not protected. Write one or two sentences explaining your reasoning.

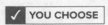 **YOU CHOOSE**

Select one of these Take Informed Action products to apply what you've learned.

A. Create a poster in which you provide drawings and/or messages that represent the freedom you chose as most important.

B. Publish a blog in which you share the facts and opinions related to the freedom you feel is most important and explain how it affects you.

C. Write a letter to a government official about what the government should do to ensure all people have the freedom you feel is most important.

Take Informed Action Rubric: Example Chart and Sentences

Self-Evaluation As you complete your fact and opinion chart and sentences, think about the following criteria. These are the criteria your teacher will use to evaluate your Take Informed Action activity.

Peer Review Use this rubric to grade the fact and opinion chart, sentences, and final product developed by another classmate or group of classmates.

	Organization	Historical Accuracy	Writing/Editing	Logic
4	The chart, sentences, and final product are exceptionally well-organized and show a thorough understanding related to the freedoms.	The chart provides strong examples, and the sentences and final product present a clear issue and strong reasons for how the freedom is being violated.	The examples, sentences, and final product are exceptionally well-written and include no errors.	The chart and reasons for how the freedom is being violated show evidence of extensive thought.
3	The chart, sentences, and final product are well-organized and show an adequate understanding related to the freedoms.	The chart provides adequate examples, and the sentences and final product present an adequate issue and reasons for how the freedom is being violated.	The examples, sentences, and final product are well-written and include few errors.	The chart and reasons for how the freedom is being violated show sufficient evidence of thought.
2	The chart, sentences, and final product are organized and show little understanding related to the freedoms.	The chart somewhat provides examples but contains some mistakes, and the sentences and final product present a weak issue and limited reasons for how the freedom is being violated.	The examples, sentences, and final product are adequately written but include a number of errors.	The chart and reasons for how the freedom is being violated show limited evidence of thought.
1	The chart, sentences, and final product lack organization and a basic understanding related to the freedoms.	The chart does not provide examples, and there are no sentences or product related to an issue and how the freedom is being violated.	The examples, sentences, and final product are not well-written and include multiple errors.	The chart and sentences show a lack of thought.
SCORE				

Copyright © McGraw Hill

TOPIC 4 • THE AMERICAN REVOLUTION, 1754–1782

Propaganda in the American Revolution

 COMPELLING QUESTION

How is propaganda used to further a cause?

Plan Your Inquiry

In this Inquiry Activity, you will develop Supporting Questions about propaganda from the Patriots and Loyalists based on the Compelling Question and examine primary sources. Finally, you will answer your Supporting Questions, communicate your research conclusions, and take action based on what you've learned.

Background Information

At first, the colonies operated fairly free of British control. Then the British began to tax the colonists to pay for the French and Indian War they had won in 1763. The taxes angered the colonists because they did not have representation in Britain's government. Some colonists, called Patriots, realized that only through fighting would they gain freedom from Britain. Colonists who still supported the British became known as Loyalists.

Both sides relied on propaganda, or biased information used to influence public opinion, to gain support. For example, the Patriots relied on speeches and printed materials to convince others of the need for liberty. They provided facts to appeal to the logic, or reasoning, of colonists. They also carefully used language to appeal to the colonists' emotions and moral beliefs. Because of this, many colonists became convinced of the need to fight for freedom.

In 1775, the first fights of the American Revolution took place. On July 4, 1776, the Declaration of Independence was approved. A turning point in the war came when colonists won the Battle of Saratoga. The British finally surrendered after a loss in the Battle of Yorktown in 1881. Signed in 1883, the Treaty of Paris made the United States an independent nation.

The first battles of the American Revolution occurred in Massachusetts at Lexington and Concord in 1775. This illustration shows Minutemen heading out for the Battle of Concord. Minutemen are Patriot colonists who formed militias to fight the British.

Develop Supporting Questions About Propaganda in the American Revolution

? COMPELLING QUESTION

How is propaganda used to further a cause?

Talk About It

Discuss with a partner what type of information you would need to know to answer this question. For example, one question might be the following: What is the purpose of propaganda?

Directions: Write down three additional questions that you need to answer to be able to determine how propaganda was used to further a cause during the American Revolution.

Supporting Question 1:

Supporting Question 2:

Supporting Question 3:

Apply Historical Concepts and Tools

Directions: As you read and work with primary sources, use the graphic organizer to take notes and organize information.

	Organizing Source Information	
Source	**Title and Author/ Creator**	**Notes**
A	"The American Crisis" by Thomas Paine	
B	Bloody Butchery by the British Troops Broadside	
C	Join or Die Cartoon under Newspaper Masthead by Paul Revere	
D	"The Glorious Seventy Four" Song	
E	"The Rebels" Song by Captain John Smyth	

Analyze Sources

Review and analyze Sources A–E. There are questions that accompany each source to help you examine the source and check for historical understanding.

"The American Crisis"

Patriot Thomas Paine proved to be a master at writing propaganda meant to inspire revolution. He is especially remembered for his pamphlet *Common Sense*, which asked colonists to fight for their beliefs. Soon after publishing *Common Sense* in 1776, Paine joined the Continental Army led by General George Washington. Washington's troops, including Paine, spent a harsh winter camped out at Valley Forge in Pennsylvania, after suffering major defeats led by British General William Howe. Paine's experience there led him to write "The American Crisis." This series of pamphlets was meant to convince others to take up arms for freedom. General Washington, touched by the language used, ordered the pamphlet to be recited aloud to his soldiers.

PRIMARY SOURCE : PAMPHLET

> 66 THESE are the times that try men's souls: The summer soldier and the sunshine patriot will, in this crisis, shrink from the service of his country; but he that stands it NOW, deserves the love and thanks of man and woman. **Tyranny**, like hell, is not easily conquered; yet we have this consolation with us, that the harder the conflict, the more glorious the triumph. What we obtain, too cheap, we esteem too lightly:—'Tis dearness only that gives every thing its value. Heaven knows how to set a proper price upon its goods; and it would be strange indeed, if so **celestial** an article as FREEDOM should not be highly rated. Britain, with an army to enforce her tyranny, has declared, that she has a right (not only to TAX) but "to BIND us in ALL CASES WHATSOEVER," and if being *bound in that manner* is not slavery, then is there not such a thing as slavery upon earth. Even the expression is **impious**, for so unlimited a power can belong only to GOD.
>
> Whether the Independence of the Continent was declared too soon, or delayed too long, I will not now enter into as an argument; my own simple opinion is, that had it been eight months earlier, it would have been much better. We did not make a proper use of last winter, neither could we, while we were in a dependent state. However, the fault, if it were one, was all our own; we have none to blame but ourselves. But no great deal is lost yet; all that Howe has been doing for this month past is rather a **ravage** than a conquest, which the spirit of the **Jersies** a year ago would have quickly repulsed, and which time and a little resolution with soon recover. 99

—Thomas Paine, "The American Crisis," December 1776

tyranny oppressive or cruel rule	**ravage** a destructive action
celestial heavenly	**Jersies** the royal colony of New Jersey, which was divided into East and West Jersey prior to 1702
impious not showing respect	

1. Explaining What does the author mean by the words "These are the times that try men's souls"? How might these words have made the audience feel?

2. Making Inferences What is implied by the terms "summer soldier" and "sunshine patriot"?

3. Identifying Paine says, "he that stands it NOW, deserves the love and thanks of man and woman." Does this appeal to the reader's emotions, logic, or moral beliefs? Explain your reasoning.

4. Analyzing Paine says, "the harder the conflict, the more glorious the triumph." What does he compare to illustrate his point? Why is this comparison persuasive?

5. Drawing Conclusions To what does Paine compare taxation without representation? Why do you think he does this?

6. Identifying the Main Idea What is the main idea of the second paragraph? Why do you think Paine makes these statements?

B

Bloody Butchery by the British Troops

Patriots used images as well as words to get their points across. The American militia faced British troops on April 19, 1775, at the Battle of Concord. The battle was the result of an order by Thomas Gage, the royal governor of Massachusetts, to seize the colonists' supply of weapons at Concord in an effort to put an end to the American rebellion. The British force was met by local militia who had been warned of the British attack and fought back fiercely. This battle, along with the Battle of Lexington that preceded it, marked the start of the American Revolution.

This broadside, or document similar to a poster, provided a record of what happened at the battle. It was also designed to increase colonial hatred toward the British through its dramatic language and imagery. For example, the coffins at the top of the broadside represented the Patriots killed in the battle. The names of the soldiers are written above the coffins. The broadside was likely posted in taverns and other places where many people gathered.

PRIMARY SOURCE : BROADSIDE

EXAMINE THE SOURCE

7. **Analyzing Perspectives** Who is the intended audience for this document, and how did the creators of the document hope it would influence that audience?

8. Interpreting How do you think the colonists most likely felt when they viewed this document? What words and graphics likely heightened their emotions?

9. Analyzing What perspective is missing from this document? Why do you think it is missing?

Need Extra Help?

To better understand what is missing, try answering the following questions first: Who took part in the battle? What might each side have said about the battle?

10. Drawing Conclusions Suppose a Loyalist saw this document. Do you think it might persuade the person to change his or her sympathies and become a Patriot? Explain your reasoning.

C

Join or Die

Colonial newspapers helped spread American patriotism through the news, opinions, and images they chose to print. One such early newspaper was *The Massachusetts Spy*, which started in 1770 by printer Isaiah Thomas. Notice that the portion of the issue shown here includes a cartoon rattlesnake. This particular image is an engraving made by the Patriot Paul Revere in 1774. However, the idea for the cartoon came from another Patriot. Benjamin Franklin first used the now-famous Join or Die cartoon in his own Pennsylvania newspaper in 1754. His goal was to encourage the colonies to join together to help prevent the French from gaining more land in North America. Despite Franklin's efforts, the colonies did not join together at that time. Later, Franklin used the same cartoon to convince colonists to unite to protest the Stamp Act, a British attempt to tax the colonists. By the time this issue of *The Massachusetts Spy* was printed, the cartoon had a new purpose. It was meant to show that the colonies had no choice but to unite to gain freedom from Britain.

PRIMARY SOURCE : NEWSPAPER

EXAMINE THE SOURCE

11. **Analyzing Visuals** Describe the images that appear on the newspaper masthead and front page. What is the significance of these images? Why might they have been included?

Need Extra Help?

To better understand the meaning of the images, think about what you already know about the following: a woman holding a torch (such as the Statue of Liberty), dragons, and rattlesnakes. Use your prior knowledge to tell why each image is significant and might have been included.

12. Interpreting What was the likely impact of the words "Join or Die"?

13. Making Connections How does knowing that the Join or Die cartoon was used other times in the colonies affect its use as a source of propaganda?

14. Speculating How might this newspaper masthead have influenced the opinions of a sympathetic Patriot audience? What about a critical Loyalist audience?

"The Glorious Seventy Four"

"The Glorious Seventy Four" was one of many protest, or liberty, songs that appeared in the American colonies. These songs were used to unite and inspire colonists in their opposition to British rule. The songwriter is unknown. However, historians believe the song was first sung in the Virginia colony in 1774. The words to the song were original, but the tune was borrowed. It comes from an existing British song celebrating the British navy. The tune would have been very familiar to a colonial audience. The song also features the line "Their tea still is driven away from our shores." This is a reference to the Boston Tea Party of 1773. In Boston, some colonists protested a British tax on tea by dumping chests of it into the harbor.

PRIMARY SOURCE : SONG

> Come, come, my brave boys, from my song you shall hear,
> That we'll crown seventy four a most glorious year;
> We'll convince **Bute and Mansfield, and North**, though they rave,
> Britons still, like themselves, **spurn** the chains of a slave.
> CHORUS:
> Hearts of oak were our **sires**,
> Hearts of oak are their sons,
> Like them we are ready, as firm and as steady,
> To fight for our freedom with swords and with guns.
>
> . . . Their tea still is driven away from our shores,
> Or presented to Neptune, or rots in our stores;
> But to awe, to divide, till we crouch to their sway,
> On brave Boston their **vengeance** they fiercely display.
> CHORUS:
> Hearts of oak, etc.
>
> Now, unasked we unite, we agree to a man,
> See our **stores** flow to Boston from rear and from van;
> Hark! the shout, how it flies, freedom's voice, how it sounds!
> From each country, each **clime**, hark, the echo rebounds!
> CHORUS:
> Hearts of oak, etc.
>
> . . . With sons, who I foster'd and cherish'd of yore,
> Fair freedom shall flourish till time is no more;
> No tyrant shall rule them, 'tis Heaven's decree;
> They shall never be slaves while they dare to be free.
> CHORUS:
> Hearts of oak, etc. "

— Anonymous, 1774

Bute and Mansfield, and North British leaders who endorsed policies disliked by colonists

spurn to turn away, reject

sires fathers

vengeance action in response to an injury or a wrong; revenge

stores supplies kept for future use

clime a region known for its climate

15. **Identifying Cause and Effect** Think about patriotic songs you know and how you react when you sing them with others. Now imagine "The Glorious Seventy Four" being sung to a familiar tune. What might have been the effect of the song on the colonists?

16. **Analyzing** What is meant by the phrase "hearts of oak"? Why do you think the author repeats this phrase in the chorus to describe fathers and sons?

17. **Interpreting** What do you think is the likely reason the author includes the phrase "Now, unasked we unite, we agree to a man"?

18. **Citing Text Evidence** What lines from the song make a claim about an authority that relates to liberty for the colonies? How might these words have affected listeners?

19. **Making Connections** This song was written before the American Revolution. Suppose a colonist heard it for the first time after the actual fighting began. What actions and place would the song bring to mind, and how might these references influence listeners?

E

"The Rebels"

The Patriots were not the only ones to spread propaganda through song before and during the American Revolution. This Loyalist song was composed by Captain John Smyth, a member of a group of American soldiers who supported the British cause. This group, first called Rogers's Rangers and then Simcoe's Rangers, fought alongside British soldiers in both the French and Indian War and the American Revolution. Unlike many American military groups of the Revolution, Simcoe's Rangers had become Loyalists and were willing to risk their lives for the British cause.

PRIMARY SOURCE : SONG

" YE brave, honest subjects, who dare to be loyal,
And have stood the brunt of every trial,
 Of hunting-shirts, and rifle-guns:
Come listen awhile, and I'll sing you a song;
I'll show you, those **Yankees** are all in the wrong,
Who, with blustering look and most awkward gait,
'Gainst their lawful sovereign dare for to **prate**,
 With their hunting-shirts, and rifle-guns.

The arch-rebels, barefooted **tatterdemalions**,
In baseness exceed all other rebellions,
 With their hunting-shirts, and rifle-guns.
To **rend** the empire, the most **infamous** lies,
Their mock-patriot Congress, do always devise;
Independence, like the first of rebels, they claim,
But their plots will be damn'd in the **annals** of fame,
 With their hunting-shirts, and rifle-guns.

. . . Come take up your glasses, each true loyal heart,
And may every rebel meet his due desert,
 With his hunting-shirt, and rifle-gun.
May Congress, Conventions, those damn'd **inquisitions**,
Be fed with hot sulphur, from **Lucifer's kitchens**,
May commerce and peace again be restored,
And Americans own their true sovereign lord.
 Then **oblivion** to shirts, and rifle-guns.
 God save the King. "

— Captain John Smyth, *Pennsylvania Ledger*, 1778

Yankees a term used by the British to insult American colonists

prate to talk foolishly and for a long time

tatterdemalion a person wearing old and torn clothing

rend to tear apart

infamous having a bad reputation

annals a record of events

inquisition an official investigation with questions that are unfriendly in nature

Lucifer's kitchens hell

oblivion the act of dying out

20. Describing How does the author describe the Patriots?

21. Analyzing How might the author's use of name-calling affect listeners?

22. Interpreting The author repeats the line "With their hunting-shirts, and rifle-guns" several times. What might be the reason for this? Why might he have varied the line near the end of the song?

23. Drawing Conclusions The author says, "May Congress, Conventions, those damn'd inquisitions, Be fed with hot sulphur, from Lucifer's kitchens." What do you think the author wanted to persuade the listener to think?

Evaluate Sources and Use Evidence

24. Citing Text Evidence Review the Supporting Questions you developed at the beginning of the topic and the evidence you gathered and recorded in the graphic organizer. Which sources will help you answer the Supporting Questions? Circle or highlight those sources in your graphic organizer. Looking at the subset of sources you have chosen, be prepared to explain why you chose each source.

	Supporting Question	Primary Source and Notes
1		
2		
3		

Challenge

Conduct research to find two additional primary sources related to the American Revolution. One should address the viewpoint of the Patriots and the other the viewpoint of the Loyalists. Then analyze how each new source uses propaganda to convey its message. Use what you have observed in the two sources to help you answer your Supporting Questions.

25. <u>Directions:</u> Now, answer the Supporting Questions that you developed at the beginning of the activity to help guide you in answering the Compelling Question.

Answer for Supporting Question 1:

Answer for Supporting Question 2:

Answer for Supporting Question 3:

Communicate Conclusions

Talk About It

26. <u>Collaborating</u> Work in a group of five. Each student should read aloud or describe a different source. Together, discuss how each source uses propaganda to convey its intended message. Take notes to record new information you learn about propaganda included in the sources.

Write About It

27. Argumentative Writing Choose two sources from the graphic organizer that helped you answer your Supporting Questions. Think about how these two sources used propaganda to convince colonists to support the Patriot cause. Also, think about what you know about the events of the American Revolution. Then write two paragraphs in which you argue whether the propaganda was effective or ineffective.

28. Answering the Compelling Question What do you think? How is propaganda used to further a cause? Use what you have learned about propaganda during the American Revolution to brainstorm a list of ways propaganda can be used to advance a cause. Then write a two-minute speech that explains how propaganda can be used to further a cause. Be sure to include evidence from at least two sources in your speech.

29. Making Connections During the time of the American Revolution, both Patriots and Loyalists used propaganda to promote their cause. Today, Americans and people throughout the world still use propaganda to further issues they care about. Modern-day propaganda can be found in advertisements for anything from consumer products to political issues and candidates. First, conduct research to find out more about propaganda as it is used today. Don't be surprised if you encounter new terms such as *bandwagon, loaded words*, and *glittering generalities*. Then choose a local, state, or national election that interests you. Find a political advertisement for each of two candidates with strongly opposing points of view. Carefully analyze both political advertisements to identify various examples of propaganda included. Record the examples in a chart, and explain why each example can be considered propaganda.

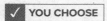 **YOU CHOOSE**

Select one of these Take Informed Action products to apply what you've learned.

A. Create a community education pamphlet. In it, describe how to identify propaganda in political advertisements. Include passages from the advertisements you analyzed to illustrate your idea.

B. Create a podcast that highlights your selected election. Discuss how propaganda might influence the election. Use examples from your research.

C. Decide which candidate seems most convincing to you. Create a Web page aimed at convincing others to support your chosen candidate. Be persuasive but truthful.

Take Informed Action Rubric: Analysis of Propaganda Techniques

Self-Evaluation As you identify and analyze examples of modern political propaganda techniques, think about the following criteria. These are the criteria your teacher will use to evaluate your Take Informed Action activity.

Peer Review Use this rubric to grade the final product related to political propaganda developed by another classmate or group of classmates.

	Organization	Writing/Editing	Historical Accuracy	Logic
4	The piece is exceptionally well organized and focused and demonstrates a thorough and deep understanding of the event or issue.	The final product is exceptionally well written and includes no errors.	The piece is well researched and is factually accurate.	The decision made shows evidence of extensive thought.
3	The piece is well organized and focused and demonstrates an adequate understanding of the event or issue.	The final product is exceptionally well written and includes few errors.	The piece is well researched but contains some factual mistakes.	The decision made shows sufficient evidence of thought.
2	The piece is organized but is inconsistent in focus and demonstrates an inadequate understanding of the event or issue.	The final product is adequately written but includes a number of errors.	The piece is not well researched and contains some factual mistakes.	The decision made shows limited evidence of thought.
1	The piece lacks organization, focus, and a basic understanding of the event or issue.	The final product is not well written and includes multiple errors.	There are many factual mistakes.	No decision has been made, showing a lack of thought.
SCORE				

TOPIC 5 • FIRST GOVERNMENTS AND THE CONSTITUTION, 1777–TODAY

The Question of the Bill of Rights

 COMPELLING QUESTION

Why was the Bill of Rights controversial?

Plan Your Inquiry

In this Inquiry Activity, you will develop Supporting Questions about the Bill of Rights and arguments for and against it being included in the U.S. Constitution based on the Compelling Question. Then you will examine primary sources related to the Bill of Rights. Finally, you will answer your Supporting Questions, communicate your research conclusions, and take action based on what you've learned.

Background Information

After declaring independence from Great Britain, a number of American colonies began writing constitutions, or written plans of government. The thirteen colonies (the original U.S. states) also loosely joined together to form a central government under the Articles of Confederation, the first written plan of government for the United States. Even after the country became an independent nation, the Articles of Confederation remained in effect.

However, the central government established under the Articles was weak and had a hard time enforcing laws. Congress could not tax the states or regulate trade. So leaders of the nation became convinced that a stronger central government was needed. A constitutional convention was held in 1787 in Philadelphia to write a new government plan for the nation. The delegates from the various states had many disagreements. Fortunately, they all agreed to many compromises, and the Constitution of the United States took shape.

Most of the delegates were pleased with the document and readily signed it. It was then time for the states to approve, or ratify, the Constitution. Some states were reluctant to approve the document because it did not include a bill of rights. A bill of rights would provide important rights and freedoms to individuals. Some feared that without a bill of rights the government might abuse its power. The issue of whether a specific guarantee of individual freedoms was needed stirred much controversy.

These teachers in Michigan protested the lack of funding for education in 2019. The right of people to peaceably assemble is protected by the Bill of Rights.

Develop Supporting Questions About the Bill of Rights

 **COMPELLING QUESTION**

Why was the Bill of Rights controversial?

Talk About It

Discuss with a partner what type of information you would need to know to answer this question. For example, one question might be: What is the purpose of a bill of rights?

Directions: Write down three additional questions that you need to answer to be able to determine what made the Bill of Rights a disputed issue.

Supporting Question 1:

Supporting Question 2:

Supporting Question 3:

Apply Historical Concepts and Tools

Directions: As you read and work with primary sources, use the graphic organizer to take notes and organize information.

Organizing Source Information		
Source	**Title and Author/ Creator**	**Notes**
A	Federalist No. 84, Certain General and Miscellaneous Objections to the Constitution Considered and Answered by Publius (Alexander Hamilton)	
B	Anti-Federalist No. 84, On the Lack of a Bill of Rights by Brutus (Robert Yates)	
C	Speech in the Virginia Convention by Patrick Henry	
D	Observations on the New Constitution, and on the Federal and State Conventions by a Columbian Patriot (Mercy Otis Warren)	
E	Letter to the *New Haven Gazette* by a Countryman (Roger Sherman)	

Analyze Sources

Review and analyze Sources A–E. There are questions that accompany each source to help you examine the source and check for historical understanding.

Federalist No. 84, Certain General and Miscellaneous Objections to the Constitution Considered and Answered

The new Constitution created a strong federal government. Those people supporting this idea became known as Federalists. They supported the idea of sharing of power between the federal and state governments. Federalists began to speak out and write about the urgent need to adopt the Constitution. James Madison, Alexander Hamilton, and John Jay wrote a series of essays that are known as the Federalist Papers. They wrote under the Publius pseudonym, or fictitious name. These 85 essays requested that the Constitution be ratified so that the idea of federalism would be supreme law for the United States. In Federalist No. 84, published in 1788, Alexander Hamilton argues against the need for a bill of rights.

PRIMARY SOURCE : ESSAY

It has been several times truly remarked that bills of rights are, in their origin, **stipulations** between kings and their subjects, abridgements of **prerogative** in favor of privilege, reservations of rights not surrendered to the prince. Such was **MAGNA CHARTA** . . . Here, in strictness, the people surrender nothing; and as they retain every thing they have no need of particular reservations. "WE, THE PEOPLE of the United States, to secure the blessings of liberty to ourselves and our posterity, do ORDAIN and ESTABLISH this Constitution for the United States of America." . . .

. . . The truth is, after all the declamations we have heard, that the Constitution is itself, in every rational sense, and to every useful purpose, A BILL OF RIGHTS. The several bills of rights in Great Britain form its Constitution, and conversely the **constitution of each State is its bill of rights**. And the proposed Constitution, if adopted, will be the bill of rights of the Union. Is it one object of a bill of rights to declare and specify the political privileges of the citizens in the structure and administration of the government? This is done in the most ample and precise manner in the plan of the convention; comprehending various precautions for the public security, which are not to be found in any of the State constitutions. . . . It certainly must be immaterial what mode is observed as to the order of declaring the rights of the citizens, if they are to be found in any part of the instrument which establishes the government. And hence it must be apparent, that much of what has been said on this subject rests merely on verbal and nominal distinctions, entirely foreign from the substance of the thing.

—Publius (Alexander Hamilton), Federalist Papers, May 28, 1788

stipulation a demand or promise in an agreement

prerogative a special right or privilege

Magna Charta (Magna Carta) the English charter listing the rights forcibly gained in 1215 by King John; includes the rights of individuals, the right to justice, and the right to a fair trial

constitution of each State is its bill of rights each state's constitution describes individual rights

1. **Summarizing** What are some of the reasons that Hamilton gives for not including a bill of rights?

2. **Explaining** Why does Hamilton reference the Magna Carta in his essay?

3. **Citing Evidence** Why does Hamilton believe the Constitution is different from the Magna Carta and therefore does not need a bill of rights? What evidence does he provide to support his belief?

4. **Analyzing Perspectives** Why does Hamilton believe the Constitution is "the bill of rights of the Union?" Explain your reasoning.

Antifederalist No. 84, On the Lack of a Bill of Rights

The Antifederalist Papers were written by the people who were opposed to or had concerns about the Constitution. The Anti-Federalists wanted state governments to remain stronger than the federal government. They were afraid of losing their individual rights. Like the authors of the Federalist Papers, they went by pseudonyms, such as Cato, Centinel, and Brutus. Authors included Patrick Henry, Samuel Adams, and George Mason. It is believed that Robert Yates was the probable author of this Anti-Federalist essay excerpt. A lawyer and judge, Yates served as a delegate representing New York at the Constitutional Convention.

PRIMARY SOURCE : ESSAY

When a building is to be erected which is intended to stand for ages, the foundation should be firmly laid. The Constitution proposed to your acceptance is designed, not for yourselves alone, but for generations yet unborn. The principles, therefore, upon which the **social compact** is founded, ought to have been clearly and precisely stated, and the most express and full declaration of rights to have been made. But on this subject there is almost an entire silence. . . .

. . . that in forming a government on its true principles, the foundation should be laid in the manner I before stated, by expressly reserving to the people such of their essential rights as are not necessary to be parted with. The same reasons which at first **induced** mankind to associate and **institute** government, will operate to influence them to observe this precaution. If they had been disposed to conform themselves to the rule of **immutable** righteousness, government would not have been **requisite**. It was because one part exercised fraud, oppression and violence, on the other, that men came together, and agreed that certain rules should be formed to regulate the conduct of all, and the power of the whole community lodged in the hands of rulers to enforce an obedience to them. But rulers have the same **propensities** as other men; they are as likely to use the power with which they are vested, for private purposes, and to the injury and oppression of those over whom they are placed, as individuals in a state of nature are to injure and oppress one another. It is therefore as proper that bounds should be set to their authority, as that government should have at first been instituted to restrain private injuries.

. . . Those who have governed, have been found in all ages ever active to enlarge their powers and abridge the public liberty. This has induced the people in all countries, where any sense of freedom remained, to fix barriers against the encroachments of their rulers. . . . this principle is a fundamental one, in all the Constitutions of our own States; there is not one of them but what is either founded on a declaration or bill of rights, or has certain express reservation of rights interwoven in the body of them.

—Brutus (Robert Yates), Antifederalist Papers, 1788

social compact a voluntary agreement among groups and the government for the mutual benefit of all

induce to persuade

institute to originate and organize

immutable unchangeable

requisite something required; essential

propensity a tendency to behave in a certain way

5. Identifying the Main Idea What is the main idea of the essay?

6. Analyzing To what does the author compare the creation of the new government? What is the most likely reason he makes this comparison?

7. Making Connections How do the author of this essay and the author of Federalist No. 84 differ in their explanations related to state constitutions? Cite evidence to support your response.

8. Analyzing Perspectives How does the author's view related to the propensities of rulers affect his reasoning about what could happen without a bill of rights?

C

Speech in the Virginia Convention

While some states eagerly accepted and ratified the Constitution as it was written, other states, such as Virginia, debated the issue of ratification. At the Virginia Ratifying Convention held in June 1788, Patrick Henry gave a series of speeches aimed at convincing others to oppose the Constitution. He believed that the document gave too much authority to the federal government at the expense of states. He also feared that it would not sufficiently protect human rights. After much debate, the delegates at the convention narrowly ratified the Constitution, but only if a bill of rights was included.

In this speech, Patrick Henry references Virginia's Declaration of Rights—a bill of rights that was included in Virginia's state constitution. Henry explains why having rights guaranteed to ensure limits to government power is essential. He highlights the difficulties individuals, particularly "common citizens," would face if they were not aware of their rights. He focuses on how even the elites of American society have doubts about a founding document that does not outline individual freedoms.

PRIMARY SOURCE : SPEECH

> Why is the trial by jury taken away? . . . Wherefore is religious liberty not secured? One Honorable Gentleman who favors adoption, said that he had had his fears on the subject. If I can well recollect, he informed us that he was perfectly satisfied by the powers of reasoning (with which he is so happily endowed) that those fears were not well grounded. There is many a religious man who knows nothing of argumentative reasoning;—there are many of our most worthy citizens, who cannot go through all the **labyrinths** of **syllogistic** argumentative deductions, when they think that the rights of conscience are invaded. This sacred right ought not to depend on constructive logical reasoning.
>
> When we see men of such talents and learning, compelled to use their utmost abilities to convince themselves that there is no danger, is it not sufficient to make us tremble? Is it not sufficient to fill the minds of the ignorant part of men with fear? If Gentlemen believe that the **apprehensions** of men will be quieted, they are mistaken, since our best informed men are in doubt with respect to the security of our rights. Those who are not so well informed will **spurn** at the Government. When our common citizens, who are not possessed with such extensive knowledge and abilities, are called upon to change their Bill of Rights (which in plain unequivocal terms, secures their most valuable rights and privileges) for construction and implication, will they implicitly **acquiesce**? Our Declaration of Rights tells us that "all men are by nature free and independent," &c. (Here Mr. Henry read the declaration of rights.) Will they exchange these Rights for logical reasons?
>
> —Patrick Henry, June 12, 1788

Copyright © McGraw Hill   Henry, Patrick, Speech in the Virginia Convention, June 12, 1788, in The Debates in the Several State Conventions of the Adoption of the Federal Constitution as Recommended by the Convention at Philadelphia in 1787, Vol 3, edited by Jonathan Elliot. Philadelphia: J.B. Lippincott Company, 1891.

labyrinth a maze

syllogistic logical argument that relies on deductive reasoning

apprehension suspicion or fear that something unpleasant will happen

spurn to reject with contempt

acquiesce to accept without protest

9. **Explaining** Why does Patrick Henry use the idea of a labyrinth in his statement, "There are many of our most worthy citizens, who cannot go through all the labyrinths of syllogistic argumentative deductions, when they think that the rights of conscience are invaded"?

10. **Identifying** What specific rights does Patrick Henry mention in the speech? What reason might he have for doing this?

11. **Interpreting** What argument does the author make related to "Gentlemen" and "common citizens"?

12. **Making Inferences** Why does Patrick Henry suggest that Virginians would be losing rights under the Constitution?

Observations on the New Constitution, and on the Federal and State Conventions

The following excerpt from a pamphlet was written in 1788 and published by Mercy Otis Warren under the pseudonym "a Columbian Patriot." Warren was a writer, historian, playwright, and political activist during the American Revolution and the debate over the Constitution. Warren did not receive a formal education but was permitted to study with her brothers. In the letter, Warren refers to a former governor. That governor was Thomas Hutchinson of Massachusetts whose unpopular and untrustworthy actions in support of Great Britain helped bring about the American Revolution.

PRIMARY SOURCE : ESSAY

There is no provision by a bill of rights to guard against the dangerous encroachments of power in too many instances to be named: . . . We are told by a gentleman of too much virtue and real probity to suspect he has a design to deceive —"that the whole constitution is a declaration of rights,"— but mankind must think for themselves, and to many very **judicious and discerning** characters, the whole constitution, with very few exceptions, appears a perversion of the rights of particular states, and of private citizens—But the gentleman goes on to tell us, "that the primary object is the general government, and that the rights of individuals are only incidentally mentioned, and that there was a clear impropriety in being very particular about them." But, asking pardon for dissenting from such respectable authority, who has been led into several mistakes, more from his **predilection** in **favour** of certain modes of governmens, than from a want of understanding or veracity, the rights of individuals ought to be the primary object of all government, and cannot be too securely guarded by the most explicit declarations in their favor. . . .

. . . After the severe conflicts this country has suffered, it is presumed, that they are disposed to make every reasonable sacrifice before the altar of peace. But when we contemplate the nature of men, and consider them originally on an equal footing, subject to the same feelings, stimulated by the same passions, and recollecting the struggles they have recently made, for the security of their civil rights; it cannot be expected that the inhabitants of the Massachusetts, can be easily **lulled** into a fatal security, by the declamatory effusions of gentlemen, who, contrary to the experience of all ages, would persuade them there is no danger to be apprehended from vesting discretionary powers in the hands of man, which he may, or may not abuse. The very suggestion, that we ought to trust to the precarious hope of amendments and redress, after we have voluntarily fixed the shackles on our own necks, should have awakened to a double degree of caution. —This people have not forgotten the artful insinuations of a former governor, when pleading the unlimited authority of parliament before the legislature of the Massachusetts;

— A Columbian Patriot (Mercy Otis Warren), 1788

judicious and discerning showing good judgment

predilection a preference for something

favour (favor) support

lull to soothe

13. Identifying What words does the author use to explain why she thinks a bill of rights is necessary?

14. Determining Context Who is the author referring to when she writes, "We are told by a gentleman. . . 'that the whole constitution is a declaration of rights'"? How do you know?

Need Extra Help?

Think about the other sources you have read in this Inquiry Activity as you answer this question.

15. Citing Evidence What does the author believe is the most important thing to be included in a plan for government? What evidence supports your response?

16. Analyzing What does the author warn against? What is the most likely reason she does this?

E

Letter to the *New Haven Gazette*

The following letter is believed to have been written by Roger Sherman, a Framer from Connecticut. It was published under a pseudonym in the period before Connecticut ratified the Constitution in January 1788. Before the American Revolution, Sherman was a member of the Connecticut colony's two-house legislative body, the General Assembly. Later, he took part in the creation of the Declaration of Independence. After American independence, Sherman attended the Constitutional Convention as a representative from Connecticut.

PRIMARY SOURCE : LETTER

No bill of rights ever yet bound the supreme power longer than the *honeymoon* of a new married couple, unless the *rulers were interested* in preserving the rights; and in that case they have always been ready enough to declare the rights and to preserve them when they were declared. The famous English **Magna Charta** is but an act of Parliament, which every **subsequent** Parliament has had just as much constitutional power to **repeal** and **annul** as the Parliament which made it had to pass it at first. But the security of the nation has always been that their government was so formed that at least *one branch* of their legislature must be strongly interested to preserve the rights of the nation.

. . . If you cannot prove by the best of all evidence, **viz.**, by the *interest of the rulers*, that this authority will not be abused or, at least, that those powers are not more likely to be abused by the Congress than by those who now have the same powers, you must by no means adopt the Constitution. No, not with all the bills of rights and all the stipulations in favor of the people that can be made.

But if the members of Congress are to be interested just as you and I are, and just as the members of our present legislatures are interested, we shall be just as safe with even supreme power (if that were granted) in Congress, as in the General Assembly. If the members of Congress can take no improper step which will not affect them as much as it does us, we need not apprehend that they will usurp authorities not given them to injure that society of which they are a part.

— A Countryman (Roger Sherman), Letter II, November 22, 1787

Magna Charta (Magna Carta)

subsequent following in time

repeal to revoke

annul to declare or make void or invalid

viz. namely; in other words

17. Identifying What argument does the author make in the first sentence of the document?

18. Interpreting What is the author's reason for saying that the Magna Carta can be repealed just as easily as it was passed?

19. Analyzing What is the implication of the author's argument about the Magna Carta?

20. Evaluating How does this source provide a limited perspective and information about the bill of rights?

Evaluate Sources and Use Evidence

21. Citing Text Evidence Review the Supporting Questions you developed at the beginning of the topic and the evidence you gathered and recorded in the graphic organizer. Which sources will help you answer the Supporting Questions? Circle or highlight those sources in your graphic organizer. Looking at the subset of sources you have chosen, be prepared to explain why you chose each source.

	Supporting Question	Primary Source and Notes
1		
2		
3		

Challenge

With a partner, conduct additional research about the Bill of Rights controversy. Each of you should then choose one side of the issue to debate. Next, imagine that you are living during the time of the creation of the Constitution. Hold an informal debate about whether a bill of rights should be added to the Constitution.

22. Directions: Now, answer the Supporting Questions that you developed at the beginning of the activity to help guide you in answering the Compelling Question.

Answer for Supporting Question 1:

Answer for Supporting Question 2:

Answer for Supporting Question 3:

Need Extra Help?

Create a T-chart with the labels *For* and *Against*. Reread each source and highlight information that identifies an argument for or against including a bill of rights. Record the information in the appropriate column. Then use the completed T-chart to answer your Supporting Questions.

Communicate Conclusions

Talk About It

23. Collaborating Work with a partner. Take turns reading each other's Supporting Questions. Compare how your Supporting Questions are alike and different. Then each of you should read aloud your answer for each question. Think about the additional information you have learned from your partner. Discuss the Compelling Question, incorporating into the discussion what each of you has discovered about the sources.

Write About It

24. Argumentative Writing Choose two sources you recorded in the graphic organizer that helped you answer the Supporting Questions you developed. Consider how these two sources demonstrate what made the idea of including a bill of rights in the Constitution debatable. Then write two paragraphs in which you describe the issue and what made it debatable and provide arguments in favor of or against it. Be sure to cite evidence from the two sources to support your position.

25. Answering the Compelling Question What do you think? Why was the Bill of Rights controversial? Use your interpretation of the primary sources to write a short statement in which you explain reasons for the controversy. Be sure to cite evidence from at least two sources in your statement.

26. Making Connections Having a bill of rights as part of the Constitution was controversial long ago. Today, however, most citizens realize its importance. Still, controversy about the Bill of Rights exists because not all citizens interpret the rights the same way. Choose one of the following amendments that make up the Bill of Rights: 1, 2, 4, 5, 6, or 8. Conduct research to identify a controversy related to your selected amendment. Take notes about the various viewpoints people hold about the amendment. Then write a statement that explains your own opinion.

✓ **YOU CHOOSE**

Select one of these Take Informed Action products to apply what you've learned.

A. Write a dialogue between two people who have opposing views about the amendment.

B. Write a newspaper editorial in which you describe the amendment's controversy and express your opinion on the issue.

C. Imagine that you are speaking at a public meeting. Give a short speech that explains your view about the amendment and why you hold that view and not the opposing view.

Take Informed Action Rubric: Identify and Compare Viewpoints of a Bill of Rights Amendment

Self-Evaluation As you complete the final product related to identifying and comparing viewpoints of a Bill of Rights amendment, think about the following criteria. These are the criteria your teacher will use to evaluate your Take Informed Action activity.

Peer Review Use this rubric to grade the viewpoint of a Bill of Rights final product developed by another classmate or group of classmates.

	Organization	Writing/Presentation	Historical Accuracy	Historical Comparison
4	The piece is exceptionally well organized and focused and demonstrates a thorough and deep understanding of the event or issue.	The final product is exceptionally executed and includes no errors.	The piece is well researched and is factually accurate.	The various viewpoints are clearly described and compared.
3	The piece is well organized and focused and demonstrates an adequate understanding of the event or issue.	The final product is well executed and includes few errors.	The piece is well researched but contains some factual mistakes.	The various viewpoints are sufficiently described and compared.
2	The piece is organized but is inconsistent in focus and demonstrates an inadequate understanding of the event or issue.	The final product is adequately executed but includes a number of errors.	The piece is not well researched and contains some factual mistakes.	The various viewpoints are somewhat described and compared.
1	The piece lacks organization, focus, and a basic understanding of the event or issue.	The final product is not adequately executed and includes multiple errors.	There are many factual mistakes.	The various viewpoints are not described and compared.
SCORE				

TOPIC 6 · THE NEW REPUBLIC, 1789–1823

Early Foreign Policy of the United States

 COMPELLING QUESTION

How did each president shape foreign policy in the early United States?

Plan Your Inquiry

In this Inquiry Activity, you will develop Supporting Questions related to issues early leaders faced regarding foreign policy and compare and contrast the issues and how they were handled based on the Compelling Question. Then you will examine primary sources related to foreign policy. Finally, you will answer your Supporting Questions, communicate your research conclusions, and take action based on what you've learned.

Background Information

In 1789, the U.S. Constitution was ratified, officially making it the supreme law of the new country. That same year, George Washington became the nation's first president. He was faced with many problems to solve in order for the new country to run smoothly. The other early presidents—John Adams, Thomas Jefferson, James Madison, and James Monroe—also encountered many issues no one had even imagined. This meant that they were setting precedents, or traditions, for the country.

The early presidents soon found they had to decide how to act toward foreign countries. In other words, they had to set foreign policy. Presidents Washington and then Adams did not want to be involved in European wars. So they followed a policy of neutrality, or not taking sides. This meant that the United States did not support either Britain or France in a 1793 war between these two countries.

At the same time, the United States wanted to trade with other countries. Neither France nor Britain was happy with the United States trading with its enemy. Staying out of European affairs would be hard for the presidents who followed Washington. Within 25 years, the United States would be negotiating land deals and even fighting a war with a foreign power.

The United States tried to maintain good relations with both France and Great Britain, who had many conflicts. However, events made this foreign policy increasingly difficult. Eventually the United States fought the British in the War of 1812. The Battle of New Orleans, shown here, was the last battle of that war.

Develop Supporting Questions About Foreign Policy Issues During the Early Republic

 COMPELLING QUESTION

How did each president shape foreign policy in the early United States?

Talk About It COLLABORATE

Discuss with a partner what type of information you would need to know to answer this question. For example, one question might be: Why did the United States need to develop a foreign policy?

Directions: Write down three additional questions that you need to answer to be able to determine how each president determined the best foreign policy for the early republic.

Supporting Question 1:

Supporting Question 2:

Supporting Question 3:

Apply Historical Concepts and Tools

Directions: As you read and work with primary sources, use the graphic organizer to take notes and organize information.

	Organizing Source Information	
Source	**Title and Author/Creator**	**Notes**
A	Farewell Address by George Washington	
B	Message to the Senate and House Regarding Reports of the Envoys to France by John Adams	
C	Ograbme, political cartoon	
D	Special Message to Congress on the Foreign Policy Crisis by James Madison	
E	The Monroe Doctrine by James Monroe	

Analyze Sources

Review and analyze Sources A–E. There are questions that accompany each source to help you examine the source and check for historical understanding.

Farewell Address

As George Washington's first term as president neared its end, the president turned to adviser James Madison to write a letter for him that bid goodbye to American citizens. However, Washington decided to seek a second term, which he won. In 1793, war in Europe compelled President Washington to issue the Proclamation of Neutrality. It made it unlawful for any Americans to take part in the war. It also prohibited foreign warships on the American coast. At the end of Washington's second term in 1796, he knew he would need a farewell address. After all, he had definitely decided not to seek a third term in the 1796 election. He returned to his original letter, revising it extensively with the help of Secretary of the Treasury Alexander Hamilton. Washington's Farewell Address was then published in the Philadelphia newspaper *American Daily Advertiser*. Of course, the address announced that Washington would not be running again. It also included a warning against the forming of alliances with foreign nations.

PRIMARY SOURCE : LETTER

. . . nothing is more essential than that permanent, **inveterate antipathies** against particular nations, and passionate attachments for others, should be excluded; and that, in place of them, just and **amicable** feelings towards all should be cultivated. . . .

As avenues to foreign influence in innumerable ways, such attachments are particularly alarming to the truly enlightened and independent patriot. How many opportunities do they afford to tamper with domestic factions, to practice the arts of seduction, to mislead public opinion, to influence or awe the public councils? . . .

. . . Excessive partiality for one foreign nation and excessive dislike of another cause those whom they actuate to see danger only on one side, and serve to veil and even second the arts of influence on the other. Real patriots who may resist the intrigues of the favorite are liable to become suspected and **odious**, while its tools and dupes usurp the applause and confidence of the people, to surrender their interests.

The great rule of conduct for us in regard to foreign nations is in extending our commercial relations, to have with them as little political connection as possible. So far as we have already formed engagements, let them be fulfilled with perfect good faith. Here let us stop. . . . Hence, therefore, it must be unwise in us to implicate ourselves by artificial ties in the ordinary **vicissitudes** of [Europe's] politics, or the ordinary combinations and collisions of her friendships or **enmities**.

inveterate firmly established	**odious** extremely unpleasant
antipathy a strong feeling of dislike	**vicissitude** change or variation
amicable friendly; agreeable	**enmities** hostilities

Our detached and distant situation invites and enables us to pursue a different course. . . .

Why forego the advantages of so peculiar a situation? Why quit our own to stand upon foreign ground? Why, by interweaving our destiny with that of any part of Europe, entangle our peace and prosperity in the toils of European ambition, rivalship, interest, humor or **caprice**?

It is our true policy to steer clear of permanent alliances with any portion of the foreign world; . . .

Taking care always to keep ourselves by suitable establishments on a respectable defensive posture, we may safely trust to temporary alliances for extraordinary emergencies. . . .

— George Washington, September 19, 1796

caprice a sudden, unpredictable change

EXAMINE THE SOURCE

1. **Summarizing** What does Washington believe about U.S. foreign policy?

2. **Interpreting** What is Washington advocating for when he says, "Our detached and distant situation invites and enables us to pursue a different course"? Explain your reasoning.

3. **Analyzing Perspectives** Why does Washington write, "the great rule of conduct for us in regard to foreign nations is in extending our commercial relations, to have with them as little political connection as possible"

4. **Drawing Conclusions** Why does Washington likely take these positions about foreign nations?

B

Message to the Senate and House Regarding Reports of the Envoys to France

Britain and France seemed determined to draw the United States into their fight. John Adams inherited these foreign affairs problems when he became the second U.S. president in 1797. France began to think that the United States favored Britain in the conflict. Because of this, the French started capturing U.S. trade ships heading to Britain. Diplomatic relations between the United States and France suffered when French leaders refused to meet with U.S. envoys, or diplomats, sent to discuss the dispute. Instead, they sent three agents who demanded a bribe and a large loan before French leaders would even consider talking to the envoys. This made Adams extremely mad. President Adams wrote the following message to Congress shortly after receiving news about the distasteful French negotiating tactics. He listed the three French agents X, Y, and Z so after the incident became public it was known as the XYZ affair. U.S. citizens were ready to go to war over the issue. However, the two sides settled the situation through diplomacy.

PRIMARY SOURCE : LETTER

While I feel a satisfaction in informing you that their exertions for the adjustment of the differences between the two nations have been sincere and **unremitted**, it is **incumbent on** me to declare that I perceive no ground of expectation that the objects of their mission can be accomplished on terms compatible with the safety, the honor, or the essential interests of the nation.

This result can not with justice be attributed to any want of moderation on the part of this Government, or to any **indisposition** to forego secondary interests for the preservation of peace. Knowing it to be my duty, and believing it to be your wish, as well as that of the great body of the people, to avoid by all reasonable concessions any participation in the **contentions** of Europe, the powers vested in our envoys were **commensurate** with a liberal and **pacific** policy . . . I can **discern** nothing which could have insured or contributed to success that has been omitted on my part, and nothing further which can be attempted consistently with maxims for which our country has contended at every hazard, and which constitute the basis of our national sovereignty.

unremitted not forgiven

incumbent on necessary

indisposition reluctance or lack of enthusiasm

contention disagreement

commensurate corresponding in extent

pacific tending to lessen conflict

discern to see or perceive by sight

5. Explaining Why does Adams believe it is "incumbent on" him to tell Congress?

6. Citing Evidence What policy does Adams describe in the second paragraph? What evidence supports this description?

7. Contrasting How is the situation Adams is facing as president different from what Washington referenced in his Farewell Address?

C

Ograbme, or The American Snapping Turtle

Not long after the American Revolution had been resolved, the French Revolution took place. Both revolutions had the same goal: to liberate the people from oppression. But the turmoil caused by the French Revolution led to the rise of French dictator Napoleon Bonaparte. Soon Napoleon looked outside of France to exert his powers and began capturing territory. A number of European nations joined together to fight back in what has become known as the Napoleonic Wars. During the wars, Napoleon boldly decreed that Great Britain would be blocked from sea trade with the European mainland. Great Britain answered with its own blockade of Napoleonic Europe. This British action hurt U.S. trade more than Napoleon's. In reality, Napoleon's small naval fleet posed little threat to U.S. trading ships. Thomas Jefferson, the U.S. president at the time, wanted a nonviolent way to prevent Britain from harming U.S. trade. He convinced Congress to pass the Embargo Act in December 1807. This act banned the United States from participating in all foreign trade. Jefferson hoped this would help the United States maintain its policy of neutrality. However, the embargo proved to be a disastrous move for the United States. American goods lay unsold, and prices tumbled. Many people lost their jobs while others turned to smuggling. New England was particularly hard hit. Its industries relied strongly on foreign trade. On top of that, the embargo did not have much negative effect on the British and French economies. In March 1809, Congress repealed the Embargo Act, opening U.S. trade with most countries. The following political cartoon was drawn while the Embargo Act was still in effect.

PRIMARY SOURCE : POLITICAL CARTOON

Alexander Anderson drew this cartoon in 1807 after the Embargo Act of 1807 was passed. The turtle is named Ograbme (embargo spelled backward).

8. Identifying What is the main idea of the political cartoon?

9. Explaining The snapping turtle symbolizes the Embargo Act of 1807. What do the other characters and the ship symbolize, and what are they trying to do?

10. Analyzing Perspectives What perspective does the cartoon represent, and how would you describe its tone?

Need Extra Help?

Think about what the artist feels and what his attitude is toward the issue. Is the cartoon serious, cheery, hopeful, biting or satirical, positive, or negative?

11. Drawing Conclusions How do you think the artist of the cartoon hoped to influence events?

12. Evaluating What information about the embargo is lacking in this source? What additional kinds of sources might be helpful?

1811, ed. J. C. A. Stagg, Jeanne Kerr Cross, Jewel L. Spangler, Ellen J. Barber, Martha J. King, Anne Mandeville Colony, and Susan Holbrook Perdue. Charlottesville: University Press of Virginia, 1999, pp. 432–439.]

Copyright © McGraw Hill   Madison, James. "From James Madison to Congress, 1 June 1812," Founders Online, National Archives, https://founders.archives.gov/documents/Madison/03-04-02-0460. [Original source: The Papers of James Madison, Presidential Series, vol. 4, 5 November 1811–9 July 1812 and Supplement 5 March 1809–19 October

D

Special Message to Congress on the Foreign Policy Crisis

The British continued to capture U.S. trade ships during the administration of James Madison, the nation's fourth president. Madison decided to stop all trade with Britain, but this did not seem enough for some Americans. A growing number of citizens began to think that it was time to give up the idea of neutrality. They wanted to go to war against Britain. For the most part, westerners and southerners wanted war while the people of New England stood against it. Following the preferences of their constituents, or voters who lived in their states, political leaders were split on the issue as well. Some Republicans, called War Hawks, spoke out strongly for war. In contrast, Federalists opposed war. President Madison began to realize that war with Britain was inevitable. On June 1, 1812, he sent the following to Congress in support of going to war. The House voted in favor of waging the war by many votes while the Senate vote was closer. On June 18, 1812, Madison signed the declaration of war, officially beginning the War of 1812. For the first time in its history, the United States had declared war on another country.

PRIMARY SOURCE : LETTER

. . . Our moderation and **conciliation** have had no other effect than to encourage perseverance and to enlarge **pretensions**. We behold our seafaring citizens still the daily victims of lawless violence, committed on the great common and highway of nations, even within sight of the country which owes them protection. We behold our vessels, freighted with the products of our soil and industry, or returning with the honest proceeds of them, wrested from their lawful destinations, confiscated by prize courts no longer the organs of public law but the instruments of arbitrary edicts, and their unfortunate crews **dispersed** and lost, or forced or **inveigled** in British ports into British fleets, whilst arguments are employed in support of these aggressions which have no foundation but in a principle equally supporting a claim to regulate our external commerce in all cases whatsoever.

We behold, in fine, on the side of Great Britain, a state of war against the United States, and on the side of the United States a state of peace toward Great Britain.

Whether the United States shall continue passive under these progressive **usurpations** and these accumulating wrongs, or, opposing force to force in defense of their national rights, shall commit a just cause into the hands of the Almighty Disposer of Events [God], . . . is a solemn question which the Constitution wisely confides to the legislative department of the government. In recommending it to their early deliberations I am happy in the assurance that the decision will be worthy the enlightened and patriotic councils of a virtuous, a free, and a powerful nation.

— James Madison, "War Message," June 1, 1812

conciliation the action of bringing to agreement

pretension false behavior meant to impress others

disperse to separate or break up

inveigle to win over by trickery

usurpation illegal seizure

13. Explaining In his message, how does Madison make the case that war is necessary?

14. Analyzing Why does Madison avoid declaring war on Great Britain? What does he do instead? Cite evidence to support your response.

15. Comparing How is Madison's approach to the issue at hand similar to Adams's handling of the French crisis? Explain your reasoning.

The Monroe Doctrine

For more than three centuries, Europeans had been interested in controlling land in the Americas. As the United States grew, the thought of European influence in the Western Hemisphere was becoming more troublesome. Americans had growing concerns that European powers would seek to gain new territory in the Americas. They wondered whether the recent independence of Latin American countries would lead to European interference in Central and South America. Perhaps, other European countries might try to help Spain regain its lost territory or take some for themselves. Russia's recent interests in northwestern North America also alarmed the United States. Such concerns led James Monroe, the fifth U.S. president, to issue the Monroe Doctrine. President Monroe first presented the doctrine during his 1823 State of the Union address before Congress. The Monroe Doctrine has served as a cornerstone of U.S. foreign policy since it was introduced. However, throughout centuries, it has been reinterpreted and applied in different ways.

PRIMARY SOURCE : DOCUMENT

. . . In the wars of the European powers in matters relating to themselves we have never taken any part, nor does it **comport** with our policy to do so. It is only when our rights are invaded or seriously menaced that we resent injuries or make preparation for our defense. With the movements in this hemisphere we are of necessity more immediately connected, and by causes which must be obvious to all enlightened and impartial observers. The political system of the allied powers is essentially different in this respect from that of America. This difference proceeds from that which exists in their respective Governments; and to the defense of our own, which has been achieved by the loss of so much blood and treasure, and matured by the wisdom of their most enlightened citizens, and under which we have enjoyed unexampled **felicity**, this whole nation is devoted. We owe it, therefore, to **candor** and to the amicable relations existing between the United States and those powers to declare that we should consider any attempt on their part to extend their system to any portion of this hemisphere as dangerous to our peace and safety. With the existing colonies or dependencies of any European power we have not interfered and shall not interfere. But with the Governments who have declared their independence and maintain it, and whose independence we have, on great consideration and on just principles, acknowledged, we could not view any **interposition** for the purpose of oppressing them, or controlling in any other manner their destiny, by any European power in any other light than as the manifestation of an unfriendly disposition toward the United States. In the war between those new Governments and Spain we declared our neutrality at the time of their recognition, and to this we have adhered, and shall continue to adhere, provided no change shall occur which, in the judgement of the competent authorities of this Government, shall make a corresponding change on the part of the United States indispensable to their security.

comport to be fitting; to act in a certain way

felicity intense happiness

candor honesty and sincerity

interposition the act of placing in an intervening position

. . . Our policy in regard to Europe, which was adopted at an early stage of the wars which have so long agitated that quarter of the globe, nevertheless remains the same, which is, not to interfere in the internal concerns of any of its powers; to consider the government **de facto** as the legitimate government for us; to cultivate friendly relations with it, and to preserve those relations by a frank, firm, and manly policy, meeting in all instances the just claims of every power, submitting to injuries from none. But in regard to those continents circumstances are eminently and conspicuously different.

It is impossible that the allied powers should extend their political system to any portion of either continent without endangering our peace and happiness; nor can anyone believe that our southern brethren, if left to themselves, would adopt it of their own accord. It is equally impossible, therefore, that we should behold such interposition in any form with indifference. If we look to the comparative strength and resources of Spain and those new Governments, and their distance from each other, it must be obvious that she can never subdue them. It is still the true policy of the United States to leave the parties to themselves, in hope that other powers will pursue the same course. . . .

— James Monroe, December 2, 1823

de facto in fact; actually

EXAMINE THE SOURCE

16. **Identifying Main Idea** What is the main purpose of the Monroe Doctrine?

17. **Determining Context** What specific events led to the writing of the Monroe Doctrine?

18. **Comparing** Does the Monroe Doctrine continue the policy President Washington set forth in his Farewell Address? Or does it represent a change from that policy or both? Explain your reasoning, and cite evidence from this source to support your response.

Evaluate Sources and Use Evidence

19. Citing Text Evidence Review the Supporting Questions you developed at the beginning of the topic and the evidence you gathered and recorded in the graphic organizer. Which sources will help you answer the Supporting Questions? Circle or highlight those sources in your graphic organizer. Looking at the subset of sources you have chosen, be prepared to explain why you chose each source.

	Supporting Question	Primary Source and Notes
1		
2		
3		

20. Directions: Now answer the Supporting Questions that you developed at the beginning of the activity to help guide you in answering the Compelling Question.

Answer for Supporting Question 1:

Answer for Supporting Question 2:

Answer for Supporting Question 3:

Communicate Conclusions

Talk About It COLLABORATE

21. Collaborating Work with a partner. Take turns reviewing your answers to your Supporting Questions. Then summarize the key foreign policies that early leaders of the United States faced. Take turns presenting your summaries to each other. Discuss the similar and different issues and the ways each leader solved the crisis he faced.

Challenge

Think about the foreign issues from the sources. Which one would you like to learn more about? Select one of the issues and the source that talks about it. Reread the source. Then identify any information, including missing perspectives, that is missing from the source.

Write About It

22. Argumentative Writing Think about the foreign crisis faced by each president in the early United States. Write a thesis statement that addresses the following question: Which crisis do you think presented the greatest problem for the country, and how well do you think the president handled that crisis? Give evidence from at least one source to support your thesis statement.

Need Extra Help?

A thesis statement is usually one sentence. For your thesis statement, state the crisis, make a claim, and say how the crisis was handled.

23. Answering the Compelling Question What do you think? How did each president shape foreign policy in the early United States? Write an essay or create a digital presentation that uses the sources to explain the foreign policy of each president, noting any similarities and differences in policy and manner of handling the crisis. Include how the foreign events affected the early United States.

24. **Making Connections** The first five presidents of the United States faced many issues related to foreign policy and had to make choices to lead the country. Foreign policy crises continued throughout the terms of later presidents, too, and the twenty-first century is no exception. Choose one foreign crisis the United States has had to deal with in recent years. Research how the president and/or Congress dealt with the crisis. What is your perspective about how the crisis was handled and whether the actions were appropriate? Write a short paragraph explaining your thoughts about the handling of the crisis and why the actions were effective or not.

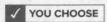 **YOU CHOOSE**

Select one of these Take Informed Action products to apply what you've learned.

A. Create a graphic organizer that compares the actions of two different presidents regarding foreign crises.

B. Write a newspaper editorial in which you describe the crisis you chose and indicate your ideas about how it was handled.

C. Create a political cartoon that shows the crisis and how it was handled.

Take Informed Action Rubric: Write About a Foreign Crisis and How It Was Handled

Self-Evaluation As you investigate a foreign crisis and how it was handled, think about the following criteria. These are the criteria your teacher will use to evaluate your Take Informed Action activity.

Peer Review Use this rubric to grade the description of the crisis and how it was handled and the final product developed by another classmate or group of classmates.

	Organization	Writing/Editing	Historical Accuracy	Logic
4	The piece is exceptionally well organized and focused and demonstrates a thorough and deep understanding of the event or issue.	The paragraph and final product are exceptionally well executed and include no errors.	The piece is well researched and is factually accurate.	The paragraph and final product show evidence of extensive thought.
3	The piece is well organized and focused and demonstrates an adequate understanding of the event or issue.	The paragraph and final product are well executed and include few errors.	The piece is well researched but contains some factual errors.	The paragraph and final product show sufficient evidence of thought.
2	The piece is organized but is inconsistent in focus and demonstrates an inadequate understanding of the event or issue.	The paragraph and final product are adequately executed but include a number of errors.	The piece is not well researched and contains some factual errors.	The paragraph and final product show limited evidence of thought.
1	The piece lacks organization and focus and does not demonstrate a basic understanding of the event or issue.	The paragraph and final product are not adequately executed and include multiple errors.	There are many factual errors.	The paragraph and final product show a lack of thought.
SCORE				

TOPIC 7 • POLITICAL AND GEOGRAPHIC CHANGES, 1828–1850

Democracy and Andrew Jackson's Presidency

? COMPELLING QUESTION

What was President Jackson's attitude toward democracy?

Plan Your Inquiry

In this Inquiry Activity, you will develop Supporting Questions about President Jackson's policies and whether they promoted or interfered with democracy based on the Compelling Question. Then you will examine primary sources related to his presidency and policies. Finally, you will answer your Supporting Questions, communicate your research conclusions, and take action based on what you've learned.

Background Information

Following the War of 1812, the United States grew geographically and economically. New states, such as Indiana, Mississippi, and Missouri, were carved out of western lands. Agriculture, as well as industry and trade, boomed. Politically, more Americans had gained a say in government. At first, only white males who could afford to pay taxes or who owned property could vote. But by the 1820s, white males in many states had gained suffrage, or voting rights. And in most states, actual voters, rather than state legislators, were choosing presidential candidates.

In 1828, candidates faced off in a fierce presidential campaign. War hero Andrew Jackson won the election by a wide margin. His support of the common man's right to take part in government helped him gain votes. Jackson himself had risen from humble beginnings on the country's western frontier. Yet he did not seek equal rights for all. In fact, Jackson held enslaved people and was known to have advertised for the return of those who had run away. Even so, people soon began calling Jackson's party the Democratic Party and the president's policies "Jacksonian Democracy."

Andrew Jackson ran for the president in 1828 for the second time. He won "popular" support, which meant the support of the common people.

Develop Supporting Questions About Democracy and Andrew Jackson's Presidency

 COMPELLING QUESTION

What was President Jackson's attitude toward democracy?

Talk About It

Discuss with a partner what type of information you would need to know to answer this question. For example, one question might be: What did voters believe about President Jackson?

Directions: Write down three additional questions that you need to answer to be able to determine what President Jackson's attitude was toward democracy.

Supporting Question 1:

Supporting Question 2:

Supporting Question 3:

Apply Historical Concepts and Tools

Directions: As you read and work with primary sources, use the graphic organizer to take notes and organize information.

Organizing Source Information		
Source	**Title and Author/ Creator**	**Notes**
A	Old Jack, the famous New Orleans mouser, clearing Uncle Sam's barn of bank and Clay rats, political cartoon	
B	The Political Barbecue, political cartoon	
C	1829 State of the Union Address by Andrew Jackson	
D	Editorial in *Cherokee Phoenix*, March 24, 1830, by Unknown Author	
E	Talk of the President of the United States by Andrew Jackson (delivered by John Eaton and General John Coffee)	

Analyze Sources

Review and analyze Sources A–E. There are questions that accompany each source to help you examine the source and check for historical understanding.

Old Jack, the famous New Orleans mouser, clearing Uncle Sam's barn of bank and Clay rats

One of Andrew Jackson's goals was to do away with the Second Bank of the United States. Jackson thought that the Bank made it too hard for Westerners to get loans. He also did not trust banks and the loans and credit they supplied. The Bank became a hot issue in Jackson's 1832 quest for a second term. Jackson believed the public supported closing the Bank. His opponents thought just the opposite. Bank supporters Henry Clay and Daniel Webster maneuvered to have Bank president Nicholas Biddle apply to renew the Bank's charter early. They thought that the public would turn against Jackson if he said no to the Bank. Jackson did in fact veto, or reject the charter, yet doing so actually made Jackson more popular. He won reelection and eventually succeeded in closing the Bank.

This political cartoon was likely drawn during the 1832 presidential campaign. In the 1830s, cartoonists often used rats to symbolize corruption. Some historians believe that the rat in the cat's mouth is Henry Clay. Another rat might be Nicholas Biddle, the president of the Bank. Jackson is shown as the cat, and he holds a rat in his mouth. His tail says "Veto." He is defending the barn (symbolizing the country), which is owned by Uncle Sam, and he is protecting it from rats, or corruption. The scared rats are saying things such as "My case is desperate!" In contrast, the men in the doorway react positively to what's happening.

PRIMARY SOURCE : POLITICAL CARTOON

1. Interpreting Why might the artist have set the cartoon in a barn with a cat and rats?

2. Explaining What is unusual about the rats? Why do you think the artist presented them this way?

3. Analyzing What is meant when the man in the back, who may be Uncle Sam, says, "Bravo my Boys! keep him in the Barn; and no doubt, but he will keep the Rats away." How does this quote relate to the rat's quote, "No chance for me while he's in the Barn"?

4. Making Inferences Why do you think the artist used rats to symbolize corruption?

5. Speculating Does this cartoon support Jackson's policy? How might it have affected the opinions of a like-minded audience? What about an audience that did not agree?

B

The Political Barbecue

Some cartoonists, such as Henry R. Robinson, made fun of Jackson for wanting to close the Bank. Easterners in particular liked the Bank. After all, they reaped the most benefit, finding it fairly easy to get loans. This Robinson cartoon presents an unflattering image of Jackson and his views on the Bank. Jackson is seen as a hog being roasted over a barbecue labeled "Public Opinion." The man kneeling at the right is former Secretary of the Treasury William Duane, and the man on the left is Jack Downing, a fictitious character that often appeared in political cartoons and commentary of the time. The men standing over Jackson disagree with his policy about the Bank. Included are Senators Henry Clay, Daniel Webster, and William Preston, bank president Nicholas Biddle, and one unknown figure. Martin Van Buren, the vice president, is seen as a small, mischievous devil taking off with treasury notes. In the cartoon, each Bank supporter is making a joke at the expense of Jackson. For example, U.S. Senator from Massachusetts Daniel Webster quips, "In Massachusetts they call it Roasting." U.S. Senator from South Carolina William B. Preston replies, "In South Carolina t'is called Barbecue only he wants a little more Basteing," which means to pour juices over the meat to keep it moist.

PRIMARY SOURCE : POLITICAL CARTOON

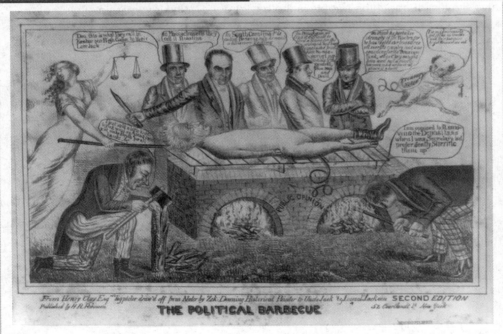

6. Comparing and Contrasting How is this cartoon similar to and different from the "Old Jack" political cartoon?

7. Analyzing What does the artist suggest about Jackson's policy toward the Bank of the United States? Explain the tone and perspective.

8. Analyzing What is significant about the people in the background? Why do you think they are included?

9. Interpreting What do the quotations tell you about the men's relationship to President Jackson?

10. Evaluating What information is missing from this source?

C

1829 State of the Union Address, Andrew Jackson

In 1824, Jackson ran for president against four candidates. Jackson received the most popular votes. However, he did not win a majority of the electoral votes so he was not named the winner. That meant the House of Representatives had to decide the outcome. The House chose John Quincy Adams. Jackson believed that he and the voters had been robbed. He was determined to win in 1828, which he did. This excerpt from his State of the Union address relates directly to what happened in the 1824 election.

PRIMARY SOURCE : ADDRESS

❝ I consider it one of the most urgent of my duties to bring to your attention the **propriety** of amending that part of the Constitution which relates to the election of President and Vice-President. Our system of government was by its framers deemed an experiment, and they therefore consistently provided a mode of remedying its defects.

To the people belongs the right of electing their Chief Magistrate; it was never designed that their choice should in any case be defeated, either by the intervention of electoral colleges or by the agency confided, under certain **contingencies**, to the House of Representatives. Experience proves that in proportion as agents to execute the will of the people are multiplied there is danger of their wishes being frustrated. Some may be unfaithful; all are liable [likely] to err. So far, therefore, as the people can with convenience speak, it is safer for them to express their own will. . . .

. . .[Y]et under the present mode of election a minority may often elect a President, and when this happens it may reasonably be expected that efforts will be made on the part of the majority to **rectify** this injurious operation of their institutions. But although no evil of this character should result from such a **perversion** of the first principle of our system—that the majority is to govern—it must be very certain that a President elected by a minority can not enjoy the confidence necessary to the successful discharge of his duties.

In this as in all other matters of public concern policy requires that as few **impediments** as possible should exist to the free operation of the public will. Let us, then, endeavor so to amend our system that the office of Chief Magistrate may not be conferred upon any citizen but in pursuance of a fair expression of the will of the majority.

I would therefore recommend such an amendment of the Constitution as may remove all intermediate agency in the election of the President and Vice-President. ❞

— Andrew Jackson, State of the Union Address, December 8, 1829

propriety the state of being suitable

contingency something that could happen but is not certain to happen

rectify to set something right

perversion something used for a corrupt purpose

impediment an obstacle or hindrance

11. Identifying Why does Jackson believe it is an "urgent duty" to amend the Constitution?

12. Summarizing Whom does Jackson say has the right of electing the president? What does he believe about their choice?

13. Analyzing Perspectives Jackson lost the 1824 presidential election when the House of Representatives had the task of choosing the winner. How did this event influence his perspective?

14. Evaluating Do you think Jackson is advocating for a more democratic approach to electing the president and vice president? Explain your reasoning.

Editorial, *Cherokee Phoenix*, Written by Unknown

In 1828 and 1829, Georgia lawmakers passed laws granting the state claim over Cherokee land. An 1829 act said that Cherokee law was no longer valid. It also declared that Georgia law would apply to all land in the state. These actions took away Cherokee rights, including land rights. Some Cherokee land was highly valued for its gold mines. To add to the Cherokee's problems, the United States Congress enacted the Indian Removal Act in 1830. This act served to back up the Georgia laws. The Cherokee hoped they could regain their land through the United States legal system. The following article, printed in a Cherokee newspaper, expresses the viewpoint of Cherokee people on the issue.

PRIMARY SOURCE : NEWSPAPER ARTICLE

❝ *Intruders.*—We have often complained of the **remissness** of the executive of the United States to remove the intruders who have settled upon Cherokee soil; in defiance of the treaties, and the **intercourse law** of the Union. Our complaints have been thus far of no avail. The President has refused, at least for a time, to employ force, because the intruders, or the settlers, as they are **stiled**, are on disputed land—Georgia claims it as having been purchased from the Creeks. The Cherokees have contended that if Georgia does claim it, that is not a sufficient reason that a lawless set of people should be encouraged to come and abuse the original inhabitants, for it is an established rule among civilized people, that a claim must first be **substantiated** before possession can be had. Why should the Indians be deprived of this rule? The Cherokees have been in peaceable possession of this disputed land—now Georgia comes in and claims it, and must they, upon that **naked** claim be deprived of their country and rights? [M]ust they with their families as a number of them have been, be turned out of doors? Is this justice? Is this protecting the Indians in their rights? Let the public judge. See also the effects of the **tacit** consent of the General Government to these intrusions. To the many injuries upon our persons, *murder*, in its most heinous, brutal, and cowardly form has been added. Who would not cry *oppression* under such treatment as this?

But what becomes of the reason given by the War Department for refusing to employ military force, indeed any measure, to remove intruders on the disputed land, when there are *thousands* on other parts of the nation? In one spot, within the circumference of a few miles, there are not less than *three thousand* employed in robbing the Cherokees of gold! . . . .

Col. Montgomery, the U. S. Agent has lately been to the place where these miners are collected, and warned them off. Some have already obeyed and removed, but others have positively refused to go, and probably will not until

remissness the quality of being neglectful

intercourse law an act passed in 1790 that said the United States would regulate trade and dealings with Native American groups and created treaties about land

stiled [styled] called

substantiate to give evidence that proves something

naked lacking support

tacit implied but not actually expressed

they are forced away. That part of the country not being within the line claimed by Georgia, we should like to know what possible excuse the executive will make, if the intercourse law is not forthwith put in force, & these people ousted. If the President does withhold the authority entrusted to him, and countenance such aggressions, then indeed, *oppression, systematic oppression,* as plain as day light will be at our doors!**"**

— Unknown, *Cherokee Phoenix,* March 24, 1830

Need Extra Help?

When reading a source that has several paragraphs, jot down the main idea of each paragraph. Consider how well the author supports those ideas and how it relates to your Supporting Questions and the Compelling Question.

EXAMINE THE SOURCE

15. Summarizing What claim does the author make about President Jackson and the "intruders"? What claim do the Cherokee make about the situation?

16. Citing Evidence What evidence does the author provide to show that ignoring the situation with the Cherokee in Georgia is more widespread?

17. Analyzing Perspectives What does the author suggest about President Jackson's policy toward Native Americans? Explain the author's tone.

Talk of the President of the United States by Andrew Jackson

In 1830, President Jackson requested that the Chickasaw people meet with United States representatives. One of these was the United States Secretary of War, John Eaton. The other was John Coffee, a friend of Jackson. Jackson had often relied on Coffee to handle matters related to Native American removal. Jackson directed the men to deliver the following message to the Chickasaw. The message delivers a stark ultimatum, or a demand to make a choice.

PRIMARY SOURCE : ADDRESS

❝ Brothers:—You have long dwelt upon the soil you occupy, and in early time before the white man kindled his fires too near to yours, and by settling around, narrowed down the limits of the chase, you were, though uninstructed, yet a happy people. Now your white brothers are around you. States have been erected within your ancient limits, which claim a right to govern and control your people as they do their own citizens, and to make them answerable to their civil and criminal codes. Your **Great Father** has not the authority to prevent this state of things; and he now asks if you are prepared and ready to submit yourselves to the laws of Mississippi, make a surrender of your ancient laws and customs, and peaceably and quietly live under those of the white man?

Brothers, listen:—The laws to which you must be subjected, are not oppressive, for they are those to which your white brothers conform, and are happy. Under them, you will not be permitted to seek private revenge, but in all cases where wrong may be done, you are through them to seek **redress**. No taxes upon your property or yourselves, except such as may be imposed upon a white brother, will be assessed against you.—The court will be open for the redress of wrongs; and bad men will be made answerable for whatever crimes or misdemeanors may be committed by any of your people, or our own.

Brothers listen:—To these laws, where you are, you must submit;—there is no preventive—no other alternative. Your great Father cannot nor can Congress, prevent it. The States only can. What then? Do you believe that we can live under those laws. That you can surrender all your ancient habits and the forms by which you have been so long controlled? If so, your Great Father has nothing to say or to advise. He has only to express a hope that you may find happiness in the determination you shall make, whatever it may be. His earnest desire, is, that you may be perpetuated and preserved as a nation; and this he believes can only be done and secured by your consent to remove to a country beyond the Mississippi, which for the happiness of our red friends was laid out by the Government a long time since, and to which it was expected ere this they would have gone. Where you are, it is not possible you can live contented and happy.

Great Father the president   **redress** an action to set something right

Besides the laws of Mississippi which must operate upon you, and which your Great Father cannot prevent, white men continually intruding are with difficulty kept off your lands, and difficulties continue to increase around you. **"**

— Talk of the President of the United States, Andrew Jackson given on August 22, 1830, by John Eaton and General John Coffee, *Cherokee Phoenix*, published October 1, 1830

EXAMINE THE SOURCE

18. Identifying Main Idea What is the message of this address?

19. Analyzing What is the tone at the beginning of the address? How does it change toward the end?

20. Drawing Conclusions How do you think Native Americans hearing this address reacted? What do you already know about Native Americans and Andrew Jackson that helps you draw your conclusion?

Evaluate Sources and Use Evidence

21. <u>**Citing Text Evidence**</u> Review the Supporting Questions you developed at the beginning of the topic and the evidence you gathered and recorded in the graphic organizer. Which sources will help you answer the Supporting Questions? Circle or highlight those sources in your graphic organizer. Looking at the subset of sources you have chosen, be prepared to explain why you chose each source.

	Supporting Question	Primary Source and Notes
1		
2		
3		

Challenge

Research further the Bank of the United States and Jackson's policy toward it. Find at least one primary or secondary source text. Analyze the source and use it to help answer one or more of your Supporting Questions. Include your research in your response.

22. Directions: Now answer the Supporting Questions that you developed at the beginning of the activity to help guide you in answering the Compelling Question.

Answer for Supporting Question 1:

Answer for Supporting Question 2:

Answer for Supporting Question 3:

Communicate Conclusions

Talk About It

23. Collaborating Work in small groups to discuss Jackson's presidency. Review each row on your graphic organizers as you discuss Jackson's policies, his reasons for those policies, and how they affected people's rights. Take notes about your discussion and choose someone to share your conclusions with the class.

Write About It

24. Argumentative Writing Choose two sources that you recorded in the graphic organizer that helped you answer your Supporting Questions. Think about how these two sources show how Jackson either worked for the benefit of the people or hindered their rights. Then write one or two paragraphs in which you argue about the effectiveness of Jackson's presidency.

23. Answering the Compelling Question What do you think? What was President Jackson's attitude toward democracy? Give an oral presentation in which you cite at least two pieces of evidence from the sources that show whether Jackson's attitude helped or hindered democracy.

26. Making Connections Many people today agree with Andrew Jackson's belief about the Electoral College. They share his view that it is undemocratic because the people do not directly elect the president. Others have a different perspective on the Electoral College and believe it shows democracy in action based on its establishment by the Constitution. With a partner, research the pros and cons of the Electoral College. Then together, make a pro and con chart with at least three pros and three cons.

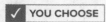 **YOU CHOOSE**

Select one of these Take Informed Action products to apply what you've learned.

A. Design a bulletin board display in which you show how the Electoral College does or does not reflect democracy.

B. Write and present a podcast to explain your point of view on the Electoral College making sure to explain its relationship to democracy.

C. Create a political cartoon that reflects your views on the Electoral College.

Take Informed Action Rubric: The Pros and Cons of the Electoral College

<u>**Self-Evaluation**</u> As you identify the pros and cons of the Electoral College and its relationship to democracy, think about the following criteria. These are the criteria your teacher will use to evaluate your Take Informed Action activity.

<u>**Peer Review**</u> Use this rubric to grade the pro and con chart and the final product developed by another classmate or group of classmates.

	Organization	Writing/Editing	Historical Accuracy	Logic
4	The piece is exceptionally well organized and focused and demonstrates a thorough and deep understanding of the event or issue.	The chart and final product are exceptionally well executed and include no errors.	The piece is well researched and is factually accurate.	The chart and final product show evidence of extensive thought.
3	The piece is well organized and focused and demonstrates an adequate understanding of the event or issue.	The chart and final product are well executed and include few errors.	The piece is well researched but contains some factual errors.	The chart and final product show sufficient evidence of thought.
2	The piece is organized but is inconsistent in focus and demonstrates an inadequate understanding of the event or issue.	The chart and final product are adequately executed but include a number of errors.	The piece is not well researched and contains some factual errors.	The chart and final product show limited evidence of thought.
1	The piece lacks organization and focus and does not demonstrate a basic understanding of the event or issue.	The chart and final product are not adequately executed and include multiple errors.	There are many factual errors.	The chart and final product show a lack of thought.
SCORE				

TOPIC 8 • LIFE IN THE NORTH AND SOUTH, 1820–1860

Early Immigration in the United States

 COMPELLING QUESTION

How did Americans react to immigrants in the mid-1800s?

Plan Your Inquiry

In this Inquiry Activity, you will develop Supporting Questions about immigration during the mid-1800s and how some groups responded to immigration based on the Compelling Question. Then you will examine primary sources related to immigration at the time. Finally, you will answer your Supporting Questions, communicate your research conclusions, and take action based on what you've learned.

Background Information

As the 1800s progressed, Americans were well on their way to populating much of the land newly acquired by the United States. Another important development occurred as well. Thanks to the Industrial Revolution that started in Great Britain, the United States's economy was changing dramatically. The economy no longer depended almost solely on agriculture. Manufacturing, or the making of products, was becoming widespread, particularly in the North. Many people began working in factories in growing cities. The United States seemed to be a good place to reside for its freedom and to earn a living. That fact did not go unnoticed by Europeans.

During the mid-1840s, many immigrants from Ireland made new homes in the eastern United States, and many Germans settled in the Midwest. The Irish came to escape famine, which is an extreme shortage of food. The Germans came to find work or to gain more rights. The immigrants brought with them their languages, religion, and customs. Some Americans were uncomfortable with the rise of this immigrant population. These Americans became known as nativists because they did not want to share their land with new groups of people. This meant they were against immigration. In particular, Protestant Americans were unhappy about the number of Roman Catholics arriving from countries such as Ireland. They also thought that immigrants would take jobs away from them. Some even claimed that immigration would bring about more crime and disease.

Americans with these beliefs formed the political party called the Know-Nothing Party. It got this name because of how its secretive members answered questions. Usually, they simply replied, "I know nothing." For a brief time, the party gained much popularity and influence in state legislatures and Congress. Despite the demise of the party, anti-immigrant feelings continued.

The Know-Nothing Party was made up of people who wanted stricter citizenship laws. It used propaganda, such as this illustrated advertising label for soap, to spread its anti-immigration beliefs. In the foreground of the label are two Native Americans, representative of the movement's prejudice against the foreign born.

Develop Supporting Questions About Immigration in the Mid-1800s

 **COMPELLING QUESTION**

How did Americans react to immigrants in the mid-1800s?

Talk About It

Discuss with a partner what type of information you would need to know to answer this question. For example, one question might be: What did the Know-Nothing Party stand for?

Directions: Write down three additional questions that you need to answer to be able to determine the reaction Americans had to immigration during the mid-1800s.

Supporting Question 1:

Supporting Question 2:

Supporting Question 3:

Apply Historical Concepts and Tools

Directions: As you read and work with primary sources, use the graphic organizer to take notes and organize information.

Organizing Source Information		
Source	**Title and Author/ Creator**	**Notes**
A	Citizen Know-Nothing, photograph	
B	Address of the Delegates of the Native American National Convention	
C	A Few Words on Native Americanism by Orestes Brownson	
D	Annual Message to the Legislature by William Seward	
E	Letter to Governor Leonard J. Farwell by Herman Haertel	

Analyze Sources

Review and analyze Sources A–E. There are questions that accompany each source to help you examine the source and check for historical understanding.

A

Citizen Know-Nothing

As more and more immigrants entered the United States, the Know-Nothing Party saw a rise in membership. Some Americans were caught up in an anti-Catholic and anti-immigrant wave and wanted more controls over who was allowed to enter the country. This lithograph, created in 1854, is a portrait of a young man believed to be Andrew Jackson Donelson. He was the nephew of Andrew Jackson's wife and was named for President Jackson. In 1856, he was nominated by the Know-Nothing Party as former president Millard Fillmore's running mate. They lost the election. This portrait is titled "Uncle Sam's Youngest Son, Citizen Know Nothing." It was meant to represent the ideal member of the Know-Nothing Party. The word *citizen* appears below the man, and above him sits an eagle in front of a bright star. An American flag surrounds the image.

PRIMARY SOURCE : PHOTOGRAPH

1. **Explaining** Think about what the man is wearing and how he looks. What might his appearance have indicated about what some people believed represented a U.S. citizen?

2. **Analyzing Perspectives** Why might the creator of the image have included the American flag surrounding the image?

3. **Drawing Conclusions** How did the increasing number of European immigrants most likely influence this image?

B

Address of the Delegates of the Native American National Convention

In 1845, members of the Native American Party, also known as the American Party, held a national convention in Philadelphia, Pennsylvania. The party set its platform, or the principles and goals of the party, at the convention. Leaders of the party outlined their nativist beliefs about the dangers of immigration to the United States in the following declaration.

PRIMARY SOURCE : DECLARATION

❝ [N]umerous societies and corporate bodies in foreign countries have found it economical to transport to our shores, at public and private expense, the feeble [weak], the imbecile [unintelligent], the idle [lazy] and **intractable**, thus relieving themselves of the burden resulting from the vices of the European social systems, by **availing** themselves of the generous errors of our own.

The **alms houses** of Europe are emptied upon our coast, *and this by our own invitation*—not casually, or to a trivial extent, but systematically, and upon a constantly increasing scale. The **Bedlams** of the old world have contributed their share to the **torrent** of immigration, and the lives of our citizens have been attempted in the streets of our capital cities by mad-men, just liberated from European hospitals, upon the express condition that they should be transported to America.

By the orders of European governments, the punishment of crimes has been **commuted** for **banishment** to the land of the free; and criminals in iron have crossed the ocean to be cast loose upon society on their arrival upon our shores. The United States are rapidly becoming the **lazar-house** and **penal colony** of Europe; nor can we reasonably **censure** such proceedings: They are legitimate consequences of our own unlimited benevolence [kindness]; and it is of such material that we profess to manufacture free and enlightened citizens, by a process occupying five short years at most, but practically, oftentimes embraced in a much shorter period of time. ❞

— American Party, Assembled at Philadelphia, July 4, 1845

intractable not easily managed or controlled

avail to take advantage of something

alms a house run by a charity where poor people live

bedlam: mahem

torrent flood

commute to change to something less harsh

banishment: exile

lazar-house a place for people with infectious diseases

penal colony a place where prisoners are sent to live

censure to find fault with

4. Explaining How does the declaration depict immigrants? Cite evidence to support your response.

5. Analyzing Perspectives According to the source, who is to blame for the immigrant situation, and why is the situation happening?

6. Drawing Conclusions According to the source, how do immigrants harm society in the United States? What are the limits to this argument?

C

A Few Words on Native Americanism

This article by activist and writer Orestes Brownson shows a more tolerant attitude toward immigration. Orestes Brownson's many writings include personal opinions on topics such as labor, social reform, democracy, emancipation, and nativism. He published a journal called *Brownson's Quarterly Review* beginning in 1838, in which he shared his religious views. In this article, Brownson is reacting to the nativist sentiments presented by a member of the Know-Nothing or Native American Party.

PRIMARY SOURCE : ARTICLE

66 [W]e would say to our countrymen that they would do well to begin by checking the **demagogical** spirit in themselves, and to be less untrue to our own American institutions. It is their fault, if they have allowed foreign radicals to corrupt them; and if danger is threatened, it is because they have lost the **integrity** and **sobriety** of our fathers. Let them remember, that it is unreasonable to expect foreigners to be transformed at once into Americans; that nationality is a stubborn thing, and is not worn out in a day, or in a single generation; that the nationality, the usages, manners, and customs, which offend us in foreign immigrants, are in themselves as respectable as our own, and that much can easily be pardoned to a poor people who have for ages been oppressed by tyrannical or incapable governments. Let them reflect on the immense advantage to material prosperity which we have gained by this influx of foreigners which alarms them. The foreign population, undeniably, has its faults, its vices even; but, though different, they are not greater than our own, often not so great. . . . Our eyes are open to their vices, and closed to our own. . . . It is easy to **declaim** against the poor, uneducated Irish crowded together in our large towns, and to find much among them that is really annoying; but it is very difficult to go among these same poor Irish people, into their houses, and enter into familiar and kindly conversation with them, and not come away charmed. . . . Place the same number of Anglo-Americans in the position of these poor and **reviled** Irish people, subject them to the same **privations** and the same usage, and we should find a difference not at all flattering to our national vanity. . . . [R]eflect that the children of the foreign population will grow up native Americans, and you may well moderate your feelings against them. They are too numerous to be massacred, too numerous to be driven from the country, . . . The immigration will soon cease or be greatly diminished, and in a few years the foreign population will be **assimilated** to the native. So, after all, with mutual **forbearance**, the evil will gradually disappear. 99

— Orestes Brownson, *Brownson's Quarterly Review*, Vol. II, No. III (Third Series), 1854

---

demogogical (demagogical) having to do with gaining power by appealing to the emotions and prejudices of the people

integrity honesty

sobriety seriousness

declaim to lecture

revile to scorn

assimilate to take in and integrate the cultural traditions of a population

forbearance self-control and tolerance

privation a necessity for living

7. Identifying What does the author believe about foreigners and foreign cultures?

8. Contrasting How does the author contrast the Irish immigrants with Anglo-Americans?

9. Analyzing Perspectives What does the author suggest about the role of immigrants?

Annual Message to the Legislature [of New York]

The writer of the following excerpt, William Henry Seward, was elected governor of New York in 1838. He later became a U.S. senator, and then secretary of state for Abraham Lincoln. After Lincoln's assassination, Seward remained in this position and is perhaps best known for recommending the purchase of Alaska from Russia in 1867. This excerpt is from Seward's Inaugural Address as governor, given on January 1, 1839. In his speech, Seward expresses the importance of equal rights for immigrants and suggests they should be welcomed and educated so they can become citizens.

PRIMARY SOURCE : SPEECH

❝ To enlarge . . . national prosperity, while we equalize its enjoyments and direct it to the universal **diffusion** of knowledge, are the great responsibilities of our age. . . .

There is another resource [through immigration] which is ours, . . . [i]t is the surplus labor, the incalculable surplus labor of the European states. This is wealth, and the moral energies of those who bring hither are an element of national greatness. They come to us under the same law which controlled the colonists in their emigration and settlement here. They force themselves upon us even though we inhospitably resist them. . . . This tide is now acquiring increased volume and velocity from the reduction of the distance between the two continents by Atlantic steam navigation. They who would roll it back, must change not merely the relations existing between this country and Europe, . . . [t]hey must **subvert** the institutions, and break down the altars of liberty in America, arrest the prosperity of the nation, deprive enterprise of its motives, and deny to labor its rewards. If all this is not done, the settlement of our western regions will go on; new states will demand admission into the Union; their trade and commerce will continue to augment our wealth; . . . The policy of this state includes every measure which tends to develop our own resources, . . . and every measure which invites the labor and capital of Europe. It requires that we welcome immigrants among ourselves, or speed them on their way to a western destination, with all the sympathy which their misfortunes at home, their condition as strangers here, and their devotion to liberty, ought to excite. If their inclination leads them to remain among us, we must assimilate their principle, habits, manners, and opinions, to our own. To accomplish this, we must extend to them the right of citizenship, with all its inestimable **franchises**. ❞

—William Seward, *The Works of William H. Seward, Vol. II,* edited by George E. Baker, 1888

Need Extra Help?

When reading a long source, read each sentence one at a time and identify its main idea. For words you do not know and that are not defined, use a print or online dictionary to find their meaning. Then paraphrase each sentence to make sure you understand the source's message.

diffusion the act of spreading

subvert to overturn

franchise a right

10. Analyzing Perspective How does Seward view immigrants? Why are they able to arrive in great numbers?

11. Drawing Conclusions What does the author suggest about the fate of the country if anti-immigration views are not diminished? Cite evidence to support your response.

12. Identifying What does the author explain about how we should treat immigrants?

E

Letter to Governor Leonard J. Farwell

During the mid-1800s, the new state of Wisconsin became home to thousands of settlers. Some were from the eastern United States, but many were new to the country, having just arrived from Europe. At first, most immigrants were from Ireland, England, Scotland, and Wales, but later, many were from Germany. By 1870, more than a million people lived in Wisconsin. By around 1852, Wisconsin had a Commission of Emigration to bring more immigrants to the state. This excerpt is a letter by Herman Haertel, the commissioner of emigration. He wrote to Wisconsin governor Leonard J. Farwell regarding how the commission had been encouraging immigrants to move to Wisconsin. Due to nativism, the commission ended in 1855.

PRIMARY SOURCE : LETTER

❝ I engaged the services of two men, whose business it is to visit all immigrant ships on their arrival at this port . . . to distribute among them descriptions of the State of Wisconsin in their respective languages. . . . I had my business card & other necessary advertisements published in several english & german papers, and besides that circulars, notices &c. printed.

It is made my duty, . . . to **induce** those who are either wholly undecided as to their place of settlement, or intend to go to other States, to choose Wisconsin for their new home. To bring about this desirable result, it is not sufficient to have distributed among them pamphlets, hand bills and business cards; but it is of the utmost importance to meet and communicate with them personally. . . .

I made it, therefore, my first object to have personal interviews with all those who have not already chosen their future residence, or intend to go to other states, in order to show them the advantages held out by our state. . . .

[M]any emigrants were sent to my office, of whom a considerable number were induced to go to Wisconsin. Up to June 1st about 200 emigrants, mostly Germans, had visited my office, and I have reason to hope that this number will increase every month. I am consulted daily by persons living in this place and other states who intend to move westward and generally show great **predilections** for Wisconsin, and also receive many letters from residents of other states asking for accurate details [regarding] Wisconsin. . . .

For the purpose of . . . inducing emigrants even before they are leaving their old country, to choose Wisconsin for their new home, I have sent my card, descriptions of the state and articles of correspondence to european newspapers of the widest circulation, to be published regularly or from time to time. ❞

—Herman Haertel, Commissioner of Emigration (Wisconsin), 1853

Copyright © McGraw Hill   TEXT: Haertel, Herman. "Letter to the governor on immigrant transportation, 1853."
Unpublished manuscript in the Wisconsin Historical Society Archives (Governor. Correspondence and Letterbooks:
Special, 1840-1914; Series 34: box 12, folder 1); online facsimile at www.wisconsinhistory.org.

induce   to convince or persuade

predilection   a set preference toward something

13. Identifying According to the excerpt, what is the "duty" of the letter writer?

14. Analyzing What is the tone of the letter? What clues in the writing help you know this?

Evaluate Sources and Use Evidence

15. <u>Citing Text Evidence</u> Review the Supporting Questions you developed at the beginning of the topic and the evidence you gathered and recorded in the graphic organizer. Which sources will help you answer the Supporting Questions? Circle or highlight those sources in your graphic organizer. Looking at the subset of sources you have chosen, be prepared to explain why you chose each source.

	Supporting Question	Primary Source and Notes
1		
2		
3		

Challenge

Research other Americans' views toward immigration in the mid-1800s. Find at least one primary or secondary source text that supports immigration and one that opposes it. Analyze the sources and use them to help answer one or more of your Supporting Questions. Include your research in your response.

16. Directions: Now answer the Supporting Questions that you developed at the beginning of the activity to help guide you in answering the Compelling Question.

Answer for Supporting Question 1:

Answer for Supporting Question 2:

Answer for Supporting Question 3:

Communicate Conclusions

Talk About It COLLABORATE

17. Collaborating Individually, rank the sources in the order of their usefulness in answering each of your Supporting Questions. Then in a group, share your Supporting Questions, answers, and rankings. Discuss the following questions:

- What attitude, or bias, does each source present, and how does it affect your understanding?

- What limitations does each source have in terms of the information provided?

- Why did you rank the sources in the way you did? Discuss any disagreements.

Write About It

18. Argumentative Writing Choose two sources that you recorded in the graphic organizer that helped you answer your Supporting Questions. Then write a letter or e-mail to the creator of each source in which you summarize the content and explain its significance. Discuss how each source helps you answer your Supporting Questions. Be sure to include key ideas from the sources and from the background information about each source.

19. Answering the Compelling Question What do you think? How did Americans react to immigrants in the mid-1800s? Give an oral presentation in which you cite two pieces of evidence from the sources that show what Americans thought about immigration in the mid-1800s.

20. <u>Making Connections</u> Compare the immigration policies of two presidents from the twenty-first century. To choose the presidents, consider what you know about them and look for presidents whose ideas may be alike on some issues but not on others. Read two articles in mainstream, reliable news media about each president's policy. Take notes on both policies.

✓ YOU CHOOSE

Select one of these Take Informed Action products to apply what you've learned.

A. Write a newspaper article in which you report your findings.

B. Create a Venn diagram to show the similarities and differences in the policies.

C. Present a slideshow explaining how the two policies are similar and different.

Take Informed Action Rubric: Immigration Policies

Self-Evaluation As you identify the similarities and differences of two twenty-first-century immigration policies, think about the following criteria. These are the criteria your teacher will use to evaluate your Take Informed Action activity.

Peer Review Use this rubric to grade the research and the final product developed by another classmate or group of classmates.

	Organization	Research	Historical Accuracy	Writing/Logic
4	The piece is exceptionally well organized and focused and demonstrates a thorough and deep understanding of the event or issue.	The research shows a thorough synthesis of information from appropriate sources about the immigration policies of two presidents.	The piece is well researched and is factually accurate.	The final product shows evidence of extensive thought.
3	The piece is well organized and focused and demonstrates an adequate understanding of the event or issue.	The research reflects an adequate synthesis of information from appropriate sources about the immigration policies of two presidents.	The piece is well researched but contains some factual errors.	The final product shows sufficient evidence of thought.
2	The piece is organized but is inconsistent in focus and demonstrates an inadequate understanding of the event or issue.	The research reflects a general discussion of information but sources are only somewhat related to immigration.	The piece is not well researched and contains some factual errors.	The final product shows limited evidence of thought.
1	The piece lacks organization and focus and does not demonstrate a basic understanding of the event or issue.	The research demonstrates a lack of effort and a failure to use appropriate sources.	There are many factual errors.	The final product shows a lack of thought.
SCORE				

TOPIC 9 • DIVISION AND CIVIL WAR, 1821–1865

The Views of Abolitionists

 COMPELLING QUESTION

Why did slavery need to be abolished?

Plan Your Inquiry

In this Inquiry Activity, you will develop Supporting Questions about arguments related to the freeing of enslaved people based on the Compelling Question. Then, you will examine primary sources written by abolitionists. Finally, you will answer your Supporting Questions, communicate your research conclusions, and take action based on what you've learned.

Background Information

By the mid-1800s, the United States had become divided both in economic activity and viewpoints about human rights. In the North, rocky soil allowed only for small farms that could easily be maintained by families. Also, large amounts of land were being used for industry. In contrast, the South had a mild climate and fertile soil that led to not only family farms, but also the creation of large, highly-profitable farms called plantations. Landowners largely forced enslaved African Americans to maintain the huge plantations. Southerners defended slavery as necessary for their economic survival. A growing number of Northerners, however, saw enslavement as against the very ideals of American democracy and its promise of freedom.

Many slaveholders treated enslaved African Americans especially inhumanely. Workers were forced to toil in fields for long hours. They could be sold at any time and thus split from their families. Beatings were common, especially if they tried to escape. Most enslaved people had little to no choice and simply endured.

Some Americans, both free African Americans and whites, took action against slavery. They became known as abolitionists. They wrote about the evils of enslavement. They spoke out at meetings with fiery speeches. Some even started newspapers devoted to the issue. African American abolitionists who had escaped slavery recounted their experiences in horrifying detail. Some abolitionists escorted runaway enslaved people out of the South, and others hid them in safe houses. These abolitionists took part in the Underground Railroad, a network of escape routes.

Many other people of the time reacted negatively to the work of abolitionists. A large number of Northerners did not want African Americans to gain a greater role in society. Southerners believed that abolitionists, if allowed to continue, would destroy their way of life and the Southern economy.

Sojourner Truth was enslaved until she was freed in New York. She was active as an abolitionist and in the women's rights movement, speaking out for both racial and gender equality.

Develop Supporting Questions About Abolitionists and Slavery

 COMPELLING QUESTION

Why did slavery need to be abolished?

Talk About It

Discuss with a partner what type of information you would need to know to answer this question. For example, one question might be the following: What led people to become abolitionists?

Directions: Write down three additional questions that you need to answer to be able to determine the reasons for abolishing slavery.

Supporting Question 1:

Supporting Question 2:

Supporting Question 3:

Apply Historical Concepts and Tools

Directions: As you read and work with primary sources, use the graphic organizer to take notes and organize information.

		Organizing Source Information
Source	**Title and Author/ Creator**	**Notes**
A	*Walker's Appeals in Four Articles*	
B	"To the Public" by William Lloyd Garrison	
C	"What to the Slave Is the Fourth of July?" by Frederick Douglass	
D	"I Am Pleading for My People" by Sojourner Truth	
E	Mothers with Young Children at Work in the Field, illustration	

Analyze Sources

Review and analyze Sources A–E. There are questions that accompany each source to help you examine the source and check for historical understanding.

Walker's Appeals in Four Articles

David Walker, born in 1796 or 1797, was the son of an enslaved father and a free mother. He founded an abolitionist organization and also wrote about the issue. In this excerpt from a pamphlet entitled *The Appeal*, Walker tries to convince enslaved people in the South to rebel. To get his pamphlets to the South, he hid them in the pockets of the secondhand clothing he sold to sailors from his waterfront shop. When the clothes resold, the pamphlets would be discovered.

PRIMARY SOURCE : PAMPHLET

❝ The Americans say, that we are ungrateful—but I ask them for heaven's sake what we should be grateful to them for—for murdering our fathers and mothers?—Or do they wish us to return thanks to them for chaining and handcuffing us, branding us, [cramming] fire down our throats, or for keeping in slavery, and beating us nearly or quite to death to make us work in ignorance and miseries, to support them and their families. . . .

And as for the greater part of the whites, it has hitherto been their greatest object and glory to keep us ignorant of our Maker, so as to make us believe that we were made to be slaves to them and their children. . . . [T]hose men tell us that . . . God put a dark stain upon us, that we might be known as their slaves!!!! . . . But the whites having made us so wretched, by subjecting us to slavery, and having murdered so many millions of us, in order to make us work for them, and out of devilishness—and they taking our wives, whom we love as we do ourselves—our mothers, who bore the pains of death to give us birth—our fathers and dear little children, and ourselves, and strip and beat us one before the other—chain, handcuff, and drag us about like rattle-snakes—shoot us down like wild bears, before each other's faces, to make us **submissive** to, and work to support them and their families. . . . [Whites] know that they have done us so much injury, they are afraid that we, being men, and [not brutes], will **retaliate**, and woe will be to them; therefore, that dreadful fear, together with an **avaricious** spirit, and the natural love in them, to be called masters, . . . bring them to the resolve that they will keep us in ignorance and wretchedness, as long as they possibly can, and make the best of their time, while it lasts. ❞

— David Walker, *Walker's Appeals in Four Articles; Together with a Preamble, to the Coloured Citizens of the World, but in Particular, and Very Expressly, to Those of the United States of America*, 1830

---

avaricious greedy and interested in gaining wealth

submissive ready to conform to the will of others

retaliate to get back at someone

Need Extra Help?

When reading a long source, read each sentence one at a time and identify its main idea. For words you do not know and that are not defined, use a print or online dictionary to find their meanings. Then paraphrase each sentence to make sure you understand the source's message.

EXAMINE THE SOURCE

1. Analyzing Perspectives Why does the author believe enslaved people have nothing to be grateful for? How might his description likely have affected the debate over slavery?

2. Interpreting How does the author describe why African Americans are submissive, and how is slavery justified?

3. Explaining Why does the author say whites continue enslavement?

B

"To the Public"

Many white Northerners accepted the fact that slavery existed in the South. The abolitionist William Lloyd Garrison was certainly not one of them. In fact, he devoted most of his life to ending slavery. Garrison used his skills as a journalist to push for the immediate emancipation of enslaved African Americans. He even started his own newspaper, printed in Boston, called *The Liberator* to promote the idea of freedom for the enslaved. The following excerpt was published in the first issue of Garrison's newspaper. In it, Garrison describes why he became convinced that a quick end to slavery rather than a gradual one was essential. His strong views angered those abolitionists who thought it best to take a series of small steps to end slavery over time.

PRIMARY SOURCE : NEWSPAPER ARTICLE

❝ Let southern oppressors tremble—let their secret **abettors** tremble—let their northern apologists tremble—let all the enemies of the persecuted blacks tremble. . . .

In defending the great cause of human rights, I wish to derive [obtain] the assistance of all religions and of all parties.

Assenting to the 'self-evident truth' maintained in the American Declaration of Independence, 'that all men are created equal, and endowed by their Creator with certain inalienable rights—among which are life, liberty and the pursuit of happiness,' I shall strenuously contend [argue] for the immediate **enfranchisement** of our slave population. In Park-street Church, on the Fourth of July, 1829, in an address on slavery, I unreflectingly assented to the popular but **pernicious** doctrine of *gradual* abolition. I seize this opportunity to make a full and **unequivocal recantation**, and thus publicly to ask pardon of my God, of my country, and of my brethren the poor slaves, for having uttered a sentiment so full of timidity, injustice, and absurdity. . . .

I am aware, that many object to the severity of my language; but is there not cause for severity? I *will be* as harsh as truth, and as uncompromising as justice. On this subject, I do not wish to think, or speak, or write, with moderation. No! no! Tell a man whose house is on fire, to give a moderate alarm; tell him to moderately rescues his wife from the hands of the ravisher; tell the mother to gradually **extricate** her babe from the fire into which is has fallen;—but urge me not to use moderation in a cause like the present. I am in earnest—I will not equivocate—I will not excuse—I will not retreat a single inch—AND I WILL BE HEARD. The **apathy** of the people is enough to make every statue leap from its pedestal, and to hasten the resurrection of the dead.

abettor someone who helps another person to do something wrong

assenting agreeing

enfranchisement setting free

pernicious harmful or destructive

unequivocal leaving no doubt

recantation a statement of denial

extricate to free or remove from difficulty

apathy lack of interest

It is pretended, that I am **retarding** the cause of emancipation by the coarseness of my **invective**, and the **precipitancy** of my measures. *The charge is not true.* On this question my influence,—humble as it is,—is felt at this moment to a **considerable** extent, and shall be felt in coming years—not perniciously, but beneficially—not as a curse, but as a blessing; and posterity will bear testimony that I was right. I desire to thank God, that he enables me to disregard 'the fear of man which bringeth a snare,' and to speak his truth in its simplicity and power. **"**

— William Lloyd Garrison, *The Liberator,* January 1, 1831

---

retarding to slow down or delay

invective harsh or critical language

precipitancy hasty action

considerable substantial, large

EXAMINE THE SOURCE

4. Explaining On what beliefs and principles does Garrison base his support for immediate abolition?

5. Drawing Conclusions What is the likely reason Garrison changed his position regarding gradual abolition?

6. Speculating Using quotes from the text, how could you argue that Garrison is going to be an important and forceful leader in the abolitionist movement?

"What to the Slave is the Fourth of July?"

The mother of abolitionist Frederick Douglass was enslaved, so he was born into slavery in 1817 or 1818. He was soon separated from his mother and forced to work as a house servant when he was eight years old. The wife of his slaveholder taught him to read and write even though it was against local law. In his twenties, he escaped and headed north. He delivered moving speeches and also wrote an autobiography. With the book's success, he was able to buy his freedom. Here is an excerpt from one of his powerful speeches, given around the Fourth of July.

PRIMARY SOURCE : SPEECH

❝ Fellow-citizens, pardon me, allow me to ask, why am I called upon to speak here to-day? What have I, or those I represent, to do with your national independence? Are the great principles of political freedom and of natural justice, embodied in that Declaration of Independence, extended to us? . . .

I am not included within . . . this glorious anniversary! Your high independence only reveals the immeasurable distance between us. The blessings in which you, this day, rejoice, are not enjoyed in common. The rich inheritance of justice, liberty, prosperity and independence, **bequeathed** by your fathers, is shared by you, not by me. The sunlight that brought light and healing to you, has brought stripes and death to me. This Fourth [of] July is yours, not mine. . . .

Fellow-citizens; above your national, **tumultuous** joy, I hear the mournful wail of millions! whose chains, heavy and grievous yesterday, are, to-day, rendered more intolerable by the jubilee shouts that reach them. . . . I shall see, this day, and its popular characteristics, from the slave's point of view. . . .

What, to the American slave, is your 4th of July? I answer: a day that reveals to him, more than all other days in the year, the gross injustice and cruelty to which he is the constant victim. To him, your celebration is a sham; your boasted liberty, an unholy license; your national greatness, swelling vanity; your sounds of rejoicing are empty and heartless. . . . [Y]our shouts of liberty and equality, hollow mockery; your prayers and hymns, your sermons and thanksgivings, with all your religious parade . . . are, to him, mere bombast, fraud, deception, impiety, and hypocrisy. . . .

But a change has now come over the affairs of mankind. . . . Intelligence is penetrating the darkest corners of the globe. It makes its pathway over and under the sea, as well as on the earth. . . . Oceans no longer divide, but link nations together. . . . Thoughts expressed on one side of the Atlantic are, distinctly heard on the other. ❞

— Frederick Douglass, July 5, 1852

bequeath to give

tumultuous involving noise and excitement

7. Analyzing Perspectives What does Douglass explain as to the enslaved person's point of view about the Fourth of July?

8. Summarizing What is the main idea of Douglass's speech?

9. Citing Evidence Which part of Douglass's speech best demonstrates the hypocrisy of the nation? Cite evidence to support your response.

D

"I Am Pleading for My People"

Like Frederick Douglass, the abolitionist who became known as Sojourner Truth escaped slavery. Unlike Douglass, however, she was born into slavery in the North, in New York. She escaped slavery just a year before the state liberated all enslaved people living there. Once free, Truth began preaching and speaking out about slavery. Although she could neither read nor write, Truth wrote her autobiography, which she dictated to a woman named Olive Gilbert. The book sold well enough to support Truth, allowing her to travel and preach. At one abolitionist event, she was scheduled to give a speech before famed speaker Wendell Phillips. In order to not be overshadowed, she did something Phillips could not do: she sang. After that, she often sang when she finished preaching or speaking.

PRIMARY SOURCE : SONG

I am pleading for my people, a poor downtrodden race
Who dwell in freedom's boasted land with no abiding place.
I am pleading that my people may have their rights restored,
For they have long been toiling, and yet had no reward.

They are forced the crops to culture, but not for them they yield,
Although both late and early, they labor in the field.

While I bear upon my body, the scores of many a gash,
I'm pleading for my people who groan beneath the lash.

I'm pleading for the mothers who gaze in wild despair
Upon the hated auction block, and see their children there. I feel for those in
    bondage-well may I feel for them.
I know how **fiendish** hearts can be that sell their fellow man.

Yet those oppressors steeped in guilt—I still would have them live;
For I have learned of Jesus, to suffer and forgive!
I want no **carnal** weapons, no machinery of death.
For I love to not hear the sound of war's **tempestuous** breath.

I do not ask you to engage in death and bloody strife.
I do not dare insult my God by asking for their life.
But while your kindest sympathies to foreign lands do roam,
I ask you remember your own oppressed at home.

I plead with you to sympathize with signs and groans and scars,
And note how base the tyranny beneath the stripes and stars.

—Sojourner Truth, 1878

fiendish extremely cruel

carnal gross or vulgar

tempestuous involving violent storms, with strong emotions

10. Explaining How do the lyrics of the song describe the plight of enslaved people? What hypocrisy does she note?

11. Interpreting How do you know Sojourner Truth is a religious person? How might her belief be related to the use of the word *pleading*?

12. Analyzing Perspectives Who is the intended audience for the song, and how does the song hope to influence that audience?

13. Making Connections How are the ideas in the song similar to those presented in Source C, "What to the Slave is the Fourth of July?"

Mothers with Young Children at Work in the Field

Abolitionists expressed their views in other ways besides speeches, newspaper articles, and pamphlets. They wrote letters, reports, songs, plays, poems, and even novels. They made posters, paintings, illustrations, and other forms of art. The woodcut print shown here comes from the illustrations of the *American Anti-Slave Almanac for 1840*. Published by the American Anti-Slave Society, these almanacs were created to give Northern viewers a terrifying look at slavery, of which they had no firsthand knowledge. Examine this illustration of enslaved workers closely to understand why this might have alarmed those who viewed it and just possibly convince them to support the abolitionist cause.

PRIMARY SOURCE : ILLUSTRATION

This illustration titled "Mothers with young Children at work in the field" comes from the American *Anti-Slavery Almanac* for 1840.

EXAMINE THE SOURCE

14. **Analyzing Visuals** What impression does the illustration give viewers about conditions faced by enslaved mothers? Explain your reasoning.

15. Interpreting Why does the mother say, "Oh my child my child"?

16. Interpreting What is significant about the child in the background? Why do you think the illustrator includes the child?

17. Analyzing Visuals Why do you think the illustrator made the shape of the whip and the snake similar?

Evaluate Sources and Use Evidence

18. **Citing Text Evidence** Review the Supporting Questions you developed at the beginning of the topic and the evidence you gathered and recorded in the graphic organizer. Which sources will help you answer the Supporting Questions? Circle or highlight those sources in your graphic organizer. Looking at the subset of sources you have chosen, be prepared to explain why you chose each source.

	Supporting Question	Primary Source and Notes
1		
2		
3		

Challenge

Research further the topic of abolitionism and abolitionists. Find at least one primary or secondary source text or image related to your topic. Analyze the source and use it to help answer one or more of your Supporting Questions. Include your research in your response.

19. Directions: Now answer the Supporting Questions that you developed at the beginning of the activity to help guide you in answering the Compelling Question.

Answer for Supporting Question 1:

Answer for Supporting Question 2:

Answer for Supporting Question 3:

Communicate Conclusions

Talk About It

20. Collaborating Work in a small group. On a large sheet of paper, draw a web with a center oval and five surrounding ovals. Write the Compelling Question in the center oval. Take turns adding source evidence to answer the question. For each piece of evidence, explain why it helps answer the question. Take turns until everyone has had at least two turns. Then work together to identify the three best pieces of evidence from your web. Select a spokesperson to share with the class how these sources help answer the Compelling Questions.

Write About It

21. Informative Writing Choose two sources you recorded in the graphic organizer that helped you best answer your Supporting Questions. Write one letter or e-mail to the author of each source in which you summarize the content and explain its importance. Include how each source helps you answer your Supporting Questions. Make certain you include facts and ideas from the sources and from the background information about each source.

22. Answering the Compelling Question What do you think? Why did slavery need to be abolished? Write one or two paragraphs in which you cite two pieces of evidence from the sources that demonstrate valid reasons for the immediate end to the practice of enslavement.

23. <u>Making Connections</u> The institution of slavery was a major violation of human rights. Today, like abolitionists, people around the world still fight against human rights abuses. Conduct research to find out more about examples of human rights abuses that take place today and about the people who work to end them. Choose one individual or organization fighting such abuse. Use a graphic organizer of your choice to summarize your findings.

✓ **YOU CHOOSE**

Select one of these Take Informed Action products to apply what you've learned.

A. Write an article about your finding that might appear in your school newspaper.

B. Create a podcast about the work of the present-day individual or organizational reformer and the issue addressed.

C. Create a brochure describing the work of the group or person that explains how people can get involved with them to help end the human rights abuse.

Take Informed Action Rubric: Immigration Policies

Self-Evaluation As you identify and describe the work of an individual or organization fighting against a human rights abuse, think about the following criteria. These are the criteria your teacher will use to evaluate your Take Informed Action activity.

Peer Review Use this rubric to grade the research and the final product developed by another classmate or group of classmates.

	Organization	Research	Historical Accuracy	Writing/Logic
4	The piece is exceptionally well organized and focused and demonstrates a thorough and deep understanding of the event or issue.	The research shows a thorough synthesis of information from appropriate sources about the individual or organization and the human rights issue being addressed.	The piece is well researched and is factually accurate.	The information provided on the graphic organizer is exceptionally well written, as is the rest of the product.
3	The piece is well organized and focused and demonstrates an adequate understanding of the event or issue.	The research reflects an adequate synthesis of information from appropriate sources about the individual or organization and the human rights issue being addressed.	The piece is well researched but contains some factual errors.	The information provided on the graphic organizer is well written, as is the rest of the product.
2	The piece is organized but is inconsistent in focus and demonstrates an inadequate understanding of the event or issue.	The research reflects a general discussion of information, but sources are only somewhat related to the individual or organization and the human rights issue being addressed.	The piece is not well researched and contains some factual errors.	Some of the product is well written, but there are mistakes.
1	The piece lacks organization and focus and does not demonstrate a basic understanding of the event or issue.	The research demonstrates a lack of effort and a failure to use appropriate sources.	There are many factual errors.	The product is poorly written, and there are many mistakes.
SCORE				

TOPIC 10 • RECONSTUCTION, 1865–1877

The Goals, Accomplishments, and Failures of the Freedmen's Bureau

 COMPELLING QUESTION

How did the Freedmen's Bureau both support and fail African Americans?

Plan Your Inquiry

In this Inquiry Activity, you will develop Supporting Questions related to the goals, accomplishments, and failures of the Freedmen's Bureau based on the Compelling Question. Then, you will examine primary sources describing the obstacles faced by freed people and the Freedmen's Bureau as well as accounts of the ways in which the bureau was meant to provide help for newly freed African Americans. Finally, you will answer your Supporting Questions, communicate your research conclusions, and take action based on what you've learned.

Background Information

Lincoln and Congress worked together to create the Freedmen's Bureau after the Northern victory of the Civil War. *Freedmen* was a term that referred to previously enslaved people. This government agency had the task of helping about 4 million people adjust to life after slavery. Among its many responsibilities was providing clothing and food. It also offered medical assistance for freed people, who might be turned away from existing hospitals. It built more than 1,000 schools for African Americans, as well as new colleges to train teachers to provide instruction in those schools. In addition, it worked to find ways for some former enslaved people to own small farms and for others to find jobs.

After President Lincoln's assassination, Congress acted to both punish the Southern states and to better the lives of African Americans. For example, the lawmakers broadened the power of the Freedmen's Bureau. It could now create courts to hear cases involving the denial of rights to African Americans. Congress also passed the Fourteenth Amendment to ensure that all Americans had both freedom and "equal protection under the law." However, as much as it tried, the Freedmen's Bureau made little headway in achieving equal rights for African Americans or gaining them ownership of property. It is perhaps best remembered for enabling former enslaved people in the South to learn to read and write.

The military built Freedmen's Village, in Washington, D.C., which eventually had 50 homes, a kitchen and dining hall, a hospital, a school, and other facilities so African Americans would find it easier to transition from slavery to freedom. The camp existed until 1900.

Develop Supporting Questions About the Freedmen's Bureau

 COMPELLING QUESTION

How did the Freedmen's Bureau both support and fail African Americans?

Talk About It

Discuss with a partner what type of information you would need to know to answer this question. For example, one question might be the following: What was the purpose of the Freedmen's Bureau?

Directions: Write down three additional questions that you need to answer to be able to determine the ways in which the Freedmen's Bureau succeeded and failed in helping African Americans.

Supporting Question 1:

Supporting Question 2:

Supporting Question 3:

Apply Historical Concepts and Tools

Directions: As you read and work with primary sources, use the graphic organizer to take notes and organize information.

	Organizing Source Information	
Source	**Title and Author/ Creator**	**Notes**
A	Letter: Freedmen's Bureau, Subdistrict Headquarters, Albany, Georgia, to Colonel John Randolph Lewis, Atlanta, Georgia	
B	The Late Convention of Colored Men: Address to the Loyal Citizens of the United States and to Congress	
C	Letter to the Assistant Commissioner, Bureau of Refugees, Freedmen, and Abandoned Lands by Joseph Tillett, et al.	
D	Howard University, a photograph	
E	Letter from Charleston, South Carolina, by Mayor Gilbert Pillsbury	

Analyze Sources

Review and analyze Sources A–E. There are questions that accompany each source to help you examine the source and check for historical understanding.

Letter: Freedmen's Bureau, Subdistrict Headquarters, Albany, Georgia, to Colonel John Randolph Lewis, Atlanta, Georgia

As a result of Reconstruction, African American men were granted the right to vote. In Georgia, some African Americans won election to the state legislature. However, white lawmakers forced their removal. The African American lawmakers then led a march to take part in a Republican rally in the small town of Camilla. Violence broke out there when white Georgians—who had been deputized by the sheriff—began shooting into the African American crowd, wounding some and killing others. A Freedmen's Bureau leader, Brevet Major Oliver Otis Howard (who later founded Howard University), wrote to John Randolph Lewis, a top official of the bureau in Georgia. In the letter, the he describes the chaos of the event and his reaction to it.

PRIMARY SOURCE : LETTER

❝ The affair at Camilla seems to have been a massacre. I enclose an accurate list of the killed & wounded so far as known.

A freedman who was a prisoner at Camilla, but who escaped during the night, states that he helped to remove one dead freedwoman, & four wounded freedmen from [the] road within a hundred yards of the Court House. The white men, his captors, boasted, to new comers, of twelve freedmen killed in one pond near Dr Dasher's, two miles from Camilla.

Another freedman took refuge in a swamp where he lay concealed all last night, with four others near him. He heard, during all the earlier part of the night, the white men scouring the woods, shouting, cursing, and shooting the freedmen. The pursuers, he says were accompanied by Bloodhounds, he heard the cries and shrieks of the fugitives as they were shot, and as they were pulled down by the dogs. . . . .

The town has been filled with freed men, they have swarmed about my office by hundreds. . . . I have addressed them counselling peace and order, I have told them that the offenders shall be punished, and that their lives should be protected, but, I have no heart for my work. I felt no assurance that my promises would ever be fulfilled. . . .

How long I shall have the heart to deceive these freedmen by false promises, & how long I shall be able to deceive them by such promises, I cannot say, but I imagine that it is not long, & when they have no confidence in my fair promises, what then? . . . Please instruct me & inform me what action will be taken, Military or Civil Authorities. ❞

— Brevet Major Oliver O. Howard, *Civil Unrest in Camilla, Georgia,* September 20, 1868

1. **Analyzing Perspectives** Why does Howard write this letter? Describe the conditions to which he responds.

2. **Identifying** Where does the former prisoner mentioned in the second paragraph indicate that he helped some of the dead or wounded? Why is this likely significant information?

3. **Drawing Conclusions** What does this source indicate about the Freedmen's Bureau?

The Late Convention of Colored Men: Address to the Loyal Citizens of the United States and to Congress

Southern African Americans became alarmed as former Confederates held political office. The newly freed worried that white Southerners would do anything to limit African American rights. As a result, they worked together to make plans. During a convention that took place in the city of Alexandria, Virginia, attendees could sign a petition to bring their cause to the attention of national leaders. This excerpt shows frustration with governmental inaction on the issue of civil rights.

PRIMARY SOURCE : PETITION

❝ Well, the war is over, the rebellion is 'put down,' and we are declared, free! Four-fifths of our enemies are paroled . . . and the other fifth are being pardoned, and the President has, in his efforts at the reconstruction of the civil government of the States, late in rebellion, left us entirely at the mercy of these **subjugated** but unconverted rebels, in everything [except] the privilege of bringing us, our wives and little ones, to the auction block. He has, so far as we can understand the tendency and bearing of his action in the case, **remitted** us for all our civil rights, to men, a majority of whom regard our devotions to your cause and flag as that which decided the contest against them! This we regard as destructive of all we hold dear, and in the name of God, of justice, of humanity, of good faith, of truth and righteousness, we do most solemnly and earnestly protest. Men and brethren, in the hour of your peril you called upon us, and despite all time-honored interpretation of constitutional obligations, we came at your call and you are saved; and now we beg, we pray, we entreat you not to desert us in this the hour of our peril!

We know these men—know them well—and we assure you that, with the majority . . . their professions of loyalty are used as a cover to [get] restored to their former relations with the Federal Government, and then, by all sorts of 'unfriendly legislation,' to render the freedom you have given us more **intolerable** than the slavery they intended for us.

We warn you in time that our only safety is in keeping them under Governors of the military persuasion until you have amended the Federal Constitution that it will prohibit the States from making any distinction between citizens on account of race or color. In one word, the only salvation for us besides the military power of the government, is in the possession of the ballot. . . .

All we ask is an equal chance with the white traitors [protected] with the oath of amnesty. Can you deny us this, and still keep faith with us? . . . [W]e thought the Freedmen's Bureau was organized and clothed with power to protect us . . . by compelling those for whom we labored to pay us, whether they liked our political opinions [through voting] or not! ❞

— from *The New York* Times, August 13, 1865

---

subjugate to bring under control

remit to refer for consideration

intolerable unable to endure

4. Explaining What are the writers of the source protesting? Why do they consider their protest justified?

5. Analyzing Perspectives How do the writers of the source believe they can remain safe from former Confederates?

6. Interpreting How do the writers expect the Freedmen's Bureau to help them when they voice their opinion through voting?

C

Letter to the Assistant Commissioner, Bureau of Refugees, Freedmen, and Abandoned Lands

During the Civil War, the North claimed the land it occupied as Union territory. One such place was Roanoke Island. Union army leaders there granted freedom to the enslaved people who the Confederates used to build forts on the island. Aware this was now Union land, other enslaved people began to move there to live in freedom since the slavery laws of the South no longer applied. In time, a colony of freed African Americans formed. The more than 3,000 colonists expected to make the land their permanent home. However, after the Civil War, the original Southern owners regained the land. The property owners tried to force the colonists off the land. This letter from some of the African American colonists of Roanoke Island explains why they think they should be allowed to remain on the land.

PRIMARY SOURCE : LETTER

❝ The undersigned freedmen, old citizens of Currituck County, State of North Carolina, born and reared upon Roanoke Island, humbly complaining respectfully **sheweth**—

That there is a **disposition** on the part of those whose lands have been restored to them by Maj. Gen. Howard . . . [to] refuse to allow the petitioners to remain upon the land . . . notwithstanding the fact that the undersigned offer to pay rent or express a desire to purchase lots.

As before stated, born and reared here, the undersigned know only how to make a living by fishing, fowling and '**progging**'—these being their means of support from their youth to the present day. They are not farmers: this is a **sterile** section, consequently, but little attention has been paid to agriculture. This being the case, the undersigned, if driven to the necessity of leaving their old home, around which cluster many pleasant recollections—would be able to earn but a poor living, being inexperienced laborers on a farm. The undersigned are sure that you will sympathize with them. They know not what to do in the matter, neither do they know where to go—indeed they here ask whether they shall be made to leave their birth-place, merely to gratify the whims of men who are not well-affected towards the government of the United States.

They therefore ask that you will take such action in this matter as will insure the undersigned justice—protect them in everything they may do in a lawful manner, or rather, see to it, that, by paying reasonable rent, they will be permitted to reside where it is their wish to spend their days, and 'when life's fitful fever's over,' lay their bones to mingle with the dust of their childhood's home. ❞

— Joseph Tillett, et al., Letters and Orders Received, Reports, and Supply Requests, Roanoke Island, Records of the Assistant Commissioner for North Carolina, Record Group 105, series 2821, National Archives, December 4, 1866

---

shewith to show

disposition temperament or nature

progging turtle hunting

sterile unable to produce vegetation

7. Interpreting How did conditions in Roanoke motivate the people to write this letter?

8. Summarizing What problem do the letter writers describe, and what solution do they hope for?

9. Drawing Conclusions How does this source help you understand how African Americans might have perceived the Freedmen's Bureau?

Howard University

Upon gaining freedom after the Civil War, African Americans leapt for the chance to get an education. Some African Americans began to open their own schools to help people become literate. The Freedmen's Bureau helped these schools succeed by providing them with money for teachers and books. The bureau also helped fund the establishment of colleges and universities devoted to furthering the education of African Americans. One of these was Howard University, in Washington, D.C., shown in the stereograph.

PRIMARY SOURCE : PHOTOGRAPH

Howard University is named for one of its founders, Major General Oliver Otis Howard, commissioner of the Freedmen's Bureau. The university opened in 1867, and today it is known as a historically black university.

10. **Analyzing Visuals** What does the image show?

11. **Analyzing Visuals** What impression does the image give viewers about Howard University and its students? Explain your reasoning.

12. **Making Connections** The university's founder, Major General O. O. Howard was the letter writer from the Freedmen's Bureau mentioned in Source A and the person to whom the letter in Source E was written. What do these facts indicate about the endurance of the Freedmen's Bureau?

13. **Drawing Conclusions** The Freedmen's Bureau provided much of the funding for Howard University. What might this tell you about the beliefs of school founder General Howard?

Letter from Charleston, South Carolina

Many Southern whites did not want freed African Americans to gain education, voting rights, and economic success. Some spread false rumors about African Americans to convince others not to allow them to gain more rights. This letter, by Gilbert Pillsbury, an abolitionist who became the mayor of Charleston, South Carolina, to J. W. Alvord, the General Superintendent of Education for the Freedmen's Bureau, answered questions Alvord had asked. Alvord forwarded the letter to the bureau's national commissioner, General Oliver Otis Howard.

PRIMARY SOURCE : LETTER

66 As to comparative **intemperance** between whites and colored, I will say that while intemperance is the crying evil in our community amongst all classes, it is evidently most [widespread] amongst the whites.

As to larceny, vagrancy, and other petty violations of the law, I can only speak with regard to the city. Here the **preponderance** is much against the colored. This fact can be readily accounted for. The colored population is not only much the largest in the city, but is crowded into the uncomfortable, unhealthy, and secluded portions. Then, the demand for labor is [low], and as a general rule preference is given to the white laborer; not because he works more willingly and earnestly, but because he is white. . . . Hence, poverty and neglect among the colored are great **inducements** to crime. . . .

I think, in the few particulars I have mentioned, the State generally is upon about the same footing as the city. It struggles against poverty and ignorance. Give us schools and fair inducements to labor, and we will cheerfully risk the consequences. The old inclination to crush and rob and keep in ignorance the colored race, is as strong as ever. . . . [I]f abandoned by their great northern deliverers to their 'old friends' of the south, their liberty, which cost the nation so dear, would not long exist, even in name.

As to your inquiry whether the colored element is dying out and wasting away, I am certain it is not the case. . . . This southern country is full of them, and I believe they are still on the increase. . . . Slavery has left them in the most **deplorable** condition; but liberty can and must restore them.

The work may be termed . . . a 'big job;' but it must be done, and that largely by the strong, benevolent arm of the north. . . .

We have made great [progress]; but don't leave us alone. . . . 99

— Mayor Gilbert Pillsbury, in a letter dated January 20, 1870, in J. W. Alvord, *Letters from the South Relating to the Condition of Freedmen, Addressed to Major General O. O. Howard, Commissioner Bureau R., F., and A. L.,* Washington, D.C., Howard University Press (1870)

Copyright © McGraw Hill   TEXT: Alvord, J. W. Letters from the South, Relating to the Condition of Freedmen Addressed to Major General O. O. Howard, Commissioner Bureau R., F., and A. L. [Refugees, Freedmen, and Abandoned Lands]. Washington: Howard University Press, 1870.

---

intemperance lack of moderation especially as it relates to excessive drinking of alcohol

preponderance distinction; dominance

inducement something that leads one to take action

deplorable wretched; disgraceful

14. Citing Evidence What evidence does Mayor Pillsbury offer as to why there is a preponderance of crime among African Americans in Charleston?

15. Comparing How does the writer compare local conditions for freed African Americans with those of the state?

16. Inferring How do the statements in this source characterize white Southerner's attitudes in Charleston toward the freed African Americans, and how can the Freedmen's Bureau help? Explain your reasoning.

Evaluate Sources and Use Evidence

17. <u>**Citing Text Evidence**</u> Review the Supporting Questions you developed at the beginning of the topic and the evidence you gathered and recorded in the graphic organizer. Which sources will help you answer the Supporting Questions? Circle or highlight those sources in your graphic organizer. Looking at the subset of sources you have chosen, be prepared to explain why you chose each source.

	Supporting Question	Primary Source and Notes
1		
2		
3		

Challenge

Research other sources related to the Freedmen's Bureau. Find at least one primary or secondary text. Analyze the source and use it to help answer one or more of your Supporting Questions. Include your research in your response.

18. Directions: Now answer the Supporting Questions that you developed at the beginning of the activity to help guide you in answering the Compelling Question.

Answer for Supporting Question 1:

Answer for Supporting Question 2:

Answer for Supporting Question 3:

Communicate Conclusions

Talk About It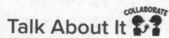

19. Collaborating In a small group, take turns sharing which of your Supporting Questions you think is most helpful in answering the Compelling Question. Share your responses to those questions. Then work together to create an infographic on the Freedmen's Bureau in which you include elements from the sources. The infographic should have to do with the Supporting Questions you identified. Share your infographic with another group or the class.

Write About It

20. Informative Writing Write a short column for a class blog or newspaper. Entitle it "Did You Know?" or give it some other short, catchy title. Explain two ways in which the Freedmen's Bureau either met its goals or did not accomplish what it set out to do.

21. Answering the Compelling Question What do you think? How did the Freedmen's Bureau both support and fail African Americans? Write one or two paragraphs in which you cite evidence from at least two sources.

Need Extra Help?

To help answer the Compelling Question, make a concept map with "Freedmen's Bureau" in the center. Add information from the sources and your prior knowledge about the subject. Record as much as you know about the bureau. Then use your concept map to help answer the question.

22. **Making Connections** The purpose of the Freedmen's Bureau was to help formerly enslaved people in the South to adjust to life in freedom. Use the Internet to find a federal, state, or local government agency that helps people today. Continue your research to discover more about how it assists people. Use a graphic organizer of your choice to take notes as you conduct research.

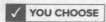 ✓ YOU CHOOSE

Select one of these Take Informed Action products to apply what you've learned.

A. Create a podcast that describes the issue the agency addresses and explains what it does to help solve the problem.

B. Create a public service announcement that alerts people in your community to the work that the agency does and how they can make use of its services.

C. Present a slideshow explaining the main responsibilities of the agency.

Take Informed Action Rubric: Government Agency

Self-Evaluation As you research and describe your selected government agency, think about the following criteria. These are the criteria your teacher will use to evaluate your Take Informed Action activity.

Peer Review Use this rubric to grade the research and the final product developed by another classmate or group of classmates.

	Organization	Research	Historical Accuracy	Writing/Logic
4	The piece is exceptionally well organized and focused and demonstrates a thorough and deep understanding of the issue and the agency.	The research shows a thorough synthesis of information from appropriate sources about the purpose and work of the agency.	The piece is well researched and is factually accurate.	The final product shows evidence of extensive thought.
3	The piece is well organized and focused and demonstrates an adequate understanding of the issue and the agency.	The research reflects an adequate synthesis of information from appropriate sources about the purpose and work of the agency.	The piece is well researched but contains some factual errors.	The final product shows sufficient evidence of thought.
2	The piece is organized but is inconsistent in focus and demonstrates an inadequate understanding of the issue and the agency.	The research reflects a general discussion of information, but sources are only somewhat related to the purpose and work of the agency.	The piece is not well researched and contains some factual errors.	The final product shows limited evidence of thought.
1	The piece lacks organization and focus and does not demonstrate a basic understanding of the issue and the agency.	The research demonstrates a lack of effort to describe the purpose and work of the agency and a failure to use appropriate sources.	There are many factual errors.	The final product shows a lack of thought.
SCORE				

TOPIC 11 • THE WEST, 1858–1896

Experiences in the American West

? COMPELLING QUESTION

Why did people move to the American West?

Plan Your Inquiry

In this Inquiry Activity, you will develop Supporting Questions related to life in the American West based on the Compelling Question. Then you will examine primary sources describing some experience of different groups who traveled there to work, live, or have religious freedom. Finally, you will answer your Supporting Questions, communicate your research conclusions, and take action based on what you've learned.

Background Information

In the mid-1800s, differences in ways of life between the North and the South exploded into civil war. Meanwhile, an entirely new way of life developed in the West. American pioneers had been making their way west since the early years of the nation. As the country grew and expanded westward, more of its population headed there. Farms and ranches dotted western land in greater numbers. New modes of transportation, such as the steamboat and the steam locomotive, allowed for the western movement of both goods and settlers. Some territories, such as Oregon and California, had large enough populations to become states within the Union.

A gold rush in California in the late 1840s further fueled western migration. Sometimes, boomtowns suddenly arose in areas that used to be barren, or deserted, land. New businesses opened in these boomtowns and in farming areas.

After the Civil War, Americans continued fulfilling their dreams of beginning a new life in the West. By 1869, a transcontinental railroad could carry goods and people across the country to its farthest western borders. The building of the railroads boosted both population growth and the establishment of industries in the West.

The railroads opened new lands, particularly in the Great Plains, to settlement. The federal government's Homestead Act offered western land cheaply, and many people quickly grabbed that opportunity. White settlers continued to flock to the West. But the attraction of the West also drew African Americans, Chinese immigrants, and others. People of various races, ethnic groups, and religions viewed the West as a new beginning.

In 1889, President Benjamin Harrison made 2 million acres of land available in the Oklahoma Territory for settlers. By 1893, settlers lined up waiting for land rushes to begin. When cannons blasted the signal, thousands of people raced to stake their land claim.

Develop Supporting Questions About the Reasons for Settling the American West

 COMPELLING QUESTION

Why did people move to the American West?

Talk About It

Discuss with a partner what type of information you would need to know to answer this question. For example, one question might be the following: Where did people live in the West?

Directions: Write down three additional questions that you need to answer to be able to determine reasons people settled in the American West.

Supporting Question 1:

Supporting Question 2:

Supporting Question 3:

Apply Historical Concepts and Tools

Directions: As you read and work with primary sources, use the graphic organizer to take notes and organize information.

	Organizing Source Information	
Source	**Title and Author/ Creator**	**Notes**
A	Buffalo Soldiers, a photograph	
B	Exodusters	
C	"Come, Come, Ye Saints" by William Clayton	
D	Chinese Leaders' Message to President Grant	
E	Sixty Years in Southern California by Harris Newmark	

Analyze Sources

Review and analyze Sources A–E. There are questions that accompany each source to help you examine the source and check for historical understanding.

Buffalo Soldiers

American settlers viewed the West as untouched territory, ready to be farmed, ranched on, and mined. However, Native Americans had called this same land home for hundreds of years. As more settlers headed west, conflicts developed between the Native Americans, who did not want to be pushed from their land, and the newcomers. Conflict became so intense that the U.S. government assigned special groups of the U.S. Army to help settlers stand their ground against the Native Americans. They also kept the peace, as needed. These regiments, made up of African American soldiers, soon became common sights in the western lands. Many of these African American fighters wore robes, or coats, made of buffalo skins. This may have led Native Americans to refer to them as "buffalo soldiers." The name stuck, and as time passed, the buffalo soldiers became well known for their devotion to their job. One of their tasks was to end unrest and help the United States claim the West from the Native Americans.

PRIMARY SOURCE : PHOTOGRAPH

Buffalo soldiers, or the African American cavalry, had the job of protecting settlers to the West from Native Americans who fought against them. The group pictured, the 25th Infantry Regiment, protected the area around Fort Keogh, Montana, beginning around 1890.

1. Analyzing Visuals What idea does the photograph present about buffalo soldiers?

2. Analyzing Think about the nickname given to these soldiers—buffalo soldiers. How might this nickname have affected their actions?

3. Drawing Conclusions What achievements likely contributed to the legacy of the buffalo soldiers?

4. Evaluating How useful is this photograph as a source about experiences in the American West? Explain your reasoning and any limitations of the source.

B

EXODUSTERS

Some African Americans saw the West as a place where they could start life anew. The African Americans who migrated to the West became known as Exodusters. The name referenced the Exodus of the Bible and the seeking of a "promised land." Settlers in some parts of the West welcomed with open arms African Americans, who were often referred to as "colored people," at that time. The 75 residents of Graham County, Kansas, wanted to increase their population, and accepting Exodusters seemed a way to do this. The white promoter of the new town lured potential residents with untrue stories of rich soil for farming. About 200 African Americans migrated to the county and started a new town called Nicodemus. Soon, it claimed renown as "The Largest Colored Colony in America." Eventually, the town prospered. By the mid-1880s, Nicodemus emerged as a bustling center of African American life, complete with a number of African American businesses. The following article about Nicodemus was published in the *Western Kansas World* newspaper, during its 12 years of existence. It describes the early days of the colony.

PRIMARY SOURCE : NEWSPAPER ARTICLE

66 The most heroic chapter in the history of colored people of Kansas was the establishment of the Nichodemus colony. In the summer of 1877, too late to make a crop, the colonists gathered on the bare prairies of Graham county. They passed the following winter in such **rude** shelters as they could construct, dug-outs and the like, their only fuel the scattered cottonwoods along the Solomon. When spring came there were 300 men, women and children, with but three horses to the party. The colonists dug up the sod [grasslands] with hoes and **mattocks**, and when

These Exodusters, African Americans who migrated west following the Civil War, settled the community of Nicodemus, Kansas, in 1877. The community included a general store and a church. Today, Nicodemus is a National Historic Site.

the grain was grown, pulled it with their hands, for want of even **sickels**. Determined to hold their lands, the men wandered near and far in search of work, some walking to Colorado, while the women held down the claims. By such toil as this the "first families" of Graham finally read their titles clear to their quarter sections and accomplished the first successful attempt by colored people to establish themselves to the public lands of the United States. 99

—*Western Kansas World*, Chronicling America: Historic American Newspapers, February 22, 1890

rude rough or unfinished state

mattock a tool shaped like a pickax used in farming

sickel (sickle) a farming tool used for cutting grain

5. Summarizing How did the people who settled in Nicodemus survive their first year?

6. Interpreting The newspaper source implies that the Exodusters came to Nicodemus to farm. What other reasons might have brought them to the colony?

7. Drawing Conclusions The excerpt explains that the men "wandered near and far in search of work." What conclusion can you draw from that statement?

8. Evaluating The source says that the forming of this colony was "the most heroic chapter in the history of colored people of Kansas." Do you agree with this statement? Explain your reasoning.

"Come, Come Ye Saints"

Some people moved west to be able to practice their religion more freely. One such group of people were the Mormons. In the mid-1830s, as many as 2,000 Mormons, or Latter-day Saints, lived and worshipped in the town of Nauvoo, Illinois. Although they had moved to Illinois to escape prejudice, they encountered unfair treatment there as well, which caused them to migrate west. They hoped that in the West they could finally achieve the religious freedom they desired. As they went west, the travelers experienced harsh conditions. William Clayton composed this hymn on his journey west with fellow Mormons. In the song, he explains to others on the trip, whom he refers to as Saints, why they should feel hopeful rather than sad. The hymn is still sung today by members of the Church of Jesus Christ of Latter-day Saints during worship.

PRIMARY SOURCE : SONG

66 Come, Come, ye Saints, no toil nor labor fear, But with joy **wend** your way; Tho' hard to you this journey may appear, Grace shall be as your day. 'Tis better far for us to strive Our useless cares from us to drive; Do this, and joy your hearts will swell—All is well! all is well!

Why should we mourn, or think our lot is hard? 'Tis not so; all is right! Why should we think to earn a great reward, If we now **shun** the fight? **Gird** up your loins, fresh courage take, Our God will never us forsake; And soon we'll have this truth to tell—All is well! all is well!

We'll find the place which God for us prepared, Far a-way in the West; Where none shall come to hurt or make a-fraid; There the Saints will be blessed. We'll make the air with music ring—Shout prais-es to our God and King; Above the rest these words we'll tell—All is well! all is well!

And should we die before our journey's through, Hap-py day! all is well! We then are free from **toil** and sor-row too; With the just we shall dwell. But if our lives are spared again To see the Saints, their rest ob-tain, O how we'll make this chorus swell—All is well! all is well! 99

— William Clayton, 1846

---

wend to move from one place to another

shun to keep away

gird to prepare for action

toil exhausting, physical labor

9. **Explaining** What is the main purpose and message of this source?

10. **Analyzing Perspectives** Consider the fact that the author was a Mormon, or Latter-day Saint. How does religious practice relate to migration that may have shaped the writing of the song?

11. **Interpreting** What does the song imply people will find in the West?

Chinese Leaders' Message to President Grant

A large number of Chinese men immigrated to the western United States for employment and a chance to start a new life. Railroad owners eagerly accepted workers who would work cheaply. However, many Americans discriminated against the Chinese for taking jobs and not assimilating to the American culture. Because of this, some Americans took action to limit or halt further Chinese immigration. Chinese people already living in the United States were also discriminated against. In response, leaders of the Chinese Consolidated Benevolent Association, a powerful organization of Chinese merchants, wrote to President Ulysses S. Grant. The authors included Lee Ming How, Lee Chee Kwan, Law Yee Chung, Chan Leung Kok, Lee Cheong Chip, Chan Kong Chew, and Lee Tong Hay.

PRIMARY SOURCE : LETTER

> We understand that it has always been the settled policy of your honorable Government to welcome emigration to your shores from all countries, without let or hindrance [obstacles]. The Chinese are not the only people who have crossed the ocean to seek a residence in this land. . . .
>
> Our people in this country, for the most part, have been peaceable, law-abiding, and industrious. They performed the largest part of the unskilled labor in the construction of the Central Pacific Railroad, and also of all other railroads on this Coast. . . . They have not displaced white laborers from these positions, but have simply multiplied the industrial enterprises of the country. . . .
>
> At the present time an intense excitement and bitter hostility against the Chinese in this land, and against further Chinese emigration, has been created in the minds of the people, led on by His Honor the Mayor of San Francisco and his associates in office, and approved by His Excellency the Governor, and other great men of the State. . . .
>
> It is charged against us that we eat rice, fish, and vegetables. It is true that our diet is slightly different from the people of this honorable country; our tastes in these matters are not exactly alike, and cannot be forced. But is that a sin on our part of sufficient gravity to be brought before the President and Congress of the United States? . . .
>
> It is charged that the Chinese are no benefit to this country. Are the railroads built by Chinese labor no benefit to the country? Are the manufacturing establishments, largely worked by Chinese, no benefit to this country? Do not the results of the daily toil of a hundred thousand men increase the riches of this country?

— Chinese Consolidated Benevolent Association, to the Chinese Consul at New York, 1885

Copyright © McGraw Hill TEXT: How, Lee Ming. "Memorial of the Six Chinese Companies to U.S. Grant, President of the United States," in The Papers of Ulysses S. Grant, Vol. 27: January 1 to October 31, 1876, edited by John Y. Simon. Carbondale (Illinois): Ulysses S. Grant Association, Southern Illinois University Press, 2005.

Need Extra Help?

When reading a source that has several paragraphs, jot down the main idea of each paragraph. Consider how well the author supports those ideas and how it relates to your Supporting Questions and the Compelling Question.

12. Explaining What originally led people to come to America from China, and how did they expect to be treated?

13. Summarizing How did Chinese immigrants impact the economy of the United States? Why are the authors of the letter writing, and how do they feel Americans see them?

E

Sixty Years in Southern California

In the 1500s, the Spanish introduced cattle to western reaches of what is now the United States. By the mid-1800s, industrious settlers of California had established ranches to raise and sell cattle. Ranching was hard work, requiring the diverse skills that only trained cowhands possessed. Spring was the time for rodeos. Back in the mid-1800s, rodeos were events where cowhands rounded up cattle running free and branded them with their ranch's symbol. They also had opportunities to show off their horseback-riding and roping skills. People from all around the area gathered to watch rodeos for entertainment and to have a chance to socialize. Writer Harris Newmark found the rodeo he attended so interesting that he included a description of it in his book of California reminiscences.

PRIMARY SOURCE : MEMOIR

❝ The third week in February witnessed one of the most interesting gatherings of *rancheros* characteristic of Southern California life I have ever seen. It was a typical *rodeo*, lasting two or three days, for the separating and re-grouping of cattle and horses, and took place at the residence of William Workman at La Puente *rancho*. . . . Under the direction of a Judge of the Plains—on this occasion, the polished **cavalier**, Don Felipe Lugo—they were examined, parted and branded, or re-branded, with hot irons impressing a mark (generally a letter or odd monogram) duly registered at the Court House and protected by the County Recorder's certificate. Never have I seen finer horsemanship than was there displayed by those whose task it was to pursue the animal and throw the lasso around the head or leg; and as often as most of those present had probably seen the feat performed, great was their enthusiasm when each **vaquero** brought down his victim. Among the guests were most of the *rancheros* of wealth and note, together with their attendants, all of whom made up a company ready to enjoy the unlimited hospitality for which the Workmans were so renowned.

Aside from the business in hand of disposing of such an enormous number of mixed-up cattle in so short a time, what made the occasion one of keen delight was the remarkable, almost astounding ability of the horseman in controlling his animal; for lassoing cattle was not his only **forte**. The vaquero of early days was a clever rider and handler of horses, particularly the bronco—so often erroneously spelled broncho—sometimes a mustang, sometimes an Indian pony. Out of a drove that had never been saddled, he would lasso one, attach a halter to his neck and blindfold him by means of a strap some two or three inches in width fastened to the halter; after which he would suddenly mount the bronco and remove the blind, when the horse, unaccustomed to discipline or restraint, would buck and kick for over a quarter of a mile, and then stop only because of exhaustion. ❞

— Harris Newmark

ranchero (Spanish) a person who farms or works on a ranch

cavalier a gentleman trained in horsemanship

vaquero (Spanish) a cowhand

forte a thing at which someone excels

14. Analyzing Perspectives Why might the author have shared this experience?

15. Making Inferences Why might people have wanted to be rancheros in the West?

16. Drawing Conclusions How is this source limited in perspective and information?

Evaluate Sources and Use Evidence

17. <u>**Citing Text Evidence**</u> Review the Supporting Questions you developed at the beginning of the topic and the evidence you gathered and recorded in the graphic organizer. Which sources will help you answer the Supporting Questions? Circle or highlight those sources in your graphic organizer. Looking at the subset of sources you have chosen, be prepared to explain why you chose each source.

	Supporting Question	Primary Source and Notes
1		
2		
3		

Challenge

Research other sources related to why people moved to the American West. Find at least one primary or secondary text. Analyze the source and use it to help answer one or more of your Supporting Questions. Include your research in your response.

18. Directions: Now answer the Supporting Questions that you developed at the beginning of the activity to help guide you in answering the Compelling Question.

Answer for Supporting Question 1:

Answer for Supporting Question 2:

Answer for Supporting Question 3:

Communicate Conclusions

Talk About It

19. Collaborating Work with a partner. Take turns reviewing your answers to your Supporting Questions. Then summarize the main reasons people had for settling in the American West. Take turns presenting your summaries to each other. Discuss the similar and different reasons and the costs and benefits of moving.

Write About It

20. Informative Writing Choose two sources that you recorded in the graphic organizer that helped you answer your Supporting Questions. Then write an e-mail to the creator of each source in which you summarize the content and explain its importance. Discuss how each source helps you answer your Supporting Questions. Be sure to include key ideas from the sources and from the background information about each source.

21. Answering the Compelling Question What do you think? Why did people move to the American West? Write one or two paragraphs in which you cite evidence from at least two sources. Write an essay or create a digital presentation that uses the sources to explain reasons people had for moving to the American West.

Need Extra Help?

To help answer the Compelling Question, make a concept map with "Settling the American West" in the center. Add information from the sources and your prior knowledge about the subject. Record as much as you know about why people moved westward. Then use your concept map to help answer the question.

22. **Making Connections** Many people moved to the American West for better opportunities or to escape some form of persecution or prejudice. Consider reasons people have for migrating from countries today. Make a list of some of these reasons. Then identify specific places where two of your reasons are the cause for groups migrating. Research sources to investigate. Use a graphic organizer of your choice to take notes as you conduct research.

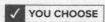 **YOU CHOOSE**

Select one of these Take Informed Action products to apply what you've learned.

A. Prepare and record a news broadcast about your findings.

B. Prepare a digital slideshow presentation to inform the public about what is happening in the countries.

C. Write a letter to someone living in one of the countries you identified and provide suggestions for ways that might make it easier for them to adapt to a new country.

Take Informed Action Rubric: Reasons for Migrating

Self-Evaluation As you research and describe reasons people in countries have for migrating, think about the following criteria. These are the criteria your teacher will use to evaluate your Take Informed Action activity.

Peer Review Use this rubric to grade the research and the final product developed by another classmate or group of classmates.

	Organization	Research	Historical Accuracy	Product
4	The piece is exceptionally well organized and focused and demonstrates a thorough and deep understanding of the issue and the agency.	The research shows a thorough synthesis of information from appropriate sources about the reasons people have for migrating and specific places from which people migrate today.	The piece is well researched and is factually accurate.	The final product addresses all criteria and provides sufficient, thoughtful reasons people migrate from specific places.
3	The piece is well organized and focused and demonstrates an adequate understanding of the issue and the agency.	The research reflects an adequate synthesis of information from appropriate sources about the reasons people have for migrating and specific places from which people migrate today.	The piece is well researched but contains some factual errors.	The final product addresses most criteria and provides some reasons people migrate from specific places.
2	The piece is organized but is inconsistent in focus and demonstrates an inadequate understanding of the issue and the agency.	The research reflects a general discussion of information, but sources are only somewhat related to reasons people have for migrating and places from which people migrate.	The piece is not well researched and contains some factual errors.	The final product addresses some criteria and provides limited reasons people migrate from specific places.
1	The piece lacks organization and focus and does not demonstrate a basic understanding of the issue and the agency.	The research demonstrates a lack of effort to describe the reasons people have for migrating and a failure to use appropriate sources.	There are many factual errors.	The final product fails to address most criteria or to attempt providing any reasons people migrate from specific places.
SCORE				

TOPIC 12 • NEW INDUSTRY AND A CHANGING SOCIETY, 1865–1914

Excluded From Reform

 COMPELLING QUESTION

How did minority groups react to discrimination and work for reform?

Plan Your Inquiry

In this Inquiry Activity, you will develop Supporting Questions related to problems faced by minority groups during the Progressive Era based on the Compelling Question. Then, you will examine primary sources describing people's experiences with discrimination, how they organized, and what they did to accomplish reform. Finally, you will answer your Supporting Questions, communicate your research conclusions, and take action based on what you've learned.

Background Information

The growth of industry changed the population distribution of the United States, with people moving from rural areas to cities and towns for work opportunities. The American economy was growing fast. Yet some Americans did not share in the prosperity.

Many groups of Americans faced discrimination. Among these were African Americans, Native Americans, Mexican Americans, and women. Immigrants also faced unfair treatment. A large number of immigrants came from eastern and southern Europe. Many were Catholic or Jewish. Immigrants from China and Mexico also arrived. Some Americans born in the United States resented immigrants for taking jobs, and as a result, the U.S. government tightened immigration requirements.

Immigrants, displaced farmers, and African Americans often settled in cities. They typically lived in cramped quarters and encountered such urban problems as poor sanitation, disease, poverty, and miserable working conditions. As time passed, reformers sought solutions to the problems faced by a growing population. Reformers worked to improve labor conditions, the state of politics, business practices, and other problems. Because of their desire to enact change, the period they lived in became known as the Progressive Era. Still, many minorities felt that not enough was being done to better their lives, so they began to organize on their own to work for political, social, and economic change.

In 1911, six women and men organized the Society of American Indians (SAI). The group shown here includes the society's first members. They met to solve issues related to disease, discrimination, and poverty faced by the Native American population.

Develop Supporting Questions About Groups Working from Reform

 COMPELLING QUESTION

How did minority groups react to discrimination and work for reform?

Talk About It

Discuss with a partner what type of information you would need to know to answer this question. For example, one question might be the following: What groups faced discrimination during the Progressive Era?

Directions: Write down three additional questions that you need to answer to be able to determine how minority groups dealt with discrimination and worked for reform.

Supporting Question 1:

Supporting Question 2:

Supporting Question 3:

Apply Historical Concepts and Tools

Directions: As you read and work with primary sources, use the graphic organizer to take notes and organize information.

		Organizing Source Information
Source	**Title and Author/ Creator**	**Notes**
A	"What Are You Going To Do About It Uncle?" a political cartoon	
B	"The Only One Barred Out," a political cartoon	
C	The Influence of Jewish Activism, newspaper article	
D	A Red Record: Tabulated Statistics and Alleged Causes of Lynchings in the United States, 1892-1893-1894 by Ida B. Wells	
E	"Lynchings at Santa Fe"	

Analyze Sources

Review and analyze Sources A–E. There are questions that accompany each source to help you examine the source and check for historical understanding.

"What Are You Going To Do About It Uncle?"

The Fourteenth Amendment to the Constitution was adopted in **1868** as one of the Reconstruction amendments after the Civil War. It states that all people born in the United States or who are naturalized are U.S. citizens and so they have the rights to due process and to equal protection under the law. The amendment clarifies that the rights of citizenship are not based on race or ethnicity. Despite constitutional protection, some groups in the United States often found that they were denied the same rights as other Americans. The following political cartoon, printed in the African American newspaper *The Kansas City Sun* in 1919, questions the fairness of this situation at the time.

PRIMARY SOURCE : POLITICAL CARTOON

Uncle Sam, a symbol of the United States, sits holding the U.S. Constitution, open to the Fourteenth Amendment.

1. Analyzing What does the cartoon show?

2. Making Connections How might your knowledge of the U.S. Constitution and the Fourteenth Amendment influence your understanding of this cartoon?

3. Drawing Conclusions What does this cartoon reveal or imply about the treatment of minority groups during the time it was drawn?

4. Evaluating What are the limitations of the information about the treatment of minority groups in the cartoon?

B

"The Only One Barred Out"

Although many Chinese immigrants helped build the nation's railroads, some Americans, called nativists, thought that immigrants—including Asians—had no place in United States society. With growing resentment, or bitterness, toward the Chinese, the U.S. government passed the Chinese Exclusion Act. This law barred, or denied, further Chinese immigration for a set period of time. Nativists cheered the law's passage, but not all Americans agreed with the law, as this cartoon shows. Some Americans believed that the work ethic of Chinese immigrants already living in the country proved that new Chinese immigrants could make positive contributions to American society. Cartoonist Frank Leslie, an immigrant himself, created the political cartoon in **1882** to appear in his own illustrated newspaper. Note that the sign says that Chinese immigrants could not enter the United States while questionable groups, in the cartoonist's opinion, could. Nihilists think life is meaningless and reject morality, while Fenians were Irish in America who organized rebellion.

PRIMARY SOURCE : POLITICAL CARTOON

THE ONLY ONE BARRED OUT.
ENLIGHTENED AMERICAN STATESMAN.—" We must draw the line *somewhere*, you know."

This cartoon reflects the passage of the Chinese Exclusion Act, which denied entry to immigrants from China for 10 years. The act was renewed two times. A Chinese immigrant is shown sitting outside the "Golden Gate of Liberty," unallowed entry, while communists, nihilists, socialists, and others are welcomed.

5. Analyzing What do you learn from the sign and caption in the cartoon?

6. Interpreting What is ironic about the words "Golden Gate of Liberty"?

7. Evaluating How useful is this cartoon as a source regarding how minority groups organize, react to discrimination, or act to get reform? Explain your reasoning.

The Influence of Jewish Activism

Both African Americans and Jewish people in the United States faced discrimination. Jewish groups formed early to combat the problem Jewish immigrants and others faced. One such group was the Anti-Defamation League, founded in the 1910s, which brought Jewish people together as a united front to fight anti-Semitic, or anti-Jewish, activities in the country. The African American writer of the following newspaper article explains that Jewish activism would be a good model for African Americans to follow to combat their own plight of mistreatment in the United States. The author notes learning in the B'nai B'rith news about an Anti-Defamation League's effort to stop the use of the William Shakespeare play *The Merchant of Venice*. This play presents an unfavorable stereotype of Jews. B'nai B'rith is a service organization, founded in the 1840s, to help improve the lives of Jewish Americans.

PRIMARY SOURCE : NEWSPAPER ARTICLE

66 A few Colored leaders, both North and South, **decry** agitation for manhood rights. They **intimate** that we must not protest against the **deprivations** basic necessitites lest we disturb the peaceful slumber and the **repose** of the South and increase racial friction. They say, 'Let our grievances and wrongs along. They will adjust themselves.' And a few of our Northern friends and sympathizers have likewise fallen into this **utopian** dream.

It has been universally conceded that the Jewish race is a gifted race. It has produced noted f[inanciers], statesmen, philosophers and poets, and it would be well to observe how that race submits to insults and **indignities**.

The B'Nai B'Rith News reports the work of the Anti-Defamation League. This League objected to the use of 'The Merchant of Venice,' in the public schools, because the play [reflected] against the Jewish race, and caricatured it.

What has been the result of this agitation on the part of the Jews. Some school superintendents have stopped the study of the play. Magazines and newspapers, [whose] articles and stories enraged the Jews[,] have apologized.

Manufacturers have destroyed moving films and theatre managers have cut out **vaudeville** acts which reflected on the Jews. This is what the Jew has gained by protesting and agitation and the Colored Americans may well profit by [their] example. 99

— *The Denver Star*, from *Chronicling America: Historic American Newspapers,*
December 26, 1914

---

decry to express disapproval

intimate to communicate indirectly

deprivations basic necessitites

repose quiet peace or rest

utopian an ideal of perfection

indignity treatment that causes one to feel shame

vaudeville comedy and song and dance shows performed in theaters

8. **Explaining** Why do some African Americans say they should not "protest against the deprivations" they face?

9. **Citing Evidence** What evidence does the source offer to support the position that African Americans should follow the example set by Jews?

10. **Analyzing** What does the newspaper article's argument imply?

D

A Red Record: Tabulated Statistics and Alleged Causes of Lynchings in the United States, 1892-1893-1894

In the late 1800s and early 1900s, some journalists, called muckrakers, used their talents to encourage reforms in the United States. For example, journalist Ida B. Wells spoke out about social ills, such as the lack of rights for women, discrimination against African Americans, and violence, especially lynching. In a lynching, a mob of white people would seize an African American and kill that person, usually by hanging, for an alleged offense—and without a trial. Lynching mostly occured in the South. As the following excerpt from her book *A Red Scare* demonstrates, Wells was particularly angry about lynching. Wells likely included "red" in the title of her statistics-based book on lynching because of the color's close association with blood. In the excerpt, she calls on readers to approach Christian organizations, including the Woman's Christian Temperance Union, or WCTU.

PRIMARY SOURCE : BOOK EXCERPT

66 What can you do, reader to prevent lynching, to **thwart** anarchy and promote law and order throughout our land?

1st. You can help **disseminate** the facts contained in this book by bringing them to the knowledge of every one with whom you come in contact, to the end that public sentiment may be revolutionized. Let the facts speak for themselves, with you as a medium.

2d. You can be instrumental in having churches, missionary societies, Y.M.C.A.'s, W.C.T.U.'s and all Christian and moral forces in connection with your religious and social life, pass resolutions of **condemnation** and protest every time a lynching takes place; and see that they are sent to the place where these outrages occur.

3d. Bring to the intelligent consideration of Southern people the refusal of capital to invest where lawlessness and mob violence hold sway. Many labor organizations have declared by resolution that they would avoid lynch **infested** localities as they would the **pestilence** when seeking new homes. If the South wishes to build up its waste places quickly, there is no better way than to uphold the majesty of the law by enforcing obedience to the same, and **meting** out the same punishment to all classes of criminals, white as well as black. 'Equality before the law,' must become a fact as well as a theory before America is truly the 'land of the free and the home of the brave.' 99

— Ida B. Wells, *A Red Record: Tabulated Statistics and Alleged Causes of Lynchings in the United States, 1892-1893-1894,* pp. 154–155

thwart to stop someone from doing something

disseminate to spread widely

condemnation strong disapproval

infest to be overrun in a troublesome way

pestilence something that is destructive

mete to give out or dispense something, such as justice or punishment

11. **Analyzing Perspectives** Why did Ida B. Wells publish this source? Describe the conditions to which she responds.

12. **Speculating** How do you think this document influenced African Americans at the time?

13. **Drawing Conclusions** How does this source help you understand the challenges that African Americans faced during the Progressive Era?

"Lynching at Santa Fe"

This newspaper account of a tragic event appeared in *The Spanish American,* a newspaper meant to keep settlers of New Mexico informed. The paper, founded in the early years of the 1900s, was published in both English and Spanish. This article offers commentary on the action of vigilantes in the region, or people who took justice into their own hands. The victim had been accused, but not convicted, of murder. Such mob violence against Mexican Americans and other minorities proved to be a common occurrence at this time and place.

PRIMARY SOURCE : NEWSPAPER ARTICLE

  66 Santa Fe was the scene of mob violence Tuesday morning when Adolfo Padilla was taken from the jail and cut to pieces with knives [in] a manner similar to that in which he had murdered his 18-year-old girl-wife a few days previously. The details of the affair are too shuddery [awful] to be repeated but the logical inference is that some citizens were so outraged by the murder committed by their victim that they gave way to the sentiment— 'An eye for an eye— A tooth for a tooth'. If these men had reason to believe the law would not properly punish this wretch there is some **extenuation** for their procedure, The law is intended to give fair and impartial justice to all and it is the ideal condition of our boasted Government of the people for the people and BY the people when justice is rendered by the courts. When courts are prostituted to the protection of some forms of crime and the persecutions of those who oppose tyranny and experience has taught that justice can not be hoped for them the tribunals of the law, then mob violence is not only to be **condoned** but encouraged. We do not know the conditions which led to this regrettable affair; we want to hope that it was unwarranted and we still live in an [enduring] faith that this form of crime may some day be banished from our fair state. **99**

    — *The Spanish American,* from *Chronicling America: Historic American Newspapers,*
April 4, 1914

---

extenuation an excuse

condone to treat as acceptable

14. Determining Context How does the newspaper article describe the events that occurred? What conditions contributed to the circumstance?

15. Interpreting What does this source indicate about beliefs some people likely had about dealing with minority groups during this time?

16. Analyzing What commentary does the article seem to make about law and vigilante justice?

Evaluate Sources and Use Evidence

17. <u>Citing Text Evidence</u> Review the Supporting Questions you developed at the beginning of the topic and the evidence you gathered and recorded in the graphic organizer. Which sources will help you answer the Supporting Questions? Circle or highlight those sources in your graphic organizer. Looking at the subset of sources you have chosen, be prepared to explain why you chose each source.

	Supporting Question	Primary Source and Notes
1		
2		
3		

Need Extra Help?

When rereading a passage, such as the excerpt from *A Red Record: Tabulated Statistics and Alleged Causes of Lynchings in the United States, 1892-1893-1894,* to find evidence for your Supporting Questions, highlight key words and ideas. Identify the main idea of each part and consider how well the author supports those ideas.

18. Directions: Now answer the Supporting Questions that you developed at the beginning of the activity to help guide you in answering the Compelling Question.

Answer for Supporting Question 1:

Answer for Supporting Question 2:

Answer for Supporting Question 3:

Communicate Conclusions

Talk About It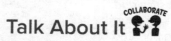

19. Collaborating With a partner, choose two Supporting Questions to write on two sheets of paper. Post your questions in the classroom. Circulate and read the other students' questions, and select two other questions to answer. Write your responses on the papers. Finally, as a class, take turns explaining which sources you found most helpful in answering the Supporting Questions and why.

Write About It

20. Informative Writing What were the causes and effects of discrimination toward minority groups? Write one or two paragraphs in which you respond to the question and cite evidence and examples from the sources to support your ideas.

21. Answering the Compelling Question What do you think? How did minority groups react to discrimination and work for reform? Write one or two paragraphs as if you were giving a speech to minority groups during the late 1800s and early 1900s. In your speech, explain how some groups have dealt with discrimination, what they have done to work for reform, and why you believe it is important for minority groups to fight for their equality and liberty.

Challenge

With a partner, research two secondary sources to learn about other ways minority groups reacted to discrimination and worked for reform. Write a summary of the two sources in which you explain how those sources helped you expand your response to the Compelling Question and explain what evidence each source uses to support its claims.

22. **Making Connections** Unfair treatment of minority groups and immigrants plagues the United States even today. African Americans, Latinos, women, and other minorities struggle with issues many other Americans do not face. Use print and digital media resources to identify two issues facing two different minority groups today. Use a graphic organizer of your choice to take notes. Include suggestions for reforms to help solve the two issues.

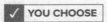 YOU CHOOSE

Select one of these Take Informed Action products to apply what you've learned.

A. Write a newspaper article in which you explain the issues facing the minority groups and possible reforms.

B. Prepare a digital slideshow presentation to inform the public of minority struggles facing groups today and suggested reforms.

C. Write and record a podcast in which you report on the issues and possible reforms.

Take Informed Action Rubric: Minority Group Issues and Reforms

Self-Evaluation As you research and describe minority group issues and reforms, think about the following criteria. These are the criteria your teacher will use to evaluate your Take Informed Action activity.

Peer Review Use this rubric to grade the research and the final product developed by another classmate or group of classmates.

	Organization	Research	Historical Accuracy	Product
4	The piece is exceptionally well organized and focused and demonstrates a thorough and deep understanding of the issue.	The research shows a thorough understanding and synthesis of information about issues related to minority groups and possible reforms.	The piece is well researched and is factually accurate.	The piece is well researched and is factually accurate.
3	The piece is well organized and focused and demonstrates an adequate understanding of the issue.	The research reflects an adequate understanding and synthesis of information about issues related to minority groups and possible reforms.	The piece is well researched but contains some factual errors.	The final product addresses most criteria and provides some information about issues related to minority groups and possible reforms.
2	The piece is organized but is inconsistent in focus and demonstrates an inadequate understanding of the issue.	The research reflects a basic understanding and synthesis of information, but sources are only somewhat related to issues that have to do with minority groups and possible reforms.	The piece is not well researched and contains some factual errors.	The final product addresses some criteria and provides limited information about issues related to minority groups and possible reforms.
1	The piece lacks organization and focus and does not demonstrate a basic understanding of the issue.	The research demonstrates a lack of effort and a failure to synthesize information about issues related to minority groups and possible reforms and a failure to use appropriate sources.	There are many factual errors.	The final product fails to address most criteria or to attempt to provide any information about issues related to minority groups and possible reforms.
SCORE				

Name _____   Date _____   Class _____

TOPIC 13 • EXPANSION AND WAR, 1865–1920

The U.S. Involvement in World War I

? COMPELLING QUESTION

What were the reasons for and against the United States entering World War I?

Plan Your Inquiry

In this Inquiry Activity, you will develop Supporting Questions related to U.S. involvement in World War I based on the Compelling Question. Then, you will examine primary sources that describe the social and political reasons both for and against the United States entering the war. Finally, you will answer your Supporting Questions, communicate your research conclusions, and take action based on what you've learned.

Background Information

In the late 1800s, the United States began to exert its influence throughout the Western Hemisphere. One result was the Spanish-American War, in which the United States took control of Cuba from Spain. In doing so, it showed the world that it was an important military force.

Meanwhile, growing nationalism and rival alliances in Europe would lead to fighting among most of the continent's nations. The assassination of Austria-Hungary's Archduke Ferdinand in 1914 ignited the conflict that became known as the Great War. On one side were the Central Powers, which included Austria-Hungary, Germany, and the Ottoman Empire. Great Britain, France, Russia, Italy, and Japan were major forces on the opposing side—the Allied Powers.

At first, the United States tried to be neutral and maintained trade with countries on both sides of the conflict. However, it lent Great Britain and France money for their war efforts, which angered Germany. The United States edged closer to the Allied side when the Germans sank the *Lusitania*, a British ship carrying some American citizens. Then, after a German plan to enlist Mexico to fight the United States came to light and Germany attacked American ships, U.S. President Woodrow Wilson asked Congress to declare war on Germany. Congress agreed. In April 1917, the United States entered the international fight that would become known as World War I.

Although the United States tried to stay out of World War I, over time, it became more difficult to remain neutral. When the country finally entered the war, recruiting posters such as this one encouraged men to fight for the country's ideals.

SPIRIT of 1917

JOIN THE
UNITED STATES MARINES
AND BE
FIRST IN DEFENSE ON LAND OR SEA
APPLY AT

Develop Supporting Questions About the United States and World War I

 COMPELLING QUESTION

What were the reasons for and against the United States entering World War I?

Talk About It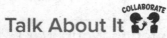

Discuss with a partner what type of information you would need to know to answer this question. For example, one question might be the following: Why did World War I begin?

Directions: Write down three additional questions that you need to answer to be able to determine the issues for and against the United States fighting in World War I.

Supporting Question 1:

Supporting Question 2:

Supporting Question 3:

Apply Historical Concepts and Tools

Directions: As you read and work with primary sources, use the graphic organizer to take notes and organize information.

	Organizing Source Information	
Source	**Title and Author/ Creator**	**Notes**
A	Translation of the Zimmermann Telegram sent by Walter Page	
B	"I Didn't Raise My Boy to Be a Soldier" by Alfred Bryan and Al Piantadosi	
C	The War Message by Woodrow Wilson	
D	Commission for Enduring Peace, Hearings Before the Committee on Foreign Affairs: Statement of Miss Jane Addams	
E	"Cousin William Said You'd Forgotten All About Them, Samuel," a political cartoon	

Analyze Sources

Review and analyze Sources A–E. There are questions that accompany each source to help you examine the source and check for historical understanding.

Translation of the Zimmermann Telegram

Great Britain intercepted a coded message from the German foreign minister, Arthur Zimmermann, to the German minister to Mexico. The contents were astonishing: Zimmermann was instructing the minister to convince Mexico to take up arms against the United States if the Americans entered the war. At first, Great Britain did not share the information in the telegram with the United States, to keep Germany from knowing Great Britain had broken Germany's code. Eventually, eager for the United States to join the Allied Powers, Great Britain shared the telegram with American government officials. The text of the actual telegram is shown. The American public was furious when the telegram's contents were published in newspapers across the United States.

PRIMARY SOURCE : TELEGRAM

66 We intend to begin on the first of February unrestricted submarine warfare. We shall **endeavor** in spite of this to keep the United States of America neutral. In the event of this not succeeding, we make Mexico a proposal or alliance on the following basis: make war together, make peace together, generous financial support and an understanding on our part that Mexico is to reconquer the lost territory in Texas, New Mexico, and Arizona. The settlement in detail is left to you. You will inform the President of the above most secretly as soon as the outbreak of war with the United States of America is certain and add the suggestion that he should, on his own **initiative**, invite Japan to immediate **adherence** and at the same time **mediate** between Japan and ourselves. Please call the President's attention to the fact that the **ruthless employment** of our submarines now offers the prospect of **compelling** England in a few months to make peace. 99

—Translation of the Zimmermann Telegram by Walter Page, London, England, February 24, 1917

endeavor try

initiative the ability to start something

adherence strict support for a rule or plan

mediate work between two others to reach an agreement

ruthless without pity

employment the use of something

compelling forcing

1. Identifying What is the German foreign minister offering? What does he expect Mexico to do in return?

2. Determining Context What purpose does this document serve? Explain its significance.

3. Speculating The telegram was intercepted before it reached Mexico's leaders so they never saw it. How do you think they would have reacted? Do you think they would have allied against the United States? Explain your reasoning.

B

"I Didn't Raise My Boy to Be a Soldier"

Before 1917, as war raged in Europe, many Americans were determined to keep their country from taking up arms as well. Those convinced that the United States should stay out of the war used propaganda to sway other Americans to share their viewpoint. These song lyrics represent the viewpoint of pacifists, or people who believe that there is never a justification for war.

PRIMARY SOURCE : SONG LYRICS

66 VERSE 1

Ten million soldiers to the war have gone,

Who may never return again.

Ten million mothers' hearts must break

For the ones who died in vain.

Head bowed down in sorrow

In her lonely years,

I heard a mother murmur thro' her tears:

CHORUS

'I didn't raise my boy to be a soldier,

I brought him up to be my pride and joy,

Who dares to place a musket on his shoulder,

To shoot some other mother's darling boy?

Let nations **arbitrate** their future troubles,

It's time to lay the sword and gun away,

There'd be no war today,

If mothers all would say,

'I didn't raise my boy to be a soldier.'

VERSE 2

What victory can cheer a mother's heart,

When she looks at her **blighted** home?

What victory can bring her back

All she cared to call her own.

Let each mother answer

In the years to be,

Remember that my boy belongs to me! 99

—Alfred Bryan and Al Piantadosi, 1915

arbitrate to settle a dispute

blighted destroyed

4. Analyzing Perspectives What is the main idea of the song lyrics?

5. Interpreting How is public sentiment about the war shown in the title?

6. Evaluating How useful are these lyrics as a source about reasons to avoid the war?

C

The War Message

In early 1917, the U.S. was still neutral. A British blockade of German ports led to the Germans' use of submarines, called U-boats, to sink any ships transporting supplies to Britain. Wilson protested, and Germany agreed it would issue warnings before attacking neutral ships. However, in 1917, Germany declared it would sink any ships traveling to Allied ports. Germany then sank four U.S. merchant ships. President Wilson then believed it was time for the U.S. to declare war on Germany. In this speech to Congress on April 2, 1917, Wilson describes why he thought this.

PRIMARY SOURCE : SPEECH

❝ On the third of February last I officially laid before you the extraordinary announcement of the Imperial German Government that on and after the first day of February it was its purpose to put aside all **restraints** of law or of humanity and use its submarines to sink every vessel that sought to approach either the ports of Great Britain and Ireland or the western coasts of Europe or any of the ports controlled by the enemies of Germany within the Mediterranean. . . . Vessels of every kind, whatever their flag, their character, their cargo, their destination, their errand, have been ruthlessly sent to the bottom: without warning and without thought of help or mercy for those on board, the vessels of friendly neutrals along with those of **belligerents**. . . . I am not now thinking of the loss of property involved, immense and serious as that is, but only of the **wanton** and wholesale destruction of the lives of noncombatants, men, women, and children, engaged in pursuits which have always, even in the darkest periods of modern history, been deemed innocent and legitimate. Property can be paid for; the lives of peaceful and innocent people cannot be. The present German submarine warfare against commerce is a warfare against mankind.

It is a war against all nations. American ships have been sunk, American lives taken, in ways which it has stirred us very deeply to learn of, but the ships and people of other neutral and friendly nations have been sunk and overwhelmed in the waters in the same way. There has been no discrimination. The challenge is to all mankind. Each nation must decide for itself how it will meet it. The choice we make for ourselves must be made with a moderation of counsel and a temperateness of judgment befitting our character and our motives as a nation. We must put excited feeling away. Our motive will not be revenge or the victorious assertion of the physical might of the nation, but only the **vindication** of right, of human right, of which we are only a single champion. ❞

— Woodrow Wilson, *War Message and Facts Behind It,* Washington, D.C.: Committee on Public Information, April 2, 1917

---

restraints limits

belligerents those waging war

wanton causing harm or damage for no reason

vindication the act of justifying or clearing someone of blame

7. **Summarizing** Why does President Wilson say that the United States is justified for entering World War I?

8. **Making Connections** Why might Wilson have outlined his reasons? How did his message shape world events at the time?

D

Commission for Enduring Peace, Hearings Before the Committee on Foreign Affairs: Statement of Miss Jane Addams

Between the war's start and America's entry into it, many people in the U.S. were strongly opposed to American involvement. Among those was Jane Addams. Addams had already gained national attention for her reform efforts relating to poverty, alcohol use, child labor, housing, and women's rights, and help for immigrants. However, it was her strong desire for world peace that led her to give the following speech regarding calling together a conference of neutral nations to discuss propositions for peace.

PRIMARY SOURCE : SPEECH

66 I think people get confused about the functions of this conference of nations. It is not that they intend to get together to make terms of peace—nobody but the nations who are fighting can make the terms—but they felt that a conference of neutrals would have coming to it all sorts of propositions for peace, and they would clear the ground, so to speak. I think no one knows how hard it is for the people in the warring countries to believe that some other method besides war is possible. . . .

[T]he English papers try to make everybody think the Germans want to fight to the bitter end, and the German papers try to make the people believe that the English want to fight to the bitter end, and so they go on fighting. . . .

[I]t is the business, so long as the fighting goes on, to keep enthusiasm at a high pitch, and the people are afraid to talk about peace for fear of lessening the enthusiasm. . . . We believe if there were a conference where such things could be proposed and discussed, although we might not bring an end to the war, it would certainly establish some sort of international opinion, and it would certainly give the various peoples within the various nations a chance to enter into communication with each other. . . . If a government is in a war, it can not do anything except go on. We were told that over and over again. Over and over again we were told that if they could save their faces—could consider peace terms without being in the position of seeming to want peace—although they do want peace—they would then be glad to consider them. That is human nature. If you get into bad position, you have got to go on to the end, unless somebody puts in a hand and gets you out.

Now, it seems to me that the United States in this turmoil of the world, being more outside than the other nations, would be **sage** to act without compromising itself and without in the least saying what the terms of the peace shall be; simply say, 'Here we are to serve you, and let you climb down, so to speak, with as much dignity as possible.' 99

— Jane Addams and others, House of Representatives, Sixty-Fourth Congress First Session, Washington, D.C., January 11, 1916

sage wise

Copyright © McGraw Hill TEXT: Addams, Jane. Testimony before Commission for Enduring Peace, Committee on Foreign Affairs, House of Representatives, January 11, 1916. Washington: Government Printing Office, 1916.

9. **Analyzing Perspectives** What approach does Jane Addams support?

10. **Drawing Conclusions** How does this source help you understand why some people were against entering World War I?

E

"Cousin William Said You'd Forgotten All About Them, Samuel"

The sinking of the *Lusitania* proved to be one of the turning points for shifting American public opinion from neutrality to pro-Allied Powers. On May 7, 1915, a German U-boat attacked the passenger ship, leading to the deaths of 1,200 passengers, including 94 children. The United States was not quite ready to enter the fight then. It would take additional German aggressions, including direct attacks on American ships, to provoke the country to war. In the meantime, this political cartoon encouraged Americans to remember what happened to the *Lusitania*.

PRIMARY SOURCE : POLITICAL CARTOON

This cartoon, by William Allen Rodgers, may have appeared in the *New York Herald* on December 18, 1915. It shows children who died in the sinking of the *Lusitania*. The figure on the left represents Franz Joseph of Austria. The figure on the right is Uncle Sam.

11. Describing Describe the drawings and text within this political cartoon.

12. Analyzing What effects might the political cartoon have had on its audience?

Evaluate Sources and Use Evidence

13. **Citing Text Evidence** Review the Supporting Questions you developed at the beginning of the topic and the evidence you gathered and recorded in the graphic organizer. Which sources will help you answer the Supporting Questions? Circle or highlight those sources in your graphic organizer. Looking at the subset of sources you have chosen, be prepared to explain why you chose each source.

	Supporting Question	Primary Source and Notes
1		
2		
3		

Challenge

Work with a partner to conduct additional research into other reasons Americans may have wanted to avoid war. Find two primary or secondary sources to help you answer at least two of your questions. Share what you learned in a short report to other pairs.

14. Directions: Now answer the Supporting Questions that you developed at the beginning of the activity to help guide you in answering the Compelling Question.

Answer for Supporting Question 1:

Answer for Supporting Question 2:

Answer for Supporting Question 3:

Communicate Conclusions

Talk About It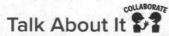

15. Collaborating In a small group, take turns describing which source you found the most helpful in answering each of your Supporting Questions. Be sure to explain why you found each source helpful. Then discuss what additional sources you might research to find out more about the reasons for and against the United States entering World War I.

Need Extra Help?

To help you analyze the sources, ask yourself the following questions: Which point of view does this source convey? What does this source tell me? What other points of view might provide additional insight or understanding? What else would I still like to know?

Write About It

16. Argumentative Writing Did Germany's actions provide sufficient justification for the United States to become involved in what was a foreign conflict? Write a letter to one of the authors or illustrators (one to two paragraphs) from the inquiry in which you answer this question. In your response, cite evidence from that source as well as one other source to support your ideas.

17. Answering the Compelling Question What do you think? What were the reasons for and against the United States entering World War I? Write a summary in response to the question.

18. **Making Connections** What conflicts between other nations or within nations exist today or existed in the last five years, and what opinions do Americans have about them? Watch or read a national or international news source and identify a current or recent conflict that people in the United States are likely to feel strongly about. Research two other appropriate sources on the conflict to learn about its historical and/or contemporary context. Decide whether you do or do not support U.S. involvement in this conflict and why. Use a graphic organizer of your choice to provide your point of view and reasons for it.

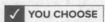 YOU CHOOSE

Select one of these Take Informed Action products to apply what you've learned.

A. Write a newspaper editorial in which you explain the conflict and your point of view about U.S. involvement in it.

B. Prepare a television or radio news broadcast in which you report on the conflict and summarize your opinion regarding U.S. involvement.

C. Draw a political cartoon that clearly expresses key aspects of the conflict and your viewpoint.

Take Informed Action Rubric: Conflict and Opinion

Self-Evaluation As you research and identify a conflict and form an opinion related to U.S. involvement in it, think about the following criteria. These are the criteria your teacher will use to evaluate your Take Informed Action activity.

Peer Review Use this rubric to grade the research and the final product developed by another classmate or group of classmates.

	Organization	Research	Historical Accuracy	Product
4	The piece is exceptionally well organized and focused and demonstrates a thorough and deep understanding of the issue.	The research shows a thorough understanding and synthesis of information about the conflict and its historical and/or contemporary context.	The piece is well researched and is factually accurate.	The final product addresses all criteria and provides sufficient and thoughtful information about the conflict and your point of view about involvement in the conflict and reasons for your viewpoint.
3	The piece is well organized and focused and demonstrates an adequate understanding of the issue.	The research reflects an adequate understanding and synthesis of information about the conflict and its historical and/or contemporary context.	The piece is well researched but contains some factual errors.	The final product addresses most criteria and provides some information about the conflict and your point of view about involvement in the conflict and reasons for your viewpoint.
2	The piece is organized but is inconsistent in focus and demonstrates an inadequate understanding of the issue.	The research reflects a basic understanding and synthesis of information, but sources are only somewhat related to the conflict and its historical and/or contemporary context.	The piece is not well researched and contains some factual errors.	The final product addresses some criteria and provides limited information about the conflict and your point of view about involvement in the conflict and reasons for your viewpoint.
1	The piece lacks organization and focus and does not demonstrate a basic understanding of the issue.	The research demonstrates a lack of effort and a failure to synthesize information about the conflict and its historical and/or contemporary context or a failure to use appropriate sources.	There are many factual errors.	The final product fails to address most criteria or to attempt providing any information about the conflict or point of view about involvement in the conflict and reasons for that viewpoint.
SCORE				

TOPIC 14 • THE 1920S AND THE 1930S, 1920–1930

Harlem Renaissance

 COMPELLING QUESTION

What were the contributions of the Harlem Renaissance?

Plan Your Inquiry

In this Inquiry Activity, you will develop Supporting Questions related to the Harlem Renaissance and the contributions made by individuals based on the Compelling Question. Then, you will examine primary sources related to this prolific artistic movement. Finally, you will answer your Supporting Questions, communicate your research conclusions, and take action based on what you've learned.

Background Information

By the early 1920s, the United States had largely recovered from its participation in World War I. Soldiers returned home to start families and find employment. In time, the economy boomed, at least for a while. New technologies, such as electricity, led to industrial growth and improved ways of living. The period of time now remembered as the Roaring Twenties also saw many social changes. Women gained new freedoms, and mass media, such as movies, newspapers, and radio, provided avenues for the spread of new cultural ideas.

Racial discrimination of African Americans remained. Some African Americans fled difficult lives in the South to head to Northern cities, a movement known as the Great Migration. Though the African Americans flocking to Northern cities still faced some forms of discrimination, they also experienced new freedoms. This was particularly true in New York City, where newcomers joined longtime African American New Yorkers in a neighborhood in northern Manhattan called Harlem. The more than 170,000 African Americans living there found many ways to explore and express African American culture in what has become known as the Harlem Renaissance. A *renaissance* is a "rebirth."

Many African American musicians called Harlem home, and their contributions to the musical genre of jazz gave the Roaring Twenties another nickname—the Jazz Age. Other creative Harlem residents expressed African American culture through painting and sculpture, literature, theater, and dance. Harlem nightclubs and theaters were packed nightly with both African Americans and whites in the audience. Sadly, as the economic happy days of the Roaring Twenties ended, so, too, did the Harlem Renaissance.

Nightly, the sound of jazz music played live by African American musicians could be heard at the Cotton Club, a Harlem nightclub. Cab Calloway and Duke Ellington were among the renowned African Americans who performed there. However, the audience consisted of white patrons only. This image appeared on a program issued for a Calloway show.

GO ONLINE   to use the Digital Inquiry Journal.

Develop Supporting Questions About the Harlem Renaissance

 COMPELLING QUESTION

What were the contributions of the Harlem Renaissance?

Talk About It

Discuss with a partner what type of information you would need to know to answer this question. For example, one question might be the following: What was the Harlem Renaissance?

Directions: Write down three additional questions that you need to answer to be able to determine ways in which the Harlem Renaissance contributed to society during the 1920s and beyond.

Supporting Question 1:

Supporting Question 2:

Supporting Question 3:

Apply Historical Concepts and Tools

Directions: As you read and work with primary sources, use the graphic organizer to take notes and organize information.

	Organizing Source Information	
Source	**Title and Author/ Creator**	**Notes**
A	"America" by Claude McKay	
B	"Enter the New Negro" by Alain Locke	
C	"Dream Variations" by Langston Hughes	
D	"The Harp," a sculpture by Augusta Savage	
E	"How It Feels to Be Colored Me" by Zora Neale Hurston	

Analyze Sources

Review and analyze Sources A–E. There are questions that accompany each source to help you examine the source and check for historical understanding.

"America"

Born in Jamaica in 1899, Claude McKay came to the United States as a young man to attend college. After first enrolling at the Tuskegee Institute, he transferred to Kansas Agricultural College. In 1914, McKay left Kansas for New York City. There, he became a regular contributor to *The Liberator,* the leading journal of art, and a leading voice in the Harlem Renaissance. While growing up in Jamaica, McKay did not experience the harsh racism that he faced in the United States.

PRIMARY SOURCE : POEM

> " Although she feeds me bread of bitterness,
>
> And sinks into my throat her tiger's tooth,
>
> Stealing my breath of life, I will confess
>
> I love this cultured hell that tests my youth.
>
> Her vigor flows like tides into my blood,
>
> Giving me strength erect against her hate,
>
> Her bigness sweeps my being like a flood.
>
> Yet, as a rebel **fronts** a king in state,
>
> I stand within her walls with not a shred
>
> Of terror, malice, not a word of **jeer**.
>
> Darkly I gaze into the days ahead,
>
> And see her might and granite wonders there,
>
> Beneath the touch of Time's **unerring** hand,
>
> Like priceless treasures sinking in the sand. "

—Claude McKay, "America," 1921

fronts confronts, faces
jeer to mock
unerring certain or sure

1. **Analyzing Perspectives** Based on the poem, how does McKay feel about the United States?

2. **Interpreting** What impressions are created by the words "bread of bitterness" and "cultured hell"?

3. **Analyzing** What future does McKay see for America?

4. **Evaluating** What might have been the impact of this poem at the time? How did it reflect the feelings of African Americans?

"Enter the New Negro"

Alain LeRoy Locke held degrees from Harvard University and was the first African American Rhodes scholar, which led him to head the philosophy department at Howard University. His book, *The New Negro: An Interpretation,* included artistic and literary works on what it meant to be African American. For this and other reasons, Locke is often referred to as the "father of the Harlem Renaissance." Printed in the magazine *Survey Graphic,* this article by Locke describes a change in African American point of view during the Harlem Renaissance.

PRIMARY SOURCE : MAGAZINE ARTICLE

❝ In the last decade something beyond the watch and guard of statistics has happened in the life of the American Negro. . . .

Could such a **metamorphosis** have taken place as suddenly as it has appeared to? The answer is no; not because the New Negro is not here, but because the Old Negro had long become more of a myth than a man. The Old Negro, we must remember, was a creature of moral debate and historical controversy. His has been a **stock** figure **perpetuated** as an historical fiction partly in innocent sentimentalism, partly in deliberate reactionism. The Negro himself has contributed his share to this through a sort of protective social mimicry [copying] forced upon him by the adverse circumstances of dependence. So for generations in the mind of America, the Negro has been more of a formula than a human being. . . . [H]e has subscribed to the traditional positions from which his case has been viewed. Little true social or self-understanding has or could come from such a situation. . . . The mind of the Negro seems suddenly to have slipped from under the tyranny of social intimidation and to be shaking off the psychology of imitation and implied inferiority. By shedding the old chrysalis of the Negro problem we are achieving something like a spiritual emancipation. . . . The multitude perhaps feel as yet only a strange relief and a new vague urge, but the thinking few know that in the reaction the vital inner grip of prejudice has been broken.

With this renewed self-respect and self-dependence, the life of the Negro community is bound to enter a new dynamic phase. . . . The migrant masses, shifting from countryside to city, hurdle several generations of experience at a leap, but more important, the same thing happens spiritually in the life-attitudes and self-expression of the Young Negro, in his poetry, his art, his education and his new outlook, with the additional advantage of course, of the poise and greater certainty of knowing what it is all about. From this comes the promise and warrant of a new leadership. ❞

—Alain Locke, "Enter the New Negro," *Survey Graphic*, Vol. 53, No. 11, March 1, 1925: 631–634

metamorphosis a change into something new

stock overused

perpetuated continued on and on

5. Analyzing Perspectives According to Locke, who was the "Old Negro," and how did the "Old Negro" act?

6. Explaining What kind of transformation has the "New Negro" undergone?

"Dream Variation"

During the Harlem Renaissance, a number of writers emerged who devoted their talents to describing the African American experience. Among them were Zora Neale Hurston, Claude McKay, Anne Spencer, and Langston Hughes. Although also a writer of plays, short stories, essays, novels, and newspaper columns, Langston Hughes is best known for exquisite poetry about African American life. Among his best remembered poems are "The Negro Speaks of Rivers," and "Harlem"—which begins with the line "What happens to a dream deferred?" The Langston Hughes poem that follows describes a vision of how life should be that other African Americans of the time might also yearn for.

PRIMARY SOURCE : POEM

Dream Variations

> To fling my arms wide
> In some place of the sun,
> To whirl and to dance
> Till the bright day is done.
> Then rest at cool evening
> Beneath a tall tree
> While night comes gently
> Dark like me.
> That is my dream.
>
> To fling my arms wide
> In the face of the sun.
> Dance! Whirl! Whirl!
> Till the quick day is done.
> Rest at pale evening,
> A tall, slim tree,
> Night coming tenderly
> Black like me.

— Langston Hughes, *The New Negro: An Interpretation,* edited by Alain Locke, New York: Albert and Charles Boni, 1925:143

7. **Summarizing** Based on the first stanza, what is Langston Hughes's dream? Based on the second stanza, what is the reality Hughes and other African Americans face?

8. **Describing** How does the tone in each stanza differ?

9. **Drawing Conclusions** How might this poem have affected African Americans during the Harlem Renaissance? Why did it remain relevant during the civil rights movement of the 1960s and still today?

D

"The Harp"

African American artists, such as Jacob Lawrence, Aaron Douglas, and Augusta Savage, contributed to the Harlem Renaissance through their visual depictions of African American life. Savage gained initial recognition with her sculptural busts of well-known figures in African American society, such as W.E.B. Du Bois. When asked to fashion a sculpture for the 1939 World's Fair held in New York, she found inspiration in James Weldon Johnson's poem "Lift Every Voice and Sing," which had been set to music. This song quickly had become an unofficial anthem for the African American community. The result of Savage's artistic endeavor was "The Harp," also known as "Lift Every Voice and Sing," shown in the image.

PRIMARY SOURCE : SCULPTURE

Unfortunately, "The Harp," a plaster-cast statue with a black basalt-like finish, was destroyed shortly after the World's Fair, along with all the art that had been displayed, due to lack of storage space. The 16-foot-tall sculpture featured 12 African American singers.

10. <u>Analyzing Visuals</u> What details do you notice in the sculpture? What are the different parts of the sculpture?

11. <u>Making Connections</u> This sculpture is also known as "Lift Every Voice and Sing." Why might this be significant? To whom might the singers be singing?

12. <u>Drawing Conclusions</u> What might the rising African American figures symbolize, and why might the figures be placed so close together?

E

"How It Feels to Be Colored Me"

Most experts on the Harlem Renaissance point to Zora Neale Hurston as one of its most outstanding writers. Her most famous work is the novel _Their Eyes Were Watching God._ In the following essay, Hurston describes that differing shades of skin affect how one was treated, but she is strong and proud of her heritage.

PRIMARY SOURCE : ESSAY

❝ But changes came in the family when I was thirteen, and I was sent to school in Jacksonville. I left Eatonville, the town of the **oleanders**, a Zora. When I disembarked from the river-boat at Jacksonville, she was no more. It seemed that I had suffered a sea change. I was not Zora of Orange County any more, I was now a little colored girl. I found it out in certain ways. In my heart as well as in the mirror, I became a fast brown—warranted not to rub nor run.

But I am not tragically colored. There is no great sorrow dammed up in my soul, nor lurking behind my eyes. I do not mind at all. I do not belong to the sobbing school of Negrohood who hold that nature somehow has given them a lowdown dirty deal and whose feelings are all but about it. Even in the helter-skelter skirmish that is my life, I have seen that the world is to the strong regardless of a little **pigmentation** more or less. No, I do not weep at the world—I am too busy sharpening my oyster knife.

Someone is always at my elbow reminding me that I am the granddaughter of slaves. It fails to register depression with me. Slavery is sixty years in the past. The operation was successful and the patient is doing well, thank you. The terrible struggle that made me an American out of a potential slave said 'On the line!' The Reconstruction said 'Get set!' and the generation before said 'Go!' I am off to a flying start and I must not halt in the stretch to look behind and weep. Slavery is the price I paid for civilization, and the choice was not with me. It is a **bully** adventure and worth all that I have paid through my ancestors for it. No one on earth ever had a greater chance for glory. The world to be won and nothing to be lost. It is thrilling to think—to know that for any act of mine, I shall get twice as much praise or twice as much blame. It is quite exciting to hold the center of the national stage, with the spectators not knowing whether to laugh or to weep.

The position of my white neighbor is much more difficult. No brown **specter** pulls up a chair beside me when I sit down to eat. No dark ghost thrusts its leg against mine in bed. The game of keeping what one has is never so exciting as the game of getting. ❞

—Zora Neale Hurston, 1929

---

oleander a poisonous bush with groupings of beautiful pink, red, or white flowers

pigmentation the coloring of a plant, animal, or person

bully great, grand

specter ghost; something that proves to be haunting to one's mind

Need Extra Help?

Zora Neale Hurston uses figurative language throughout this essay. That is, she does not always use words as they are normally used. Instead, she uses and combines them in unusual ways to make her writing more interesting. Reread this essay. Pause after each sentence and look for the different ways Hurston combines words to give her writing extra meaning.

EXAMINE THE SOURCE

13. Identifying How does Hurston describe her move from Eatonville to Jacksonville? Why does this change occur?

14. Interpreting Why might Hurston say that she is not "tragically colored"? What evidence does she provide to support her belief?

15. Analyzing Why does Hurston say that her white neighbors have reasons to be worried?

Evaluate Sources and Use Evidence

16. <u>**Citing Text Evidence**</u> Review the Supporting Questions you developed at the beginning of the topic and the evidence you gathered and recorded in the graphic organizer. Which sources will help you answer the Supporting Questions? Circle or highlight those sources in your graphic organizer. Looking at the subset of sources you have chosen, be prepared to explain why you chose each source.

	Supporting Question	Primary Source and Notes
1		
2		
3		

Challenge

Work with a partner to find another creative work by an artist or writer of the Harlem Renaissance. Study that work and determine how it can help you answer your Supporting Questions.

17. Directions: Now answer the Supporting Questions that you developed at the beginning of the activity to help guide you in answering the Compelling Question.

Answer for Supporting Question 1:

Answer for Supporting Question 2:

Answer for Supporting Question 3:

Communicate Conclusions

Talk About It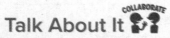

18. Collaborating In a small group, take turns describing which source you found the most helpful in answering each of your Supporting Questions. Be sure to explain why you found each source helpful. Then discuss what additional sources you might research to find out more about the contributions made during the Harlem Renaissance.

Write About It

19. <u>Argumentative Writing</u> In which creative field did African Americans make the biggest contributions not only to African American culture of the time but also to American culture as a whole? Write an editorial for an online magazine in which you answer this question. In your editorial, cite evidence from at least two sources to support your ideas.

20. <u>Answering the Compelling Question</u> What do you think? What were the contributions of the Harlem Renaissance? First, think about contributions of individual African Americans. Then, think about how the creativity of the Harlem Renaissance changed people's attitudes. Make a poster that illustrates the contributions of the Harlem Renaissance.

Take Informed Action

21. **Making Connections** During the Harlem Renaissance, African Americans made many contributions that are still remembered today. Think about the different groups of people who call your state or community home today. Find out about two people of diverse backgrounds in the state or community who have made outstanding contributions. Use a graphic organizer of your choice to outline each person's accomplishments. Be sure to explain why and how they should be remembered in history.

✓ **YOU CHOOSE**

Select one of these Take Informed Action products to apply what you've learned.

A. Write a resolution for one of these individuals as to why that person deserves to be honored.

B. Create a pamphlet that describes the achievements of the people you selected.

C. Form a class achievers club that has as its purpose to explain why various people at the state and local levels should be honored for their achievements. Prepare a presentation about the contributions of those you selected that you might give at a future club meeting.

Take Informed Action Rubric: People's Contributions

Self-Evaluation As you research and identify people's contributions, think about the following criteria. These are the criteria your teacher will use to evaluate your Take Informed Action activity.

Peer Review Use this rubric to grade the research and the final product developed by another classmate or group of classmates.

	Organization	Research	Historical Accuracy	Product
4	The piece is exceptionally well organized and focused and demonstrates a thorough and deep understanding of the contributions of the selected individuals.	The final product shows evidence of in-depth research into the contributions of diverse people in the state or community.	The piece is well researched and is factually accurate.	The final product addresses all criteria and provides sufficient, thoughtful information about the contributions of individuals in the state or community.
3	The piece is well organized and focused and demonstrates an adequate understanding of the contributions of the selected individuals.	The final product shows evidence of adequate research into the contributions of diverse people in the state or community.	The piece is well researched but contains some factual errors.	The final product addresses most criteria and provides some information about the contributions of individuals in the state or community.
2	The piece is organized but is inconsistent in focus and demonstrates an inadequate understanding of the contributions of the selected individuals.	The final product shows little evidence of research into the contributions of diverse people in the state or community.	The piece is not well researched and contains some factual errors.	The final product addresses some criteria and provides limited information about the contributions of individuals in the state or community.
1	The piece lacks organization and focus and does not demonstrate a basic understanding of the contributions of the selected individuals.	The final product shows no evidence of research into the contributions of diverse people in the state or community.	There are many factual errors.	The final product fails to address most criteria or to attempt providing any information about the contributions of individuals in the state or community.
SCORE				

TOPIC 15 · WORLD WAR II, 1939–1945

Japanese Internment Camps

 COMPELLING QUESTION

How did the United States treat Japanese Americans during WWII?

Plan Your Inquiry

In this Inquiry Activity, you will develop Supporting Questions related to the treatment of Japanese Americans during World War II based on the Compelling Question. Then you will examine primary sources related to the controversial actions the United States took related to this group of people. Finally, you will answer your Supporting Questions, communicate your research conclusions, and take action based on what you've learned.

Background Information

The year was 1941, and the United States was still trying to stay neutral in World War II. Across the ocean, the Allies—Great Britain, France, and Russia—fought the Axis nations in Europe—mainly Germany and Italy—because they sought control of much of the continent. Meanwhile, in Asia, the Chinese battled the Japanese, who had aligned with Germany. Though sympathetic to the Allies, the United States hoped to avoid joining the war. Yet the United States did take some actions against the Axis nations, such as loaning money to the Allies and limiting trade with the Japanese.

In retaliation, the Japanese staged a surprise attack on the United States at Pearl Harbor, Hawaii, on December 7, 1941. Immediately, the United States declared war on Japan. Soon after, Germany and Italy declared war on the United States in support of Japan. Americans rushed to support the war effort. A number of Japanese Americans joined the U.S. Army. Others remaining on the home front contributed labor, time, and money to help, just as other Americans did.

Many Americans, however, questioned the loyalty of Japanese Americans and believed that they might act in support of Japan. As a result, the U.S. government ordered more than 100,000 Japanese Americans to move to internment camps. They had not been accused or convicted of a crime: They were placed in the camps simply because they were Japanese. At the camps, men, women, children, and babies lived in crowded, unfamiliar, and uncomfortable quarters. More than two-thirds of those in the camps were American citizens, having been born in the United States. In addition to being forced to relocate, many Japanese American citizens of the United States had to sell their land, businesses, and possessions before they moved to the camps.

These Japanese American boys entertain themselves in the Japanese internment camp near Tule Lake, California. Tule Lake served as a holding place for almost 19,000 Japanese Americans in the early 1940s.

Develop Supporting Questions About the U.S. Government's Treatment of Japanese Americans During World War II

 COMPELLING QUESTION

How did the U.S. treat Japanese Americans during WWII?

Talk About It

Discuss with a partner what type of information you would need to know to answer this question. For example, one question might be: What were Japanese internment camps?

Directions: Write down three additional questions that you need to answer to be able to determine what life was like for Japanese Americans in the United States during World War II.

Supporting Question 1:

Supporting Question 2:

Supporting Question 3:

Apply Historical Concepts and Tools

Directions: As you read and work with primary sources, use the graphic organizer to take notes and organize information.

	Organizing Source Information	
Source	**Title and Author/ Creator**	**Notes**
A	Memorandum to the President by Attorney General Francis Biddle	
B	A letter to Norio Higano from Camp Harmony by Kenji Okuda	
C	100th Infantry Battalion, a photograph	
D	"To Undo a Mistake is Always Harder Than Not to Create One Originally" by Eleanor Roosevelt	
E	*Korematsu* v. *United States*, a Supreme Court dissenting opinion	

Analyze Sources

Review and analyze Sources A–E. There are questions that accompany each source to help you examine the source and check for historical understanding.

"Memorandum to the President"

Most people who emigrated from Japan to the United States settled on the West Coast. When war broke out against Japan, many Americans questioned the loyalty of Japanese Americans. The U.S. military had suggested internment, or confinement, and many members of Congress and everyday Americans supported it. Influential newspaper columnists Walter Lippman and Westbrook Pogler also called for the detention of Japanese Americans. President Franklin D. Roosevelt stood poised to intern Japanese American as the fear of Japanese spies grew even stronger. Even so, some members of the executive branch of the U.S. government maintained that this was not the right course of action. In the following excerpt from a memorandum to President Roosevelt, Attorney General Francis Biddle explains why action against Japanese Americans is not necessary.

PRIMARY SOURCE : MEMORANDUM

> 66 For several weeks there have been increasing demands for **evacuation** of all Japanese, **aliens** and citizens alike, from the West Coast states. A great many of the West Coast people distrust the Japanese, various special interests would welcome their removal from good farm land and the elimination of their competition, some of the local California radio and press have demanded evacuation, the West Coast Congressional Delegation are asking the same thing and finally, Walter Lippman and Westbrook Pogler recently have taken up the evacuation cry on the ground that attack on the West Coast and widespread **sabotage** in **imminent**. My last advice from the War Department is that there is no evidence of imminent attack and from the F. B. I. that there is no evidence of planned sabotage. 99
>
> —U.S. Attorney General Francis Biddle, February 7, 1942

evacuation the process of moving a person to another location

alien a person who is not a citizen of the country where they live

sabotage destructive action carried on by a civilian or an enemy that works against a country's war effort

imminent about to happen

1. **Identifying** What is the main idea of this memorandum?

2. **Explaining** For what reasons does Biddle say people want Japanese Americans evacuated?

3. **Analyzing Perspectives** Francis Biddle was the Attorney General and therefore had access to high levels of military intelligence. What does this indicate about the reasons other people had to say that Japanese Americans were ready to sabotage and attack the United States? What does it tell about the validity of the reasons supporting the removal of Japanese Americans?

4. **Speculating** In addition to the reasons stated in the memorandum supporting removal, what other reason might have been causing the unreasonable fear or suspicion that seemed to be coming from West Coast citizens?

A Letter from Camp Harmony

The Japanese Americans living in the United States fell into two groups. The *Issei* consisted of first-generation Japanese Americans, who had immigrated to the country. Children of the *Issei*, known as the *Nisei,* had been born in the United States and were therefore American citizens. *Issei* and *Nisei* alike found their loyalty questioned even though many were willing to risk their lives defending American democracy. Both groups faced difficult times living in internment camps during World War II. Kenji Okuda, a *Nisei* and writer of this letter, was forced to relocate at age 20 from Seattle, Washington, to Camp Harmony in Puyallup, Washington. Doing so required him to postpone his college studies. Later, he would be transferred to a camp in Colorado.

PRIMARY SOURCE : LETTER

66 On this first Memorial Day after our fateful entrance into a frightening, devastating war . . . thousands of young Americans have already perished and other thousands are fighting furiously dying and killing. . . . [T]here is nothing in this camp to remind us of that occasion except a memorial service this evening at 7. No military parade will we see; no **valiant** or half-hearted display of armed might . . . . just a quiet service for those Japanese pioneers who have died striving that we, their children, might inherit something of that Great American ideal, Democracy.

But how **futile** and **hypocritical** this all sounds . . . in concentration camps in a Democracy . . . to be kept here in at the sole **discretion** of the military . . . and yet to be expected to be willing to do our best to [ensure] the defeat of a nation with which so many of us are connected only by facial and racial characteristics. But the strange twists and turns life takes . . . perhaps to remind us that thru this very variety comes the occasions for the tragedy and the brightness of living. 99

—Kenji Okuda, from a letter to Norio Higano, May 30, 1942

valiant heroic

futile useless

hypocritical behavior that goes against what one claims to believe

discretion ability to judge or decide

5. Drawing Conclusions What does the first paragraph indicate about how Japanese Americans were treated in internment camps?

6. Explaining What is ironic about the statements "who have died striving that we, their children, might inherit something of that Great American ideal, Democracy" and "concentration camps in a Democracy"?

7. Making Connections What is the likely reason the writer refers to his location as "concentration camps"?

8. Analyzing Perspectives What makes the writer so angry at his situation?

C

100th Infantry Battalion

The bombing of Pearl Harbor sparked anger in the United States toward Japanese Americans. Many Americans viewed them with suspicion because of their Japanese ancestry. In reality, many Japanese Americans were patriotic. Some had enlisted in the armed forces before the United States declared war on Japan. Others quickly enlisted or readily accepted being drafted after Pearl Harbor. Some joined the military to escape life in an internment camp. In any case, many Japanese Americans served in segregated units, such as the 100th Infantry Battalion and the 442nd Regimental Combat Team. These Japanese American fighters became renowned for their bravery and skill in battle. Other Japanese Americans served as translators and interpreters because of their fluency in both English and Japanese. In all, more than 30,000 Japanese Americans fought to ensure victory for the Allies.

PRIMARY SOURCE : PHOTOGRAPH

Members of the 100th Infantry Battalion stand at attention as Lt. Gen. Mark Clark (left of man in tie) and Commanding General of the Fifth Army James V. Forrestal (in tie) inspect them. Forrestal was the Secretary of the Navy and the 100th was serving as an honor guard for his visit.

9. **Explaining** What might the photograph show about Japanese Americans?

10. **Identifying** What does the way these soldiers are equipped tell you about the U.S. Army's attitude toward these troops?

11. **Comparing and Contrasting** How does this photograph demonstrate a similarity and a difference to the previous source?

12. **Making Connections** What purpose does this image serve? What does it indicate about the members and methods of the U.S. Army?

"To Undo a Mistake Is Always Harder Than Not to Create One Originally"

Some Americans believed that the Japanese Americans who were in internment camps were being treated too well. They criticized the War Relocation Authority, the federal agency overseeing the internment process, for ensuring that the basic needs of Japanese Americans were adequately met. They argued that the money spent to buy supplies for the Japanese Americans could be better spent elsewhere. At the same time, other Americans began to speak out against Japanese internment. In 1943, First Lady Eleanor Roosevelt paid a visit to an Arizona relocation center to witness the conditions there for herself. She then wrote a magazine article that vividly described life in a Japanese internment camp. This excerpt is from the original draft of that article.

PRIMARY SOURCE : ARTICLE

❝ To undo a mistake is always harder than not to create one originally but we seldom have the foresight. Therefore we have no choice but to try to correct our past mistakes and I hope that the recommendations of the staff of the War Relocation Authority, who have come to know individually most of the Japanese Americans in these various camps, will be accepted. Little by little as they are checked, Japanese Americans are being allowed on request to leave the camps and start independent and productive lives again. Whether you are a taxpayer in California or in Maine, it is to your advantage, if you find one or two Japanese American families settled in your neighborhood, to try to regard them as individuals and not to condemn them before they are given a fair chance to prove themselves in the community.

'A Japanese is always a Japanese' is an easily accepted phrase and it has taken hold quite naturally on the West Coast because of fear, but it leads nowhere and solves nothing. A Japanese American may be no more Japanese than a German-American is German, or an Italian-American is Italian, or of any other national background. All of these people, including the Japanese Americans, have men who are fighting today for the preservation of the democratic way of life and the ideas around which our nation was built. ❞

—Eleanor Roosevelt, from "To Undo a Mistake is Always Harder Than Not to Create One Originally," 1943, from *Confinement and Ethnicity: An Overview of World War II Japanese American Relocation Sites* by J. Burton, M. Farrell, F. Lord, and R. Lord. (Seattle, WA: University of Washington Press), 19–24.

13. Analyzing Perspectives What point of view does Eleanor Roosevelt appear to have about the internment of Japanese Americans? Why is holding and expressing this point of view somewhat challenging for her?

14. Drawing Conclusions Why does Eleanor Roosevelt caution against accepting the phrase "A Japanese is always a Japanese"?

15. Making Inferences Why does Roosevelt point out that the connection Japanese Americans have to Japan may not be any different from the connection German Americans have to Germany or Italian Americans have to Italy?

16. Identifying What does Roosevelt remind Americans of at the end of the source? Why is this important?

E

Korematsu v. *United States*, 323 US 214 – Supreme Court, 1944

Most Japanese Americans had little choice but to accept the U.S. government's demand that they relocate to a Japanese internment camp. However, some, such as Fred Korematsu of California, refused to leave their homes. Korematsu was convicted of violating Executive Order 9066, which had authorized the forced removal of Japanese Americans. He sued, alleging that such a demand to move violated his Fifth Amendment rights. In time, the case went to the U.S. Supreme Court. Ultimately, the Supreme Court ruled that the removal of Japanese Americans was justified as a way to safeguard the country. Justice Hugo Black wrote the majority opinion, a statement explaining the thinking behind the Supreme Court's decision on a case. Justice Frank Murphy wrote one of the dissenting opinions, or opposing views. A portion of his dissenting opinion appears below.

PRIMARY SOURCE : DISSENTING OPINION

MR. JUSTICE MURPHY, dissenting.

66 This exclusion of 'all persons of Japanese ancestry, both alien and non-alien,' from the Pacific Coast area on a plea of military necessity in the absence of **martial law** ought not to be approved. Such exclusion goes over 'the very brink of constitutional power' and falls into the ugly abyss of racism.

In dealing with matters relating to the prosecution and progress of a war, we must **accord** great respect and consideration to the judgments of the military authorities who are on the scene and who have full knowledge of the military facts. The scope of their discretion must, as a matter of necessity and common sense, be wide. And their judgments ought not to be overruled lightly by those whose training and duties ill-equip them to deal intelligently with matters so vital to the physical security of the nation.

At the same time, however, it is essential that there be definite limits to military discretion, especially where martial law has not been declared. Individuals must not be left **impoverished** of their constitutional rights on a plea of military necessity that has neither substance nor support. Thus, like other claims conflicting with the asserted constitutional rights of the individual, the military claim must subject itself to the judicial process of having its reasonableness determined and its conflicts with other interests reconciled. 'What are the allowable limits of military discretion, and whether or not they have been overstepped in a particular case, are judicial questions.' [according to] *Sterling* v. *Constantin*, 287 U.S. 378, 401. 99

—U.S. Supreme Court Justice Frank Murphy, *Korematsu* v. *United States*, 1944

martial law the law temporarily applied on an area by the military, usually during an emergency

accord give recognition

impoverished completely without

17. Identifying What is the main argument of Justice Murphy's dissenting opinion?

18. Analyzing Perspectives Why does Justice Murphy believe that the internment of Japanese Americans was not a military necessity?

19. Evaluating The majority opinion in the case upheld that the removal of Japanese Americans was justified as a way to safeguard the country. Justice Murphy contended that racial discrimination in any form was not justifiable in our democratic society. Which perspective most matches what you believe? Provide support for your point of view.

Evaluate Sources and Use Evidence

20. Citing Text Evidence Review the Supporting Questions you developed at the beginning of the topic and the evidence you gathered and recorded in the graphic organizer. Which sources will help you answer the Supporting Questions? Circle or highlight those sources in your graphic organizer. Looking at the subset of sources you have chosen, be prepared to explain why you chose each source.

	Supporting Question	Primary Source and Notes
1		
2		
3		

Challenge

Search the Internet to find firsthand accounts of Japanese Americans required to live in an internment camp. Take notes as you look through the accounts. Identify specific details that help you better understand how the Japanese were treated while living in these camps. Add any information to help answer your Supporting Questions.

21. <u>Directions:</u> Now answer the Supporting Questions that you developed at the beginning of the activity to help guide you in answering the Compelling Question.

Answer for Supporting Question 1:

Answer for Supporting Question 2:

Answer for Supporting Question 3:

Communicate Conclusions

Talk About It

22. <u>Collaborating</u> Work with a partner to further analyze each source. Together, can you find additional details that help you understand how Japanese Americans were treated by other Americans or by the U.S. government? Add those details to the answers to your Supporting Questions. Then share them with another pair of students.

Write About It

23. Informative Writing Write a short "Did You Know?" column for a class blog or newspaper article. In your column, explain how fear and racism were the main reasons for the treatment of Japanese Americans.

24. Answering the Compelling Question What do you think? How did the United States treat Japanese Americans during World War II? Create a political cartoon with both graphics and words that provides a visual answer to this question.

25. Making Connections Throughout U.S. history, some Americans have expressed fears about an influx of foreigners to the country. In the 2000s, people from Latin American countries have headed to the United States in search of job opportunities or to flee persecution. Many have entered the country through legal means but others have done so illegally. In the late 2010s, the U.S. government established a policy of incarcerating individuals identified as being illegal immigrants. Attitudes about this policy of detention vary. Conduct research to learn more about the policy from its use in the late 2010s to the present day. Use a compare-contrast graphic organizer to take notes about two different perspectives on the issue. Then make an informed decision about how illegal immigrants should be treated.

✓ **YOU CHOOSE**

Select one of these Take Informed Action products to apply what you've learned.

A. Write a letter that you might send to a government official, such as a member of the U.S. Congress, in which you outline your position on the issue.

B. Prepare arguments to support your side of the issue that you might present in a debate about the issue with another classmate or an invited guest.

C. Create a podcast about this issue to help others learn more about it, being sure to present the different perspectives on the issue.

Take Informed Action Rubric: Government Policy on Illegal Immigrants

Self-Evaluation As you research and evaluate the U.S. government's policy on illegal immigrants, think about the following criteria. These are the criteria your teacher will use to evaluate your Take Informed Action activity.

Peer Review Use this rubric to grade the research and the final product developed by another classmate or group of classmates.

	Organization	Research	Historical Accuracy	Product
4	The piece is exceptionally well organized and focused and demonstrates a thorough and deep understanding of the issue.	The final product shows evidence of in-depth research into the issue of the detention of illegal immigrants.	The piece is well researched and is factually accurate.	The final product addresses all criteria and provides sufficient, thoughtful information about the issue of detaining illegal immigrants.
3	The piece is well organized and focused and demonstrates an adequate understanding of the issue.	The final product shows evidence of adequate research into the issue of the detention of illegal immigrants.	The piece is well researched but contains some factual errors.	The final product addresses most criteria and provides some information about the issue of detaining illegal immigrants.
2	The piece is organized but is inconsistent in focus and demonstrates an inadequate understanding of the issue.	The final product shows little evidence of research into the issue of the detention of illegal immigrants.	The piece is not well researched and contains some factual errors.	The final product addresses some criteria and provides limited information about the issue of detaining illegal immigrants.
1	The piece lacks organization and focus and does not demonstrate a basic understanding of the issue.	The final product shows no evidence of research into the issue of the detention of illegal immigrants.	There are many factual errors.	The final product fails to address most criteria or to attempt providing any information about the issue of detaining illegal immigrants.
SCORE				

TOPIC 16 • THE COLD WAR, 1945–1976

Space Race and the Cold War

? COMPELLING QUESTION

How did the Space Race affect the United States?

Plan Your Inquiry

In this Inquiry Activity, you will develop Supporting Questions related to the Space Race during the Cold War based on the Compelling Question. Then you will examine primary sources about the Space Race, reactions about the Soviet Union's attempts in space, and U.S. plans to pursue a space program of its own. Finally, you will answer your Supporting Questions, communicate your research conclusions, and take action based on what you've learned.

Background Information

After World War II, the growing rivalry of the United States and the Soviet Union to become the world's dominant superpower would lead to the Cold War. This war was waged without actual combat (thus the term "cold"). Both sides took actions to try to instill fear in the other by increasing their military, stockpiling nuclear weapons, and aiding other countries allied with them. At stake was which was superior. The United States and its allies were determined to prevent the Soviets from spreading communism to other parts of the world.

This rivalry extended into space. Both sides competed to be the first and the best in space exploration, beginning what became known as the Space Race. Americans were horrified when the Soviet Union succeeded in launching the human-made, satellite *Sputnik* into space in 1957. To be competitive, the United States established the National Aeronautics and Space Administration (NASA) in 1958. When Soviet cosmonaut Yuri Gagarin became the first person to orbit Earth in 1961, President John F. Kennedy and Congress decided that the U.S. needed to lead space exploration.

Only 23 days after the Soviet mission, the United States witnessed astronaut Alan Shepard Jr. making the first American spaceflight. Then, in early 1962, Americans applauded when U.S. astronaut John Glenn successfully orbited Earth. By 1969, astronaut Neil Armstrong had taken the first steps on the moon. Clearly, the United States had proved itself competitive with the Soviet Union in claiming what had become known as the last frontier.

During the Space Race, American astronauts made a number of voyages to the moon, planting an American flag on its surface each time. During the Apollo 17 mission of 1972, astronauts used the Lunar Module (left) to land on the moon. The Lunar Roving Vehicle (right) provided ground transportation in their explorations there. The Apollo 17 astronauts are remembered as the last people to take moonwalks.

Develop Supporting Questions About the Space Race During the Cold War

 **COMPELLING QUESTION**

How did the Space Race affect the United States?

Talk About It

Discuss with a partner what type of information you would need to know to answer this question. For example, one question might be: What was the Space Race?

Directions: Write down three additional questions that you need to answer to be able to determine the effect of the Space Race on the United States.

Supporting Question 1:

Supporting Question 2:

Supporting Question 3:

Apply Historical Concepts and Tools

Directions: As you read and work with primary sources, use the graphic organizer to take notes and organize information.

Organizing Source Information		
Source	**Title and Author/ Creator**	**Notes**
A	Reaction to the Soviet Satellite: A Preliminary Evaluation by White House Office of the Staff Research Group	
B	Memorandum for the President by T. Keith Glennan and Thomas S. Gates	
C	Man in Space, Victory for Russia	
D	Space Race, a political cartoon	
E	Address at Rice University on the Nation's Space Effort by John F. Kennedy	

Analyze Sources

Review and analyze Sources A–E. There are questions that accompany each source to help you examine the source and check for historical understanding.

Reaction to the Soviet Satellite: A Preliminary Evaluation by White House Office, Staff Research Group

Knowing that the Soviet satellite *Sputnik* circled Earth terrified many Americans. Many became convinced that the Soviet Union, or the Union of Soviet Socialist Republics (USSR) as it was formally called, were more technologically advanced than the United States. That is exactly what the Soviets wanted them to think. The Staff Research Group prepared summaries of the activities of various government agencies, for President Eisenhower, Vice President Richard Nixon, and Chief of Staff Sherman Adams, among others.

PRIMARY SOURCE : MEMORANDUM

66 [E]ven temporary Soviet possession of a clear lead in missile research and technology underlines Soviet potential capacity to compete successfully in fields in which U.S. leadership has been generally taken for granted. The pattern may have changed, from one in which the USSR was seen as seeking to catch up, to one in which the USSR and the U.S. are viewed as in more or less level competition. This is clearly one of the aims of Soviet propaganda treatment, which can be expected to make a very strong effort to create and deepen the impression that the satellite marks a new era, and to make its launching a sort of Great Divide. . . .

The peculiar nature and dramatic appeal of the *Sputnik*, making its passes over every region of the earth, are likely to give it greatest impact among those least able to understand it. It will generate myth, legend and enduring superstition of a kind peculiarly difficult to **eradicate** or modify, which the USSR can exploit to its advantage, among backward, ignorant, and apolitical audiences particularly difficult to reach. . . .

[T]he U.S. itself set the stage for assuring the impact of the *Sputnik* — first by the fanfare of its own announcement of its satellite plans, second by creating the impression that we considered ourselves to have an **invulnerable** lead in the scientific and technological area, and third by the nature of the reaction within the U.S. All this has served to underscore the importance, implications, and presumed validity of Soviet performance and Soviet claims. ring the responses of other people. 99

—White House Office of the Staff Research Group, Box 36, Special Projects: *Sputnik, Missiles and Related Matters; NAID #12082706, October 16, 1957*

eradicate to remove completely

invulnerable impossible to harm

1. **Analyzing Perspectives** What ideas does this memorandum seek to cast doubt on?

2. **Identifying** What concerns are expressed in the memorandum?

Memorandum for the President

U.S. leaders soon realized that a concentrated effort would be necessary for their country to keep up with and surpass the Soviet Union in regard to space exploration. This memo, sent to President Dwight D. Eisenhower, recommends plans for organizing governmental activities related to space. It also set the stage for NASA becoming the main agency responsible for such activities.

PRIMARY SOURCE : MEMORANDUM

❝ The Secretary of Defense and the Administrator of NASA have agreed upon, and recommend to the President, certain action designed to clarify responsibilities, improve coordination, and enhance the national space effort. The actions recommended below are consistent with the steps taken by the Secretary of Defense to clarify responsibilities and assignments in the field of military space applications within the Department of Defense [DOD].

The Secretary of Defense and the Administrator have agreed upon and recommend to the President the following actions:

A. The assignment to NASA of sole responsibility for the development of new space booster vehicle systems of very high thrust. Both the DOD and NASA will continue with a coordinated program for the development of space vehicles based on the current **ICBM** and **IRBM** missiles and growth versions of those missiles.

B. The transfer from the Department of the Army to NASA of the Development Operations Division of the Army Ballistic Missile Agency, including its personnel and such facilities and equipment which are presently assigned and required for the future use of NASA at the transferred activity, and such other personnel, facilities and equipment for administrative and technical support of the transferred activity as may be agreed upon.

C. The provision by the Army to NASA of such administrative services as may be agreed upon to effect a smooth transition of management and funding responsibility of the transferred activity. . . .

The Secretary of Defense and the Administrator of NASA have reached agreement and recommend approval of the above actions in the firm belief that the national space effort requires a strong civilian agency and program and a strong military space effort by the Department of Defense, and clear lines of responsibility and authority if the U.S. is to employ its best efforts in the exploration of outer space and to assure the defense of the nation. ❞

—T. Keith Glennan and Thomas S. Gates, DDE's Records as President, Official File, Box 770, OF 342 NASA (7), October 21, 1959

ICBM intercontinental ballistic missile

IRBM intermediate-range ballistic missile

3. Identifying What is the purpose of this memorandum?

4. Drawing Conclusion What is the likely reason for using a separate civilian agency for the Space Race?

Man in Space, Victory for Russia

Before 1957, much of world thought of the Soviet Union as lagging behind the United States in technology. However, the successful launch of *Sputnik* on October 4, 1957, changed everything. Suddenly, the Soviet Union had gained status on the world stage. Then, the Soviets' launch of the first man into space on April 12, 1961, helped cement the idea of the USSR as a leader of scientific advancement. The following newspaper article, published several months later in 1961, explains the significance of these Soviet technological accomplishments.

PRIMARY SOURCE : ARTICLE

66 On October 5, 1957, the Soviet news agency Tass made the following announcement:

'The first satellite was successfully launched in the U.S.S.R. on October 4.'

Thus Russia announced her first great victory in the race into space. The propaganda effects, exploited to the full, were great.

Last Wednesday morning, Moscow radio made the following announcement:

'Russia has successfully launched a man into space.'

Thus again the Soviet had outdistanced the United States and again she had won a great propaganda victory.

The new Soviet triumph, no less spectacular for the fact that it had long been predicted, represented an outstanding breakthrough—in the exploration of space, in man's capacity to exist there and in the possibilities of interplanetary travel.

Militarily, the feat demonstrated again the Soviet lead in massive rocket boosters and brought a step nearer the possible **utilization** of space as a launching area for nuclear weapons. 99

—*New York Times*, April 16, 1961 and, October 21, 1959

utilization making effective use of something

Need Extra Help?

It may be helpful to know that *propaganda* means "the spreading of ideas about an institution or individual for the purpose of influencing opinion." During the Cold War, both the Soviet Union and the United States used propaganda to show how well they were progressing in space exploration.

5. __Analyzing__ Why do you think that the article includes the statement, "The propaganda effects, exploited to the full, were great"?

6. __Interpreting__ What is meant by the statement, "Thus again the Soviet had outdistanced the United States and again she had won a great propaganda victory"?

7. __Describing__ How does the article depict the Soviet accomplishments?

Space Race

In the fall of 1960, political candidate John F. Kennedy was well on his way to winning the presidency of the United States, but Dwight D. Eisenhower was still chief executive of the United States. Eisenhower had never really embraced space exploration as a necessary course of action for the country. At the same time, thousands of miles away, the Soviet Union's premier Nikita Khrushchev glowed over his nation's successes in space. The Soviets had no problem acknowledging that space technology could help them gain greater military strength as well as advance scientific knowledge. This political cartoon from the time illustrates how many Americans thought the United States compared to the Soviet Union in terms of space exploration.

PRIMARY SOURCE : POLITICAL CARTOON

The artist pictures a weakling Dwight D. Eisenhower, whose nickname was Ike, with strongman Nikita Khrushchev. The weights on the barbell Khrushchev is lifting are drawn as little Sputniks. The Soviet leader is standing on a platform that features a Soviet symbol, the hammer and sickle.

10. Analyzing Notice the physical characteristics of President Eisenhower and Nikita Khrushchev. What does the cartoonist suggest about the two men? What inference can you make?

11. Drawing Conclusions What might the cartoonist have hoped to achieve with this cartoon?

12. Evaluating What are the limitations of the information in the cartoon about the Space Race?

E

Address at Rice University on the Nation's Space Effort

John F. Kennedy took the oath of office as president of the United States on January 20, 1961. From the start, he proved to be a strong supporter of space exploration. On September 12, 1962, he spoke about the topic at Rice University in Houston, Texas. He explained why the United States needed to be a leader in space exploration.

PRIMARY SOURCE : SPEECH

❝ We meet at a college noted for knowledge, in a city noted for progress, in a State noted for strength, and we stand in need of all three, for we meet in an hour of change and challenge, in a decade of hope and fear, in an age of both knowledge and ignorance. The greater our knowledge increases, the greater our ignorance unfolds. . . .

The exploration of space will go ahead, whether we join in it or not, and it is one of the great adventures of all time, and no nation which expects to be the leader of other nations can expect to stay behind in the race for space. . . .

[T]his generation does not intend to **founder** in the backwash of the coming age of space. We mean to be a part of it—we mean to lead it. For the eyes of the world now look into space, to the moon and to the planets beyond, and we have vowed that we shall not see it governed by a hostile flag of conquest, but by a banner of freedom and peace. We have vowed that we shall not see space filled with weapons of mass destruction, but with instruments of knowledge and understanding.

Yet the vows of this Nation can only be fulfilled if we in this Nation are first, and, therefore, we intend to be first. . . . .

We set sail on this new sea because there is new knowledge to be gained, and new rights to be won, and they must be won and used for the progress of all people. . . . Whether it will become a force for good or ill depends on man, and only if the United States occupies a position of **pre-eminence** can we help decide whether this new ocean will be a sea of peace or a new terrifying theater of war. . . .

We choose to go to the moon. We choose to go to the moon in this decade and do the other things, not because they are easy, but because they are hard, because that goal will serve to organize and measure the best of our energies and skills, because that challenge is one that we are willing to accept, one we are unwilling to postpone, and one which we intend to win . . . .

To be sure, we are behind, and will be behind for some time in manned flight. But we do not intend to stay behind, and in this decade, we shall make up and move ahead. ❞

—John F. Kennedy, September 12, 1962

---

founder sink or drown
pre-eminence uperiority

8. **Analyzing Perspectives** What does President Kennedy believe about space exploration? What evidence does he provide to support his belief in U.S. involvement?

9. **Identifying** What is the president's purpose in delivering this speech? What appeals does he make to secure his audience's support?

Evaluate Sources and Use Evidence

13. **Citing Text Evidence** Review the Supporting Questions you developed at the beginning of the topic and the evidence you gathered and recorded in the graphic organizer. Which sources will help you answer the Supporting Questions? Circle or highlight those sources in your graphic organizer. Looking at the subset of sources you have chosen, be prepared to explain why you chose each source.

	Supporting Question	Primary Source and Notes
1		
2		
3		

Challenge

Search the Internet to find out more about how average Americans were affected by the Space Race. How did it affect their attitudes? their view about the United States and its place in the world? their day-to-day activities? Use what you have learned to add to your answers to your Supporting Questions.

14. Directions: Now answer the Supporting Questions that you developed at the beginning of the activity to help guide you in answering the Compelling Question.

Answer for Supporting Question 1:

Answer for Supporting Question 2:

Answer for Supporting Question 3:

Communicate Conclusions

Talk About It 👥

15. Collaborating Work in a small group. Draw a concept web and write the Compelling Question in the center. Take turns adding source evidence that helps answer the question until everyone has had at least two turns. Explain why each source helps answer the question. Then, as a group, identify the three most helpful pieces of evidence. Write a paragraph explaining how these sources help answer the Compelling Question. Select a spokesperson to share your conclusions with the class.

Write About It

16. Argumentative Writing Not everyone in America agreed on the value of the Space Race. Write an essay that first explains positive effects of the Space Race on the United States and its citizens. Then, provide arguments for how the Space Race had negative effects. Cite evidence from the sources as appropriate.

17. Answering the Compelling Question What do you think? How did the Space Race affect the United States? Make an illustrated poster that shows your thoughts.

18. **Making Connections** Many experts point out that another space race is taking place today. This time, more countries are taking part, as are private companies. Conduct research to find out more about the present-day space race. Why is a new space race taking place? Who are the major players? What are their purposes and goals? What roles do competition and cooperation play? How might the modern space race affect prospects for peace? How is the United States taking part in the twenty-first-century space race? Take notes as you conduct research to help you answer these questions.

✓ **YOU CHOOSE**

Select one of these Take Informed Action products to apply what you've learned.

A. Create an article for the school newspaper that describes important details about the present-day space race. Conclude with an explanation of why knowing this information is important.

B. Write a newspaper editorial that explains what you believe the U.S. domestic and foreign policies should be on the issue of space exploration today.

C. Compose and perform a song that describes the possible risks and benefits of the modern-day space race.

Take Informed Action Rubric: Government Policy on Illegal Immigrants

Self-Evaluation As you research the present-day space race, think about the following criteria. These are the criteria your teacher will use to evaluate your Take Informed Action activity.

Peer Review Use this rubric to grade the research and the final product developed by another classmate or group of classmates.

	Organization	Research	Historical Accuracy	Product
4	The piece is exceptionally well organized and focused and demonstrates a thorough and deep understanding of the subject.	The final product shows evidence of in-depth research into the subject of the present-day space race.	The piece is well researched and is factually accurate.	The final product addresses all criteria and provides sufficient, thoughtful information about the present-day space race.
3	The piece is well organized and focused and demonstrates an adequate understanding of the subject.	The final product shows evidence of adequate research into the subject of the present-day space race.	The piece is well researched but contains some factual errors.	The final product addresses most criteria and provides some information about the present-day space race.
2	The piece is organized but is inconsistent in focus and demonstrates an inadequate understanding of the subject.	The final product shows little evidence of research into the subject of the present-day space race.	The piece is not well researched and contains some factual errors.	The final product addresses some criteria and provides limited information about the present-day space race.
1	The piece lacks organization and focus and does not demonstrate a basic understanding of the subject.	The final product shows no evidence of research into the subject of the present-day space race.	There are many factual errors.	The final product fails to address most criteria or to attempt providing any information about the present-day space race.
SCORE				

TOPIC 17 • CIVIL RIGHTS AND AMERICAN SOCIETY, 1954–1968

Nonviolent Protests of the Civil Rights Movement

 COMPELLING QUESTION

How did nonviolent protest help African Americans gain civil rights?

Plan Your Inquiry

In this Inquiry Activity, you will develop Supporting Questions related to nonviolent protest of the American civil rights movement based on the Compelling Question. Then you will examine primary sources about the history of the civil rights movement, its leaders, its goals, and its protests. Finally, you will answer your Supporting Questions, communicate your research conclusions, and take action based on what you've learned.

Background Information

The U.S. Declaration of Independence proudly proclaims that "All men are created equal." However, African Americans were long denied equality—the basic principle of democracy. Despite the results of the Civil War and attempts at Reconstruction to help formerly enslaved people, African Americans did not have equal rights. They began to more actively seek their civil rights after World War II because they were tired of policies of discrimination and the persistence of segregation. After all, African Americans had fought in the war too. They believed this proved they should be treated the same as other Americans.

The National Association for the Advancement of Colored People (NAACP) led civil rights efforts in the 1950s. One early success was a favorable decision in the Supreme Court case *Brown* v. *Board of Education*. After hearing compelling arguments by NAACP lawyer Thurgood Marshall, the court decided that separating school children by race was unconstitutional. Some school districts began integration in their schools, but many Southerners did not want desegregation.

African American leaders organized nonviolent protests during the 1950s and 1960. Their acts of civil disobedience included bus boycotts, sit-ins, freedom rides, and marches. Slowly, the civil rights movement led to changes in federal and state law and policy. Over time, African Americans have made progress through the recognition of their equal rights under the law, however, the struggle continues for fair and equal treatment in society.

To protest the fact that African Americans were not allowed to be seated at the F.W. Woolworth Co.'s lunch counter in Greensboro, North Carolina, the students staged a sit-in in 1960. Over time, more people joined in and protests began in other places in the South. This six-month protest resulted in the store's decision to integrate its lunch counters.

Develop Supporting Questions About Protests During the Civil Rights Movement

 COMPELLING QUESTION

How did nonviolent protest help African Americans gain civil rights?

Talk About It COLLABORATE

Discuss with a partner what type of information you would need to know to answer this question. For example, one question might be: What is meant by nonviolent protest?

Directions: Write down three additional questions that you need to answer to be able to determine how nonviolent protest helped African Americans gain civil rights.

Supporting Question 1:

Supporting Question 2:

Supporting Question 3:

Apply Historical Concepts and Tools

Directions: As you read and work with primary sources, use the graphic organizer to take notes and organize information.

Organizing Source Information		
Source	**Title and Author/ Creator**	**Notes**
A	Emmett Till's Mother, a photograph and quote by Mamie Till Mobley	
B	John F. Kennedy Speech, "June 11, 1963: Address on Civil Rights"	
C	"Letter from Birmingham Jail" by Dr. Martin Luther King, Jr.	
D	Interview with Malcolm X by Kenneth Clark	
E	March on Washington Speech by John Lewis	

Analyze Sources

Review and analyze Sources A–E. There are questions that accompany each source to help you examine the source and check for historical understanding.

Emmett Till's Mother

Some brave African Americans willingly risked their lives to lead civil rights protests in the 1950s and 1960s. Others became participants in the civil rights movement because of a tragic event in their personal life. For example, the kidnapping and murder of 14-year-old Emmett Till in 1955 placed the teen in the forefront of the civil rights movement. While visiting relatives in a small town in Mississippi, townspeople claimed that the young African American from Chicago whistled at a white female store clerk. Two white men killed him for this alleged act. At trial, a white jury found the men not guilty of any crime. The verdict horrified African Americans and made Till a symbol of the lack of justice for African Americans in the United States. Thousands of mourners attended the slain boy's funeral held in Chicago. Mamie Till Mobley, Emmett's mother, had her life changed forever by this event. She become an outspoken civil rights activist, beginning with a moving speech at a 1955 NAACP rally.

Emmett Till's mother, Mamie Till Mobley, stands next to the open casket of her murdered son at his funeral. Photos of Emmett lined the inside of the casket so the more than 100,000 mourners could see what Emmett looked like before his brutal murder.

66 When people saw what had happened to my son, men stood up who had never stood up before. People became vocal who had never vocalized before. Emmett's death was the opening of the civil rights movement. He was the sacrificial lamb of the movement. 99

—Mamie Till Mobley, at the NAACP rally, September 1955

1. **Analyzing Perspectives** Why do you think Mamie Till Mobley wanted an open casket for Emmett's funeral?

2. **Drawing Conclusions** What feelings might the photo have brought up in people?

3. **Interpreting** What does Mamie Till Mobley mean by her words "He was the sacrificial lamb of the movement"?

B

Address on Civil Rights

Frustrated with continuing segregation in Birmingham, Alabama, local civil rights activist and minister Fred Shuttlesworth asked for help from people beyond his state's borders. In 1963, Dr. Martin Luther King, Jr., and the Southern Christian Leadership Conference (SCLC) came to the minister's aid. They worked closely with local civil rights groups and churches in an organized effort to end segregation in Birmingham. Protests in the city included mass meetings, sit-ins, boycotts, and other nonviolent actions. The protests and the reactions to them caught the nation's attention. The Birmingham protests in part contributed to President John F. Kennedy's belief that the time was right for federal action to help eliminate discrimination against African Americans. He called upon the U.S. Congress to take action on national civil rights legislation. A portion of his speech announcing his challenge to Congress to address civil rights and segregation appears below.

PRIMARY SOURCE : SPEECH

❝ The events in Birmingham and elsewhere have so increased the cries for equality that no city or State or legislative body can **prudently** choose to ignore them. The fires of frustration and discord are burning in every city, North and South, where legal remedies are not at hand. **Redress** is sought in the streets, in demonstrations, parades, and protests which create tensions and threaten violence and threaten lives. We face, therefore, a moral crisis as a country and as a people. It cannot be met by **repressive** police action. It cannot be left to increased demonstrations in the streets. It cannot be quieted by **token** moves or talk. It is a time to act in the Congress, in your State and local legislative body and, above all, in all of our daily lives. . . .

[T]here are . . . necessary measures which only the Congress can provide, and they must be provided at this session. The old code of equity law under which we live commands for every wrong a remedy, but in too many communities, in too many parts of the country, wrongs are inflicted on Negro citizens and there are no remedies at law. Unless the Congress acts, their only remedy is in the street.

I am, therefore, asking the Congress to enact legislation giving all Americans the right to be served in facilities which are open to the public—hotels, restaurants, theaters, retail stores, and similar establishments. **❞**

—John F. Kennedy, "Address on Civil Rights," June 11, 1963

---

prudently wisely

redress relief or a means for solving a problem

repressive controlling, often by force

token minimal, hollow, or largely symbolic

4. Summarizing What does President Kennedy say the events in Birmingham highlight?

5. Analyzing Perspectives Why does President Kennedy think the time is "now" to address the issue?

6. Identifying the Main Idea What is the main idea of the speech?

7. Drawing Conclusion What made President Kennedy's action toward improving civil rights historic?

C

"Letter from Birmingham Jail"

Dr. King and the other protest leaders defied the city government's order to stop the protests in Birmingham. He was arrested and jailed. The next day, the local newspaper published a letter written by eight white members of the clergy in Birmingham. They called for patience and said that local African Americans should negotiate with the city and wait to see what happens. While in jail, Dr. King wrote a thoughtful response to the clergy's letter, a portion of which is excerpted below.

PRIMARY SOURCE : LETTER

❝ Injustice anywhere is a threat to justice everywhere. We are caught in an inescapable network of mutuality, tied in a single garment of destiny. Whatever affects one directly affects all indirectly. Never again can we afford to live with the narrow, provincial "outside agitator" idea. Anyone who lives inside the United States can never be considered an outsider anywhere in this country.

You **deplore** the demonstrations that are presently taking place in Birmingham. But I am sorry that your statement did not express similar concern for the conditions that brought the demonstrations into being. . . . I would not hesitate to say that it is unfortunate that so-called demonstrations are taking place in Birmingham at this time, but I would say in more **emphatic** terms that it is even more unfortunate that the white power structure of this city left the Negro community with no other alternative. . . .

My friends, I must say to you that we have not made a single gain in civil rights without determined legal and nonviolent pressure. History is the long and tragic story of the fact that privileged groups seldom give up their privileges voluntarily. Individuals may see the moral light and voluntarily give up their unjust posture; but . . . groups are more immoral than individuals.

We know through painful experience that freedom is never voluntarily given by the oppressor; it must be demanded by the oppressed. Frankly, I have never yet engaged in a direct action movement that was "well timed," . . . For years now I have heard the word 'Wait!' It rings in the ear of every Negro with piercing familiarity. This 'Wait' has almost always meant "Never." . . . We must come to see . . . that 'justice too long delayed is justice denied.' We have waited for more than three hundred and forty years for our constitutional and God-given rights. . . . I guess it is easy for those who have never felt the stinging darts of segregation to say, 'Wait.' . . . There comes a time when the cup of endurance runs over, and men are no longer willing to be plunged into an abyss of injustice where they experience the bleakness of corroding despair. I hope, Sirs, you can understand our legitimate and unavoidable impatience. ❞

—Dr. Martin Luther King, Jr., "Letter from Birmingham Jail," April 16, 1963

deplore express strong disapproval

emphatic strong emphasis

Copyright © McGraw Hill   TEXT: Martin Luther King, Jr., "Letter from Birmingham Jail, 16 April 1963 . Reprinted by arrangement with The Heirs to the Estate of Martin Luther King Jr., c/o Writers House as agent for the proprietor New York, NY. Copyright 1963 Dr. Martin Luther King Jr; copyright renewed 1991 Coretta Scott King.

8. **Identifying the Main Idea** In the second paragraph, what does Dr. King argue to support his view that the demonstrations are necessary?

9. **Interpreting** Why does Dr. King believe that it is necessary to put pressure on the whites in Birmingham?

D

Malcolm X Interview

Some African Americans became increasingly dissatisfied with the slow progress the civil rights movement appeared to be making. New leaders arose who sought more radical change and desired such change to take place sooner than later. One such leader was Malcolm X, who in dynamic speeches, expressed the flaws of a society dominated by whites and encouraged African Americans to show "Black Pride." Although he was assassinated in 1965, Malcolm X's actions would inspire the Black Power Movement of the late 1960s and 1970s. The following primary source is from an interview with Malcolm X that was done by the well-respected African American scholar and activist Dr. Kenneth Clark in 1963. Here, Malcolm X explains why he believes African Americans should take a radical approach to gaining equal rights, including defending themselves with violence if necessary. A year later Malcolm X changed his views, supporting a less violent direction, yet his desire for equality never wavered. In this interview, Malcolm X refers to the Honorable Elijah Muhammad who led the radical group Nation of Islam, which advocated that African Americans rise up, separate from the United States, and form their own nation.

PRIMARY SOURCE : INTERVIEW

   66 **Malcolm X:** [T]he black people in this country have been the victims of violence at the hands of the white man for four hundred years. And following the ignorant Negro preachers, we have thought that it was godlike to turn the other cheek to the brute that was brutalizing us. And today, the Honorable Elijah Muhammad is showing black people in this country that just as the white man and every other person on this earth has God-given rights, natural rights, civil rights, any kind of rights that you can think of, when it comes to defending himself, black people should have—we should have the right to defend ourselves also. And, because the Honorable Elijah Muhammad makes black people brave enough, men enough, to defend ourselves no matter what the odds are, the white man runs around here with the philo-- with the doctrine that we are—Mr. Muhammad is advocating violence when he's actually telling Negroes to defend themselves against violent people.

Kenneth Clark: I see. Well, Reverend Martin Luther King preaches a doctrine of non-violent insistence upon the rights of the American Negro. What is your attitude toward this philosophy?

Malcolm X: The white man pays Reverend Martin Luther King, subsidizes Reverend Martin Luther King, so that Reverend Martin Luther King can continue to teach the Negroes to be defenseless. That's what you mean by non-violent: be defenseless. Be defenseless in the face of one of the most cruel beasts that has ever taken a people into captivity. That's this American white man. And they have proved it throughout the country by the police dogs and the police clubs. A hundred years ago they used to put on a white sheet and use a bloodhound against Negroes. Today they've taken off the white sheet and put on police uniforms, they've traded in the bloodhounds for police dogs, and they're still doing the same thing. **99**

—Kenneth Clark, Interview with Malcolm X from "Perspectives: Negro and the American Promise," June 24, 1963

10. Analyzing Perspectives For what does Malcolm X advocate in this interview? What does he condemn?

11. Comparing and Contrasting How does Malcolm X view Dr. Martin Luther King, Jr.'s philosophy of nonviolence?

March on Washington Speech by John Lewis

At the March on Washington held on August 28, 1963. Dr. King gave his now famous "I Have a Dream" speech. A young civil rights leader named John Lewis also spoke that day. Lewis's speech criticized the federal government's approach to addressing civil rights. He applauded the proposed Civil Rights Act endorsed by President John F. Kennedy, but wanted to include the prevention of discrimination in public facilities, known as Title III. The next year, the Civil Rights Act of 1964 became law—complete with Title III. In 1986, he successfully ran for a seat in the U.S. House of Representatives. Through winning reelections, he was still in office at the time of his death in 2020.

PRIMARY SOURCE : SPEECH

❝ We come here today with a great sense of misgiving. It is true that we support the administration's Civil Rights Bill. We support it with great reservation, however. Unless title three is put in this bill, there's nothing to protect the young children and old women who must face police dogs and fire hoses in the South while they engage in peaceful demonstration. . . .

As it stands now, the voting section of this bill will not help the thousands of people who want to vote. It will not help the citizens of Mississippi, of Alabama and Georgia who are unqualified to vote for lack of sixth grade education. One man, one vote is the African cry. It is ours too. It must be ours. . . .

My friends let us not forget that we are involved in a serious social revolution. By and large, politicians who build their career on immoral compromise and allow themselves an open forum of political, economic and social exploitation dominate American politics.

There are exceptions, of course. We salute those. But what political leader can stand up and say, 'My party is a party of principles'? . . .Where is the political party that will make it unnecessary to march on Washington? Where is the political party that will make it unnecessary to march in the streets of Birmingham? Where is the political party that will protect the citizens of Albany, Georgia? . . .

To those who have said, 'Be patient and wait,' we must say that we cannot be patient. We do not want our freedom gradually but we want to be free now.

We are tired. We are tired of being beat by policemen. We are tired of seeing our people locked up in jail over and over again, and then you holler 'Be patient.' How long can we be patient? We want our freedom and we want it now. . . .

They're talking about slow down and stop. We will not stop. . . .

By the forces of our demands, our determination and our numbers, we shall send a desegregated South into a thousand pieces, put them together in the image of God and Democracy. We must say wake up America, wake up! For we cannot stop, and we will not and cannot be patient. ❞

—John Lewis, March on Washington speech, August 28, 1963

12. **Identifying** What statement does Lewis make against politicians and political parties? What does he call for?

13. **Drawing Conclusions** What does the tone of Lewis's speech indicate about his feelings?

Challenge

Find the original version of John Lewis's March on Washington speech, which older civil rights leaders asked him to "tone down" for the event. As you analyze this original speech, consider any differences you notice in language and tone. How was his message modified? Make a presentation that summarizes the differences and explains why older civil rights leaders asked for a less-radical version.

Evaluate Sources and Use Evidence

14. <u>Citing Text Evidence</u> Review the Supporting Questions you developed at the beginning of the topic and the evidence you gathered and recorded in the graphic organizer. Which sources will help you answer the Supporting Questions? Circle or highlight those sources in your graphic organizer. Looking at the subset of sources you have chosen, be prepared to explain why you chose each source.

	Supporting Question	Primary Source and Notes
1		
2		
3		

Need Extra Help?

To help you analyze each source, enter key information into a three-column chart with the headings *Source, Likely Audience,* and *Main Message* or *Subject* at the top of the columns. Record details for each source in the rows below.

15. Directions: Now answer the Supporting Questions that you developed at the beginning of the activity to help guide you in answering the Compelling Question.

Answer for Supporting Question 1:

Answer for Supporting Question 2:

Answer for Supporting Question 3:

Communicate Conclusions

Talk About It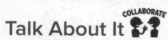

16. Collaborating With a partner, take turns posing one of your Supporting Questions. Listen to the other student's response. Then, share your answer. When you have finished, decide which two Supporting Questions (and their answers) as well as which two to three sources most help you understand the value of nonviolent protest during the civil rights movement. Share your conclusions with the class.

Write About It

17. **Argumentative Writing** How effective has the civil rights movement been in achieving its goals? Write a short letter (one to two paragraphs) to one of the authors from the inquiry in which you answer this question. In your response, cite evidence from that source as well as one other source to support your ideas.

18. **Answering the Compelling Question** What do you think? How did nonviolent protest help African Americans gain civil rights? In response to the question, write jacket copy (the description on the back or inside cover of a book) for a nonfiction book about the civil rights movement.

Need Extra Help?

To help answer the Compelling Question, make a concept map with "civil rights" in the center. Add information from the sources and your prior knowledge about the subject. Be sure to add information about nonviolent protest. Record as much as you know about this type of protest. Then use your concept map to help answer the question.

19. <u>Making Connections</u> Some people today may know little about the civil rights movement of the 1950s and 1960s and the men and women who played a part in it. Imagine that you are a writer for a historical society. Your current assignment is to find ways to inform teenagers about people, places, and events of the civil rights movement and help them understand why the struggle for civil rights is still important today. You have been asked to research people and events of the movement and select one to demonstrate its relevance to youth today.

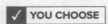 **YOU CHOOSE**

Select one of these Take Informed Action products to apply what you've learned.

A. Write an article for your school newspaper that explains the significance of the person or event you have chosen as representative of the civil rights movement.

B. Write and read aloud a poem that relates the contribution of your chosen person, place, or event to the civil rights movement.

C. Write a newspaper editorial that argues why your selected person or event should be remembered in your community and the actions to be taken to ensure that this happens.

Take Informed Action Rubric: Civil Rights Movement

<u>Self-Evaluation</u> As you research debatable issues related to civil rights, think about the following criteria. These are the criteria your teacher will use to evaluate your Take Informed Action activity.

<u>Peer Review</u> Use this rubric to grade the research and the final product developed by another classmate or group of classmates.

	Organization	Research	Historical Accuracy	Product
4	The piece is exceptionally well organized and focused and demonstrates a thorough and deep understanding of the subject.	The final product shows evidence of in-depth research into the selected civil rights movement person, place, or event.	The piece is well researched and is factually accurate.	The final product addresses all criteria and provides sufficient, thoughtful information about the person, place, or event focused on.
3	The piece is well organized and focused and demonstrates an adequate understanding of the subject.	The final product shows evidence of adequate research into the selected civil rights movement person, place, or event.	The piece is well researched but contains some factual errors.	The final product addresses most criteria and provides some information about the person, place, or event focused on.
2	The piece is organized but is inconsistent in focus and demonstrates an inadequate understanding of the subject.	The final product shows little evidence of research into the selected civil rights movement person, place, or event.	The piece is not well researched and contains some factual errors.	The final product addresses some criteria and provides limited information about the person, place, or event focused on.
1	The piece lacks organization and focus and does not demonstrate a basic understanding of the subject.	The final product shows no evidence of research into the selected civil rights movement person, place, or event.	There are many factual errors.	The final product fails to address most criteria or to attempt providing any information about the person, place, or event focused on.
SCORE				

TOPIC 18 • AMERICA SINCE THE 1970S, 1970–PRESENT DAY

Immigration in the United States

? COMPELLING QUESTION

What are the experiences of immigrants to the United States?

Plan Your Inquiry

In this Inquiry Activity, you will develop Supporting Questions related to immigration in the twenty-first century in the United States based on the Compelling Question. Then you will examine primary sources about United States immigration policies, reasons people immigrate illegally, experiences of undocumented immigrants, and roles of immigrants in society. Finally, you will answer your Supporting Questions, communicate your research conclusions, and take action based on what you've learned.

Background Information

Many who come to here from other countries dream of a better life. As such, immigration to the United States has continued during the 1900s and 2000s. Today, fewer people immigrate from Europe than they did in the past, and many more people come from Latin America or Asia.

Many immigrants come to the United States through legal channels by receiving visas that allow them to enter the country. However, some of these people stay on after their visas have expired. Other people enter the country illegally, slipping in without visas or permission. These people are considered undocumented and therefore illegal immigrants. Today, more than 11 million individuals live in the United States illegally.

During the last decades of the 1900s, many Americans seemed open to the idea of increased immigration and to amnesty, or forgiveness, for those who entered the country illegally. In the 2000s, however, some American citizens and leaders began to look for ways to keep people from illegally entering the United States and to remove, or deport, undocumented immigrants already in the country.

In recent years, presidents have looked for ways to reduce illegal immigration and fix the problem of undocumented immigrants in the country. President Obama increased enforcement efforts at the border and introduced DACA to help children who had been brought into the United States illegally. President Trump emphasized securing the border by building a wall and prosecuting undocumented immigrants. President Biden stopped work on the wall and said he would reduce illegal immigration by giving aid to countries people were trying to flee so that they wouldn't have to migrate to the United States.

These new citizens proudly wave the flag of the country to which they just pledged allegiance at a naturalization ceremony in Los Angeles in 2018.

Develop Supporting Questions About Immigration

 **COMPELLING QUESTION**

What are the experiences of immigrants to the United States?

Talk About It

Discuss with a partner what type of information you would need to know to answer this question. For example, one question might be: Why do people immigrate to the United States?

Directions: Write down three additional questions that you need to answer to be able to identify experiences of immigrants to the United States.

Supporting Question 1:

Supporting Question 2:

Supporting Question 3:

Apply Historical Concepts and Tools

Directions: As you read and work with primary sources, use the graphic organizer to take notes and organize information.

Organizing Source Information		
Source	**Title and Author/ Creator**	**Notes**
A	"DREAM Act: I'm an Illegal Immigrant at Harvard" by Anonymous	
B	Thousands Join "Defend DACA" March in Los Angeles, a photograph	
C	"Actor: I'm a DACA Recipient. Please Don't Deport Me" by Bambadjan Bamba	
D	Immigration and the Food System by Jessica Kurn	
E	"I Might Finally See My Sons Again" by Ashitha Nagesh	

Analyze Sources

Review and analyze Sources A–E. There are questions that accompany each source to help you examine the source and check for historical understanding.

"DREAM Act: I'm an Illegal Immigrant at Harvard"

Some undocumented immigrants are children who entered the United States along with their parents or alone. As these children grow up in the United States, they think of it as home. Since 2001, some members of Congress have introduced legislation to ensure these young people can stay in the U.S. legally. The proposed act is officially called the Development, Relief, and Education for Alien Minors, or the DREAM Act. The young, undocumented immigrants to whom the act would apply are called "DREAMers." In the following article, one DREAMer describes her experiences.

PRIMARY SOURCE : ARTICLE

❝ I was born in South America and lived there until I was 4 but I've lived here since I started kindergarten. . . . School has always been my sanctuary, a place where I could be alone with my books and words, a **respite** from reality, a place where I could be loved and appreciated for my mind and my heart. Opponents of the DREAM Act say citizenship is not a right, it's a privilege. . . .

Immigration law has never been straightforward, and 9/11 made it impossible to do anything about it. I am 21 years old and this is a burden I've had to carry for most of my life. I'm emotionally exhausted from living my life in a perpetual state of **purgatory** and I now know I am expected to also live in a perpetual state of **penance**. We broke the law and deserve to be punished, the argument goes. So why haven't we been punished?

I don't have an answer to that question, but **in lieu of** an answer, I could tell you that perhaps we have been [punished]—daily, privately, painfully. Punishment isn't made legitimate by the presence of an audience. . . .

I can tell you that I spent my first two years at Harvard paralyzed by fear and **self-loathing**. I can tell you about the day my father's driver's license was suspended. . . . Our family's only government-issued identification card was suddenly gone. . . . He buried his face in my hair and sobbed violently—it remains the only time I've seen him cry. . . .

I am terrified because I know I might once again have to live with a decision that is not mine to make. It would hurt to be forced to leave, but it hurts to stay the way I'm staying now. I belong to this place but I also want it to belong to me. ❞

—Anonymous, "Dream Act: I'm an Illegal immigrant at Harvard," *The Daily Beast*, updated July 14, 2017

respite a short period of rest or relief

purgatory suffering

penance showing sorrow

in lieu of instead of

self-loathing a feeling of disgust about oneself

1. **Analyzing Perspectives** What makes school so important to the author? What words from the source demonstrate these feelings?

2. **Drawing Conclusions** Why does the author feel that she and her family have already been punished, although the punishment has not been through legal means?

B

Thousands Join "Defend DACA" March in Los Angeles

Impatient with the slow progress of the DREAM Act, President Barack Obama started Deferred Action for Childhood Arrival, or DACA, in 2018. This program provided a way for about 800,000 young undocumented immigrants to get work permits and avoid being deported. Not long into his presidency, Obama had used an executive order to create DACA. Trump thought this was unconstitutional. He wanted Congress to deal with immigration. After four states said they would sue to shut down DACA, Trump shut it down, but he gave Congress six months to act. They failed to do so. While some Americans cheered the news, many others were dismayed. A number of lawsuits were filed and many protests were held. One such protest is shown below.

PRIMARY SOURCE :PHOTOGRAPH

In attendance at the march pictured here are DREAMers, naturalized citizens, and other American citizens who support the DREAM Act and want DACA to be fully reinstated. The signs they carry, some written in English and others in Spanish, explain some of the reasons the protesters support the DREAM Act and DACA.

3. **Analyzing Perspective** Consider the subjects and perspective of the image. What does the photographer want to show with this image? What significance does the photographer want to convey?

4. **Identifying** To what conditions was this protest responding?

5. **Interpreting** What might this image indicate about immigrants and their knowledge of the principles the United States was founded on?

6. **Evaluating** How useful is this photograph as a source about immigrant response to the DREAMer situation?

C

Actor: I'm a DACA Recipient. Please Don't Deport Me

There is no one way to characterize DREAMers. They are men and women from around the globe, ranging in age from toddlers to individuals in their 20s and 30s. They may follow any religion. They may be fairly uneducated or hold a master's degree. The author of this editorial is an actor who came to the U.S. with his parents from Cote d'Ivoire, in West Africa. He describes how despite his status as an undocumented immigrant, he persevered to become successful.

PRIMARY SOURCE : ARTICLE

❝ In 1992, when I was 10 years old, my family was fleeing political persecution and found refuge in the South Bronx. . . . We came in with a visitor's visa and applied for political asylum. . . .

[A]s I was trying to adjust to my new surroundings, my parents were trying their best to understand this complicated immigration system. Oftentimes, the willingness and struggles of immigrants to obtain or keep legal status is left out of the media's coverage. They fell prey to **unscrupulous** immigration lawyers who ripped them off because resources for black immigrants were limited—especially for **Francophone** Africans and Africans who only speak African languages.

It wasn't until my senior year in high school that I found out what having my asylum case 'pending' meant for me: I was undocumented. I didn't qualify to receive any financial aid or college scholarships, even if I was granted them.

It felt like my dream to become an actor was over. . . .

So I picked myself up and worked my way through drama school without financial aid, avoiding auditions for any role that would require me to work internationally because I knew I couldn't travel. If I left, there were no guarantees I'd be let back in.

While I was trying to maneuver through life without legal status, I was also dealing with the realities of being black in America. To be black without papers meant that I was walking on an additional layer of eggshells—never wanting to appear too aggressive or suspicious.

In my case and the case of many black immigrants, it could have also led to criminalization and deportation proceedings. . . .

DACA was a lifeline. . . . I applied, was accepted and worked my way up in Hollywood. I am here legally until my DACA status expires. My life has not been defined by my immigration status, but, like so many, it is something that now looms large with the current political fight in Congress over immigration laws. ❞

—Bambadjan Bamba, CNN, January 23, 2018

unscrupulous not honest or fair

Francophone a person who speaks French as a first language

7. **Identifying the Main Idea** What message does this source convey?

8. **Interpreting** What does the author mean when he writes he was "walking on an additional layer of eggshells"?

D

Immigration and the Food System

The following article describes the crucial role that legal and undocumented immigrants have in bringing food from the farm field to the table of all Americans. It also describes the challenges farmers face in hiring undocumented workers.

PRIMARY SOURCE : ARTICLE

66 [A] waiter carries a salad bowl through a restaurant. This is not just a bowl of greens—these spinach leaves and romaine hearts represent a vast network of labor: from farmers planting the seeds and farmworkers harvesting the greens, to drivers trucking them across state lines, and kitchen staff washing them, and many layers in between.

Immigrants are deeply involved in this complex journey from seed to plate. They are an essential link in the chain of our food system, and are an **indelible** part of rural America, contributing to the economic and cultural fabric of these communities. It's hard to picture our food system without them.

Farmer Randy Mooney, Chairman of the Board of the Dairy Farmers of America, knows this all too well. After losing his main farmhand due to illness, Randy tried tirelessly to recruit workers for his farm. Randy . . . went through the usual channels: local universities (three of them), newspaper postings, and word of mouth, all of which resulted in only one response (that didn't work out). But, just down the road, his neighbor had consistent, reliable help from immigrant farmworkers.

This phenomenon is not unique. . . . Farm help is needed from coast to coast, border to border, and among all agricultural sectors. Estimates of farmworkers in this country vary greatly. On the one hand, Farmworker Justice, estimates that 70–80% of farmworkers are immigrants (between half and three-quarters of whom are undocumented). The USDA however, has a slightly lower number, citing that about 60% of all agriculture workers are foreign born. These **discrepancies** speak to the **veiled** nature of the work, number of undocumented workers, and power **inequities embedded** in the industry. Crop production employs the most immigrants, as 85% of fruits and vegetables are harvested by hand.

Randy explains that the main legal route for most farmers to employ foreign labor is through the H-2A visa program. . . . [T]hese visas allow farmers to hire non-citizens for seasonal, temporary work. The nature of dairy farming, with its year-round schedule, means farmers like Randy are out of luck when it comes to employing legal immigrant labor. 99

—Jessica Kurn, August 24, 2018

Copyright © McGraw Hill TEXT: Kurn, Jessica. "Immigration and the Food System." Farm Aid. August 24, 2018. https://www.farmaid.org/blog/fact-sheet/immigration-and-the-food-system/

indelible lasting

discrepancy a difference between things that should be the same

veiled not openly or directly expressed; disguised

inequity injustice or unfairness

embedded part of; within

9. Summarizing What is the main problem described in the source?

10. Identifying Why is the legal route to find workers impractical?

11. Analyzing Perspectives Why does the author say immigrants are "an essential link in our food system"?

"I Might Finally See My Sons Again"

Not long after taking the oath of office as president of the United States, Donald Trump set about fulfilling campaign promises to restrict immigration as a way he believed he might protect the country from terrorism. He issued several executive orders limiting travel to the United States from countries experiencing high levels of terrorism and civil unrest, including the nations of Iran, Iraq, Syria, Somalia, Sudan, and Yemen. For the same reason, he banned refugees fleeing Syria's civil war from entering the United States. Civil rights groups called the orders discriminatory against Muslims and succeeded in blocking them. However, the U.S. Supreme Court narrowly upheld the legality of a later court order that expanded the ban to include the non-Muslim majority countries of North Korea and Venezuela. Additional countries would face travel restrictions in 2020. One of President Joe Biden's first acts as incoming president in January 2021 was to overturn the travel restriction executive orders by Trump. The following article describes the personal ordeal of one Somali immigrant separated from his family because of a travel ban in effect during the time of the Trump presidency.

PRIMARY SOURCE : ARTICLE

❝ 'My child turned five yesterday. We have been apart his whole life. . . .' When he first moved to Ohio in 2015, Afkab Hussein planned for his pregnant wife to join him the following year. But while his wife and children now live in Kenya, they are Somali citizens—and Somalia was one of the countries on the first **iteration** of the travel ban. Since he moved, he has only been able to pay a couple of very short visits to his family—and missed the births of his two young children. . . . He has missed all of the major milestones in his sons' lives so far: 'Yesterday was my first son's fifth birthday—and I wasn't there.' ❞

—Ashitha Nagesh, BBC News, December 2, 2020

iteration a version of something

12. Identifying The author is writing about Afkab Hussein's experiences. What did Hussein hope would happen when he moved to Ohio? What prevented this from happening?

13. Drawing Conclusions Why might Hussein's story be considered especially sad?

14. Analyzing How does this source help you understand the hardships faced by many immigrants?

15. Evaluating What are the limitations of the information in the source related to the reason for Hussein's situation?

Evaluate Sources and Use Evidence

16. **Citing Text Evidence** Review the Supporting Questions you developed at the beginning of the topic and the evidence you gathered and recorded in the graphic organizer. Which sources will help you answer the Supporting Questions? Circle or highlight those sources in your graphic organizer. Looking at the subset of sources you have chosen, be prepared to explain why you chose each source.

	Supporting Question	Primary Source and Notes
1		
2		
3		

Need Extra Help?

To help you analyze each source, enter key information into a three-column chart with the headings *Source, Likely Audience,* and *Main Message* or *Subject* at the top of the columns. Record details for each source in the rows below.

17. Directions: Now answer the Supporting Questions that you developed at the beginning of the activity to help guide you in answering the Compelling Question.

Answer for Supporting Question 1:

Answer for Supporting Question 2:

Answer for Supporting Question 3:

Communicate Conclusions

Talk About It

18. Collaborating Individually, rank the sources in the order of their usefulness in answering each of your Supporting Questions. Then in a group, share your Supporting Questions, answers, and rankings. Discuss the following questions:

- What bias does each source present, and how does it affect your understanding?
- What limitations does each source have in terms of the information provided?
- Why did you rank the sources in the way you did?

Write About It

19. Informative Writing How can you find out more about the experiences of undocumented immigrants? What do you think should be the solution for DREAMers? Write an essay to provide your response.

20. Answering the Compelling Question What do you think? What are the experiences of immigrants to the United States? Imagine that you are interviewing two of the authors of the sources in the lesson. Write two different questions to ask each person. Then provide possible answers to each question. Base your answers on the information contained in the sources.

Challenge

With a partner, research two primary or secondary sources to learn about other ways people are affected by immigration policies. Write a summary of the two sources in which you explain how those sources helped you expand your response to the Compelling Question and explain what evidence each source uses to support its claim.

18. **Making Connections** In recent years, Americans have debated many issues related to immigration and particularly to illegal immigration. These include the following: whether a border wall should be built along the U.S.-Mexico border, the creation of sanctuary cities, the use of detention camps, the treatment of immigrants in those camps, separation of families, the need for a DREAM Act as law, the usefulness of DACA, whether immigration should be based on skill-level of applicants, whether refugees should be granted asylum, and whether the United States should provide financial assistance to Central American countries. Select one of these issues or another related to immigration to research further. Using a graphic organizer, take notes that describe the various sides of the issue.

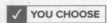 **YOU CHOOSE**

Select one of these Take Informed Action products to apply what you've learned.

A. Create a podcast about the issue that describes it and objectively presents the various views people hold about the issue.

B. Create a story, song, or poem that describes how someone may feel in that situation.

C. Create a multi-media presentation that explains the issue and possible solutions.

Take Informed Action Rubric: Government Policy on Illegal Immigrants

Self-Evaluation As you research debatable issues related to immigration, think about the following criteria. These are the criteria your teacher will use to evaluate your Take Informed Action activity.

Peer Review Use this rubric to grade the research and the final product developed by another classmate or group of classmates.

	Organization	Research	Historical Accuracy	Product
4	The piece is exceptionally well organized and focused and demonstrates a thorough and deep understanding of the subject.	The final product shows evidence of in-depth research into the selected immigration issue.	The piece is well researched and is factually accurate.	The final product addresses all criteria and provides sufficient, thoughtful information about the immigration issue it is focused on.
3	The piece is well organized and focused and demonstrates an adequate understanding of the subject.	The final product shows evidence of adequate research into the selected immigration issue.	The piece is well researched but contains some factual errors.	The final product addresses most criteria and provides some information about the immigration issue it is focused on.
2	The piece is organized but is inconsistent in focus and demonstrates an inadequate understanding of the subject.	The final product shows little evidence of research into the selected immigration issue.	The piece is not well researched and contains some factual errors.	The final product addresses some criteria and provides limited information about the immigration issue it is focused on.
1	The piece lacks organization and focus and does not demonstrate a basic understanding of the subject.	The final product shows no evidence of research into the selected immigration issue.	There are many factual errors.	The final product fails to address most criteria or to attempt providing any information about the immigration issue it is focused on.
SCORE				

Instructions for Inquiry Journal Study Guide

1. Carefully remove the Inquiry Journal Foldables Study Guide pages.

2. Cut the pages in half along the dark middle line marked with a scissors icon.

3. Cut away all grey sections from the ten half-sheets. Note, extended anchor tabs will remain on the left side of each page. Fold along the dashed lines to form the anchor tabs.

4. Stack the anchor tabs of sections 1, 2, 3, 4, and 5 on top of each other. Align the left anchor tabs so the numbers 1-5 are seen along the TOP edge. Staple or glue them together.

5. Stack the anchor tabs of sections 6, 7, 8, 9, and 10 on top of each other. Align the left anchor tabs of each so the numbers 6-10 are seen along the BOTTOM edge. Staple or glue the anchor tabs together.

6. Place the thick anchor tab of the 1-5 section on top of the anchor tab of the 6-10 section. Staple or glue the two thick sections together. Make sure the numbers 1-10 are visible around the top and bottom edges of the booklet.

7. Glue or staple the cover anchor tab on top of the other anchor tabs to finish the booklet. The Table of Contents will be visible on the front.

Anchor Tab

 by Dinah Zike

Types of Primary and Secondary Sources

1A	Advertisement	**1B**	Poster, Handbill
2A	Artifact	**2B**	Fine Arts, Sculpture
3A	Song, Poem	**3B**	Folktale, Fable
4A	Book, Novel, Biography	**4B**	Autobiography, Memoir
5A	Graph, Table, or Chart	**5B**	Survey, Questionnaire
6A	Diary, Journal	**6B**	Letter
7A	Map	**7B**	Government Document, Law
8A	News Article	**8B**	Editorial
9A	Architecture	**9B**	Photograph
10A	Political Cartoon	**10B**	Speech, Sermon

1

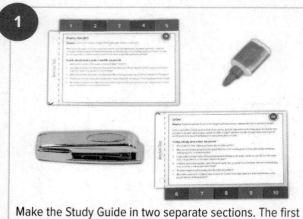

Make the Study Guide in two separate sections. The first section will have five tabs across the top, and the second will have five tabs along the bottom.

2

When the anchor tabs are placed on top of each other all ten numbers will be visible. Glue or staple them together to form one booklet.

3

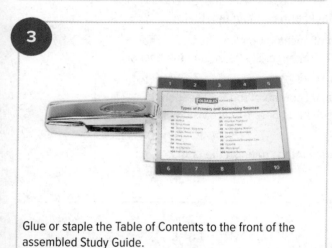

Glue or staple the Table of Contents to the front of the assembled Study Guide.

4

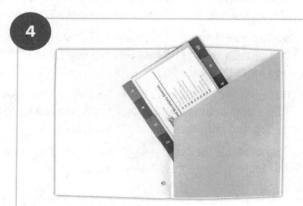

Cut an envelope to form a pocket and glue it on the inside back cover of the Inquiry Journal. Allow the glue to dry. Store the Study Guide in this pocket and remove it as needed to study the Primary and Secondary Sources in your Inquiry Journal.

Advertisement

1A

Purpose: To analyze visual techniques that are used to promote a certain action or way of thinking

Advertisements usually have two main purposes: to inform and to persuade. Usually before people buy a product or use a service, they need to be persuaded that it is something they should do. Carefully observe the advertisement. What is your first impression: is it a manipulative tool, a creative tool, or both?

To think critically about an advertisement, ask yourself:

1. What is the purpose of the advertisement? Who do you think created it? What group of people are they trying to influence?

2. What techniques were used to attract attention to the product? Who was the target audience for whom it was designed? For example, would the graphics appeal more to a young audience or an older audience?

3. Is any evidence given to support the information that is being presented? Do you think claims or details have been exaggerated?

4. Is there any other information or points of view that have been ignored? If so, why?

5. How do you think consumers would respond to the advertisement today?

6. What other primary or secondary sources could be used to understand the advertisement as it relates to the cultural, economic, and business environment of the time?

Poster, Handbill

1B

Purpose: To learn how images and text influenced people to think a certain way

Posters are often used to inform, remember, motivate, promote awareness, or present political or corporate messages. Posters or handbills have been used for hundreds of years to encourage people to support a cause, join an organization, attend an event, travel to a location, or promote a political candidate.

To think critically about a poster or handbill, ask yourself:

1. What is the purpose of the poster or handbill? Who created it?
2. How does it spread information or raise awareness about something? Does the poster create an emotional response? Does it ask people to do something?
3. Where do you think the poster was displayed? What techniques were used to attract attention to the poster?
4. How do you think the poster was received when it was produced? How do you think it would be received today?
5. What other primary or secondary sources could be used to understand the poster as it relates to the cultural, social, and political environment of the time?

Fine Arts, Sculpture

2B

Purpose: To learn about the culture and values of people as reflected in the objects they created

Closely observe the art object. Describe it in a way to someone who hasn't seen it. Is it two- or three-dimensional? Is it made from paint, stone, wood, clay, bone, metal, or leather? What can you infer about its size, shape, color, texture, and weight? Describe the level of craftsmanship, skill, and talent of the artist or artisans who created it.

To think critically about an art object, ask yourself:

1. Why was the art object created? Was it created for artistic, religious, or economic purposes?
2. Is the artist known to us today? Do you think the artist was popular during his or her lifetime?
3. What does the art object reveal about the historical time period and society that created it?
4. Why is this art object important today?
5. What other primary or secondary sources could be used to learn more about this or similar art?

Artifact

Purpose: To learn about physical objects that were created and used by humans in their daily lives

Artifacts include tools, eating utensils, clothing, jewelry, oil lamps, and pottery, as well as objects from religious ceremonies, hunting or military activities, and economic transactions (coins and objects of trade). Analyze and describe the artifact's age, size, shape, color, texture, weight, or design. What might its appearance indicate about who made it and how it was used?

To think critically about an artifact, ask yourself:

1. What materials were used in its construction—clay, wood, metal, stone, leather, shells, beads, gems? Was it made by hand or by a machine?

2. What is the purpose of the artifact?

3. Can this artifact be compared to something from a different culture, geographic location, or time period? What similarities and/or differences exist between the two artifacts?

4. Why is the artifact important today? What does it reveal to us?

5. What other primary or secondary sources could be used to learn more about this and similar artifacts?

Song, Poem

Purpose: To learn how music and words reflect people's thoughts and experiences

What is the title of the poem or song? Read the song or poem silently. Read the work aloud. What is the work about? Listen to someone else read it or sing it. What words or phrases do you think are the most important? Does it refer to events or feelings that you have learned about or experienced? Use reference materials to familiarize yourself with unknown terms or concepts.

To think critically about a song or poem, ask yourself:

1. Why was the song or poem written? What is the theme of the song or poem?

2. Analyze the theme of the song or poem. Is the theme easy to understand, or are figurative forms of speech used to communicate it?

3. Who was the intended audience? What did the artist want the audience to experience?

4. What does the song or poem reveal about the time in which it was written? Does it give insight into what life was like during this time in history?

5. What other primary or secondary sources could be used to understand the cultural, social, and political environment of the time period that the song or poem was popular?

3B

Folktale, Fable

Purpose: To learn about the values and character traits important to people

Folktales and fables are stories that have been preserved and passed on to generations. The characters typically make decisions that are not thought through, and something negative happens as a result. Folktales have humans as the main characters and often indicate that making a better decision would have resulted in a better outcome. Fables usually have animals with human characteristics as the main characters, and they often teach a moral lesson.

To think critically about a folktale or fable, ask yourself:

1. What conflict does the main character encounter? What decision does the character make and why? What actions does the character take to address the conflict?

2. What are the consequences of the character's decision and/or actions?

3. What happens when the character does not act in a manner that meets the expectations of the community?

4. Does the story give insight into values of the time in which it was written? List specific examples.

5. What other primary or secondary sources could be used to understand the cultural, social, and political environment of the time the folktale or fable was written?

4B

Autobiography, Memoir

Purpose: To learn about an event or period of time through the writings of someone who experienced it

An autobiography and a memoir are similar in that they both are written by a person who is sharing public and private information about his or her life. An autobiography usually describes a person's entire life, while a memoir focuses on a limited period of time or a few related experiences.

To think critically about an autobiography or memoir, ask yourself:

1. What was the author's purpose in writing the autobiography or memoir— to inform, persuade, or entertain? Is it written as a historical narrative or an emotional account of an event or time period?

2. From what you know about the time period and the author, does the autobiography or memoir seem realistic? Do you suspect that events have been exaggerated to make them more interesting?

3. Are there instances when the author shares something private that would be difficult to reveal to the public?

4. Compare and contrast your life with the life of the author. What does the comparison reveal about the culture, technology, and events of the two periods of time?

5. What other sources could be used to understand the author, the time in which her or she lived, and the accuracy of his or her account?

Anchor Tab

Book, Novel, Biography

Purpose: To analyze how people write an account about a person, event, or series of events

Some written works, such as textbooks, are secondary sources that are based on research from primary and secondary sources. The authors did not personally experience what they are writing about, but they have analyzed data, examined documents, and interviewed experts. They then summarize the information in one written work. Novels are works of fiction that might include historical details to tell a story. Biographies are accounts of someone's life written by someone else.

To think critically about a book, novel, or biography, ask yourself:

1. Why was the book written? Describe the book. Is it a reference book, historical novel, or biography? What does it reveal about the time period?

2. Is the author also known for something other than writing this book?

3. Is there a forward or preface to the book? Is there back matter such as an appendix, bibliography, or index? What do these tell you about the book?

4. Was the book popular when it was written? If so, why? Why is the book important today?

Graph, Table, or Chart

Purpose: To analyze data using a visual format

Data is a collection of facts or statistics that can be analyzed to make conclusions, predictions, and decisions. Historically, data has been collected by the military, government, corporations, and special interest groups. Knowing what data was available during a historical time period helps us understand why certain decisions were made and why certain actions were taken. Data is often presented in visual formats, including graphs, tables, or charts, so that it is easy to understand.

To think critically about data, ask yourself:

1. Who collected and reported the data? When was the data collected?

2. Observe the tools—graphs, tables, or charts—used to report the data. If it is a graph, what type of graph—line graph, bar graph, circle graph, picture graph? How does the tool help you understand the data?

3. Is the source of the data reliable? Does the source have any biases?

4. Who was the primary audience who used the data? What other audiences might be interested in the data?

5. How was the data used? Was it used to show positives and negatives of something, to report trends, or to document progression or decline?

6. What other sources could be used to understand why the data was collected and reported at this point in history?

Survey, Questionnaire

Purpose: To understand how people gather information

In order to learn about people's beliefs, thoughts, or preferences, researchers often have people answer a list of questions on a questionnaire. Then, once the questionnaire is completed, the answers are collected, analyzed, and interpreted. This entire process is known as a survey. Questionnaires and surveys are used by governments, companies, and special interest groups. For example, one type of survey is the U.S. Census, which counts the number of people living in the United States; once citizens complete the Census questionnaires, the data is analyzed to make sure that each state is properly represented in Congress.

To think critically about a survey or questionnaire, ask yourself:

1. What was the purpose of the survey or questionnaire?

2. Who was the target population that took the survey? What larger population did they represent?

3. Who do you think collected and reported the data?

4. What was learned from the information gathered? How was the data used to make conclusions about it?

5. How were the results reported? Do you think the data was reported in a neutral manner or with biases?

6. What other sources could be used to understand why the data was collected and how it might have been used?

Letter

6B

Purpose: To gain insight into the personal thoughts and experiences communicated by one person to another

Letters are written from the point of view of one person, but they also tend to reflect the culture of a specific time period. For example, when someone wrote the letter, it might have been socially improper to mention a specific health problem or impolite to bluntly state one's views about an issue.

To think critically about a letter, ask yourself:

1. Who wrote the letter? Where and when was the letter written?

2. What was the primary purpose of the writer? Was he or she sharing personal news, describing something, making inquiries, or something else?

3. Is it possible to know if other letters had been written between the writer and the recipient? Does the writer refer to topics that he or she wrote about in the past?

4. Is historic information available about the writer and/or the recipient? Does the letter indicate a sense of duty, trust, curiosity, or intimacy between them?

5. What was happening historically when the letter was written?

6. What other primary or secondary sources could be used to learn more about this letter and the lives of the people who wrote to each other?

Diary, Journal

Purpose: To provide insight into the daily life during a specific time period based on one person's remembrances

Diary or journal entries might include a person's feelings, worries, hopes, concerns, activities, or opinions. The author of the diary is its primary audience. Diaries or journals might be private or shared with family or friends. Some famous diaries have been published as books or made into movies.

To think critically about a dairy or journal, ask yourself:

1. Who wrote it? Where and when was it written?

2. Is historic information available about the writer of the diary or journal?

3. What are the author's thoughts and feelings about the time period in which he or she is living?

4. Why do you think the author kept a diary or journal? What information was the author revealing or concealing?

5. What physical and emotional benefits might be associated with keeping a diary or journal? How are diaries and journals similar to or different from today's blogs?

6. What other primary or secondary sources could be used to learn more about the world at the time the diary or journal was written?

Map

Purpose: To analyze visual information about a geographic location or historical event

Throughout history, maps have been created by geographers, explorers, military forces, governments, businesses, and universities. To understand a map's purpose, you must know what the map is showing. You might also think about why the map was important for the people who used it.

To think critically about a map, ask yourself:

1. Who made the map? When and why was it made? What was happening in history at this time?

2. What type of map is it—physical, political, climatic, thematic, economic, military, or a road map?

3. What is represented on the map? Use the title, map key, labels, and personal observations to determine the subject, time period, and purpose of the map. If there are symbols on the map, what do they mean?

4. Where do you think the map maker acquired the map's information—reports, research, personal experience, interviews with others, military or naval excursions, or other maps?

5. What other primary or secondary sources could be used to understand why the map was made and how it was used?

Government Document, Law

Purpose: To learn how official records represent a society's beliefs and values

Government documents and laws are official documented records of a society during a specific period of time. Often, they reflect issues that people are concerned about and how they try to resolve challenges. Government documents and laws include: court transcriptions, press releases, financial reports, court records, informational papers, committee recommendations, executive orders, Congressional testimonies, text of a bill or a law, and reports of statistical data.

To think critically about a government document or law, ask yourself:

1. Was the document or law generated by local, state, or federal government? When and why was it made?

2. Who created or sponsored the document—an elected official, an appointed official, a committee, or a state or federal agency?

3. Observe and describe the document. Is it handwritten or typed? Is it a paper copy or is it digital? Are there any seals, stamps, or dates visible?

4. What was happening in history when this document was written? What information can be learned from these primary sources?

5. What other primary or secondary sources could be used to understand the government document or law and their purpose?

Editorial

Purpose: To provide an opinion about events or political issues and to inform/persuade the public

Editorials are often written by one person and published in a news source or magazine. They reflect the point of view of the writer. Editorials often include facts to support opinions. In order to persuade the reader to support a certain way of thinking, editorial writers use language that is often emotionally charged. Some examples of this type of language include words such as *scandalous, vicious, heartwarming, unrealistic, revolutionary, controversial,* and *sensational*.

To think critically about an editorial, ask yourself:

1. What is the editorial about?

2. Can you determine the author's background? What is his or her point of view?

3. What emotionally charged words and phrases does the author use? How does this language help reveal his or her point of view?

4. Does the author present factual information? How are facts used to sway the reader's opinion?

5. What other primary or secondary sources could be used to learn more about the world at the time the editorial was written?

News Article

Purpose: To inform a large audience about a person, an event, or issue

News or magazine articles summarize information about local, national, or global events. Many news articles also interpret events. This type of analysis, however, can reflect a reporter's biases. Look for biases as you read or listen to news stories. When you read a newspaper or magazine article, think about its information. News articles that reveal how they acquired the information are more reliable than those that do not. If you know where the source information is from, you can evaluate whether it is trustworthy. In addition, news articles might contain facts that can be checked for accuracy.

To think critically about a news article, ask yourself:

1. What is the topic of the article? When was it written? Who was the intended audience?

2. Does the article mention sources or use quotations? Are any of the following cited: experts, specialists, organizations, government reports, university studies, or research centers?

3. Does the writer exhibit any bias or use language intended to persuade the reader to think a certain way?

4. What point is the news article trying to make? Is the report thorough? What other questions would you ask?

5. What other primary or secondary sources could be used to learn more about the world at the time the news article was written?

Architecture

Purpose: To learn about the cultures that created permanent structures

Architecture is the result of the historic change from living a nomadic life based on hunting and gathering to a settled life supported by agriculture. Originally, people clustered in areas and built structures for shelter and protection. These structures served a functional purpose. Over time, as people settled into communities and their basic needs were met, architecture became more artistic and appealing. In addition, architecture began to reflect the culture in which it was created.

To think critically about architecture, ask yourself:

1. Does the structure still exist? What is/was its purpose? Where is the site located? What is the climate of the area?

2. What does the structure's design tell us about the materials and technology that were available when it was built? Note any unique details on the structure and think about why they were designed.

3. Is the architect known? Did he or she build the structure to be functional or visually appealing or both?

4. If the structure still exists, how and why has it survived? Determine if the structure is a historic example of a particular style or period.

5. What other primary or secondary sources could be used to place the architecture within historic context?

Photograph

Purpose: To capture a specific moment in time with a visual image

Photography emerged in the early 1800s C.E. Photographs record events, people, places, and objects. They often capture details of an event in a dramatic way better than an oral account of the same event.

To think critically about a photograph, ask yourself:

1. Who is the photographer? Where and when was the photograph taken?
2. What is the subject of the photograph?
3. Is there any information written or stamped on the photograph?
4. Is the subject posing in the photograph or is it an action shot? What do you think happened before and after the photo was taken? Why?
5. Does the photograph indicate the photographer's point of view about something?
6. Is there any indication the content of the photograph has been manipulated or the photo edited?
7. What other primary or secondary sources could be used to place the photograph into context?

Speech, Sermon

Purpose: To learn more about the thoughts and opinions communicated orally by a speaker to an audience

Speeches are often given by public officials, whereas sermons are spoken by religious leaders. As you read speeches and sermons, determine what the topic of the speech or sermon is and who is intended to hear it. Is the goal of the speaker to educate, motivate, persuade, or entertain? Think about how the speaker uses language or inflection to make the audience listen to him or her.

To think critically about a speech or sermon, ask yourself:

1. Where and when was the speech or sermon given? Is it possible to know if there were other speakers before or after this speech? If so, did they have the same purpose and objective?
2. What was the objective of the speech or sermon? Did the speaker focus on the objective?
3. Do you know how many people were in attendance to hear the speech? How do you think people responded to it? How do you think the speaker sounded to the audience: knowledgeable, opinionated, dull, inspirational, folksy, unifying, divisive?
4. Do you think the speaker was also trying to communicate with people other than the live audience? Why is the speech important today?
5. What other primary or secondary sources might be used to learn more about the time in which the speech or sermon was given?

Political Cartoon

Purpose: To illustrate a point of view about a current event while informing, persuading, and possibly amusing the viewer

Political cartoons are found in printed newspapers, magazines, and online. They are drawings that reflect the viewpoints of an artist and are meant to persuade or poke fun at an event or person. The artist, or cartoonist, often exaggerates a person's physical features or appearance in a special effect called *caricature*. Cartoonists also use symbols to represent people or topics. For example, the bald eagle and Uncle Sam are symbols of the United States and often appear in political cartoons because they are easily recognized by the viewer. Sometimes cartoonists help readers interpret the message of their illustration by including labels.

To interpret a political cartoon:

1. Quickly examine the cartoon. What is happening? Read the caption and any other words printed in the cartoon.

2. Do you recognize the people, places, or things with exaggerated characteristics? Why do you think the cartoonist drew them this way?

3. What symbols do you see? What larger concepts or ideals do the symbols represent?

4. What statement is the cartoon making, and how has the cartoonist communicated his or her point of view in the cartoon?

5. What other primary or secondary sources could be used to understand the political cartoon?

Name: _____

Class: _____

Cut out speech bubbles one at a time as needed. Fold the anchor tab back and forth along the dotted line and glue the anchor tab on any page where you would like to ask a question, make a comment, or state an opinion. Notes or research can be recorded on the back.

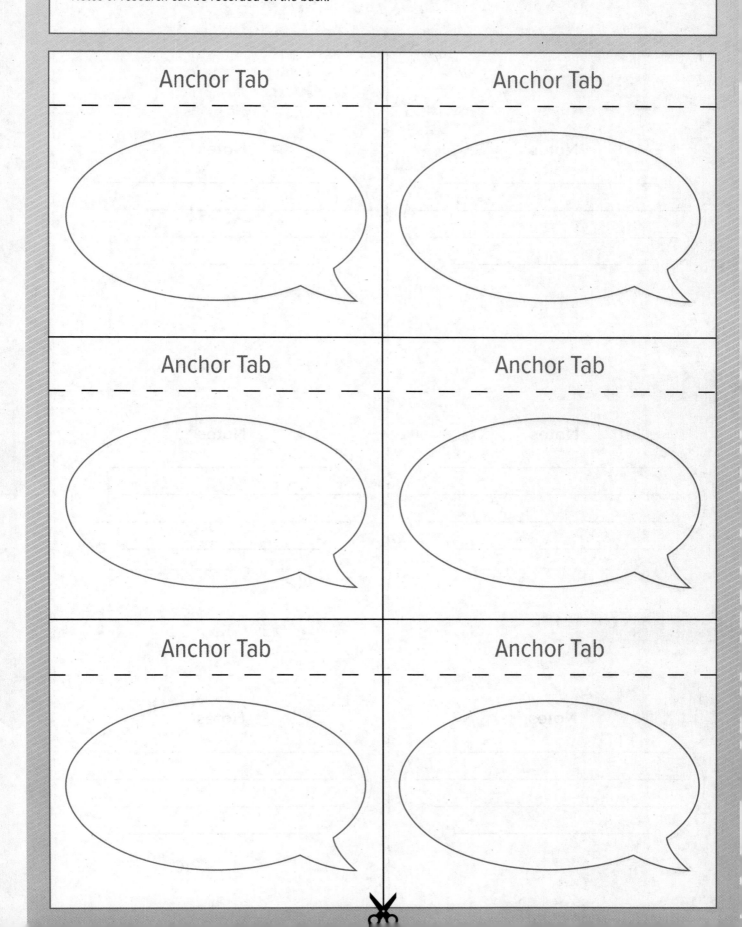

Notes

Notes

Notes

Notes

Notes

Notes